"I AM A DEMOCRAT"

The Political Career of David Bennett Hill

"I AM A DEMOCRAT"

The Political Career of David Bennett Hill

☆ ☆ ☆

Herbert J. Bass

SYRACUSE UNIVERSITY PRESS

1961

For Barbara

Preface

"Is the once great David Bennett Hill so soon forgotten?" asked a *New York Times* reader in a letter to the editor on August 14, 1928. The reader was taking the newspaper to task for omitting Hill's name from a list of two-term governors of New York. "Nothing is more unaccountable in political history," he wrote, "than the complete oblivion into which this once great national figure has fallen." Recalling the high points in Hill's career, the writer asserted that for a time Hill's name "filled the public mind from one coast to the other. . . ." "And now," he lamented, "he is so completely forgotten that he is not even a name."

The statement is perhaps a bit extravagant, the tone a bit too scolding for what quite possibly was a mere editorial oversight. Yet it is largely true that David Bennett Hill is, relative to the position he once occupied on the political stage, only a dimly recollected and poorly understood figure.

Why this is so is difficult to say. It may well be that while the accomplishments of his governorship were substantial, they did not sufficiently anticipate the future to arrest the attention of present-minded historians; or that Hill's frequent blindness to moral considerations in politics was of insufficient magnitude to qualify him as a curio, a prototype of the rogue in politics, in whom many might later find a perverse attraction. He offered no grand scheme or vision of the future, as did our Georges and Bellamys; he did not possess the singular quality of character of our Clevelands; he lacked the captivating charm and personality of our Roosevelts.

Yet in his age, and perhaps in any other, these qualities were not essential to either political success or historical importance. And Hill was both successful and important. As twice-elected governor and head of what was probably New York's most important administration during the last half of the nineteenth century, and as a major contender for the Democratic presidential nomination of 1892, Hill deserves greater attention than he has thus far received.

This study centers on that period of Hill's career when, as governor, master of the state Democratic party, emerging national figure, and presidential aspirant, his power and importance were at their zenith. The paucity of material extant on Hill's early years dictates the relatively slight attention given in this work to Hill's pre-gubernatorial career; his declining importance in the years after his unsuccessful bid for the presidency (though his influence in state party councils remained high for another decade) led to the decision to deal only in summary fashion with his post-1892 career. Hill's role in the Democratic party during the 1890's and early 1900's will be treated more fully in a later study dealing with New York and national politics of that period.

One further note is in order. Some time after the completion of this manuscript and only shortly before typesetting was to begin, a new body of Hill material came to light. Originally in the possession of the family of Peter J. Manweiler, a private secretary and confidant of Hill in his later years, the material is now in the New York State

Library at Albany. The bulk of these new papers deal with the senatorial and post-senatorial years of Hill's life. Although no reference to these papers is made in the notes to this book, I have consulted them.

I would like to thank the following publishers for granting permission to quote from their publications: Appleton-Century-Crofts, Inc., *Recollections of Grover Cleveland*, by George F. Parker; Houghton Mifflin Co., *The Letters of Grover Cleveland, 1850–1908*, edited by Allan Nevins; Holt, Rinehart, and Winston, Inc., *Four Famous New Yorkers*, by De Alva Stanwood Alexander; and Dodd, Mead & Co., *Grover Cleveland: A Study in Courage*, by Allan Nevins, copyright 1932, 1960, by Allan Nevins. Portions of chapters V, VI, and VII have appeared previously in *New York History* and are reprinted with permission.

HERBERT J. BASS

Orono, Maine
Autumn, 1961

Acknowledgments

I WOULD like to express my thanks to some of the many people whose kind assistance contributed substantially to whatever merits this study may have. I am deeply indebted to Professor Glyndon G. Van Deusen of the University of Rochester for his numerous and valuable suggestions, his continuous interest and encouragement, and all those many kindnesses which authors must so inadequately sum up in the words "friendly counsel." A very dear friend and colleague, Professor George Billias of the University of Maine, gave freely of his time and wisdom in reading and criticizing the entire manuscript. That an obstinate pride of authorship which opposed the wise but relentless use of his red pencil tried his patience, I cannot doubt; that it never tried his friendship, I can only marvel. I have also benefited from the helpful comments of Professors Glen G. Wiltsey and Richard C. Wade of the University of Rochester, both of whom read the work in an early stage. Professors Harold C. Syrett of Columbia University and Robert York of the University of Maine have taken a friendly interest in the progress of the manuscript.

My indebtedness to a number of librarians, those indispensable helpers in research, is considerable. Miss Edna Jacobsen and Miss Juliet Wolohan of the Manuscript Section of the New York Library at Albany were extremely helpful, as were Miss Margaret Butterfield and the staff of the University of Rochester Library and Mr. Louis T. Ibbotson of the University of Maine Library. In addition, the staffs of the manuscript divisions of the New York Public Library and the Library of Congress extended many courtesies. I wish also to acknowledge the timely financial assistance of the Coe Research Fund of the University of Maine, made available at a critical point in the research for this work.

And finally, my deepest debt is to my wife, Barbara. I shall not try to elaborate upon it in this space; it is a debt which she herself will best understand.

Contents

"I AM A DEMOCRAT"

The Political Career of David Bennett Hill

. . . *All politicians can be divided into three classes: the moral, the unmoral, and the immoral. The moral politician honestly makes some effort, however feeble, to do right, even at the risk of personal or party interests, while the unmoral politician has no ideal of right before him, or intention to do wrong, but aims only at success of self or party, and the immoral politician does wrong by practice and preference, knows he is wrong and brags of it; breaks every commandment of the decalogue and is proud of it.*

The moral politician is a reformer of the body politic, the unmoral politician is a conformer to the body politic, the immoral politician is a deformer of the body politic. . . . The first is a statesman, the second a politician, the third a political parasite and demagogue. . . . To which of these three classes of politicians does David B. Hill belong? This is exactly my dilemma when in the past I have tried to name Mr. Hill. No sooner does he exhibit a symptom of being a reformer, than he does something that as plainly indicates he is a conformer, on the heels of which will come some dastardly act that stamps him a deformer. I hesitate to call him either, I want to call him all three, I can't think of a name that means so much, and yet so little, unless it be the name he already bears, David Bennett Hill.

ADDRESS OF DR. C. S. CARR OF COLUMBUS, OHIO, TO THE THURMAN CLUB, MARCH 8, 1892

CHAPTER I

The Apprenticeship

THE CATHERINE Creek winds its way lazily northward
through Chemung and Schuyler counties in New York's
southern tier, and empties its murky waters into Seneca
Lake. Along its banks rise alternately high bluffs and gentle
slopes of gravelly loam and clay which, with the lowlands
bordering the creek, form the Catherine Valley. Nature
has been generous to this valley. At its opening, almost
touching the shores of the lake, is scenic Watkins Glen.
Some three miles to the south is the lesser known but
equally picturesque Havana Falls. Both of these spectacular
formations are set against a contrasting backdrop of rolling,
placid countryside. It is perhaps one of the lesser paradoxes
of history that this valley, whose most striking character-
istic is its pastoral serenity, should cradle one of the most
turbulent political careers of the late nineteenth century. For it was in this valley that David Bennett Hill spent
his early years and served his political apprenticeship.

David Hill was born in the village of Havana,[1] New York,
on August 29, 1843. The Hills were a family of moderate
means. Caleb, the father, earned enough as a skilled car-
penter to support his family comfortably, though by no
means lavishly. Their home was a modest dwelling on
Genesee Street, shaded by the tall elms which lined the

street, and close enough to the falls to be occasionally sprayed when its fine mists were caught up by a shifting breeze.[2]

Little is known of Hill's early years in Havana. The youngest of five children, David received his formal education at a ten-grade public school, where he was apparently a somewhat better than average student. Upon graduation, he decided upon a career in law, and promptly went to work in the office of Marcus Crawford, one of the two local attorneys. There, when he was not filing papers, sweeping floors, and tidying up the office, he studied law with his employer. To supplement his meager income, he also acted as the local agent for two New York insurance firms.[3]

When twenty years old, David Hill moved to Elmira, some fifteen miles from Havana. There he continued his work and studies in the offices of Thurston, Hart, and McGuire, receiving an annual salary of one hundred dollars plus board. David learned quickly, and within one year was admitted to the bar. That his diligence, application, and firm grasp of the law had not gone unnoticed was evidenced by an immediate offer of a partnership with Judge Gabriel L. Smith, an attorney of established reputation. Hill accepted with alacrity.[4]

The firm of Smith and Hill prospered from its inception, and within a few years rose to a position of prominence in the southern tier. This was no mean accomplishment, for the bar of that region included such distinguished men as Lucius Robinson, soon to become governor of New York, and H. Boardman Smith, later state Supreme Court justice.[5]

The rapid rise of the firm was due in no small part to the energies and abilities of its junior partner. Hill did not exhibit that brilliance of mind which distinguished such legal giants as Samuel Tilden and Joseph Choate; his success was attributable instead to thorough preparation of cases and meticulous attention to detail, and, in court, cogent arguments based upon a realistic understanding of human nature. Indeed, so thorough was Hill's presentation in one case that his promising career was almost literally cut short. An irate defendant in a marital suit, frustrated by Hill's presentation of the plaintiff's case, attacked Hill with a penknife and slashed him just under the left ear. Hill later joked about the incident but the scar remained with him through life.[6]

But law was not Hill's only interest, for he had already begun to serve a second master. The youthful attorney, who even as a lad in Havana had shown an interest in politics, had now completely succumbed to its fascinations. Soon after his arrival in Elmira, he began to take an active part in Elmira's political life. Within a year of his entrance to the bar, Hill was appointed counsel for the newly incorporated city. Before long, he was devoting all his after-work hours to politics. Lights in his Water Street law offices burned brightly well into the night, as local politicians dropped in to chat or to map strategy with "Davey." After closing the office, Hill would stroll the few blocks to his boardinghouse room on Lake Street in Elmira's Third Ward. Never at ease in large social gatherings, nor in the company of ladies, Hill retreated to politics as his chief, and almost only, social activity. The routine of law practice and political discussion soon became an almost daily ritual.[7]

Hill's political prospects were enhanced by his alliance with the wealthy Arnot brothers, acknowledged leaders of Democratic politics in the southern tier. With their support, he rapidly emerged as the leader of the younger Democrats. In 1868 he was selected as Chemung County's delegate to the state convention; the following year he became secretary of the new county committee. Only twenty-

six, Hill was already recognized as one of the prominent
party leaders in his region.[8]

Hill was able to play an even larger role in local and
state politics after he and several other investors purchased
a floundering printing company in the summer of 1870, and
began publication of a daily newspaper. The circumstances
of the purchase were later to bring embarrassment, and
almost disaster, to Hill in his quest for the governorship.[9]
At the time, however, the *Elmira Gazette* offered splendid
opportunities for the aspiring politician. It afforded a
vehicle for the regular expression of his own political views,
for Hill determined the staunchly Democratic policy of
the newspaper, and penned many of the important editorials
himself. Moreover, ownership of the *Gazette* afforded many
opportunities to meet and cultivate the friendship of newspaper people throughout the state.

At his district convention a few months later Hill's growing prominence and service to the party were recognized
with the nomination for state assemblyman. Elected to the
legislature in an easy victory in 1870, he was returned the
following year for another one-year term. When Hill took
his seat in the assembly at the age of twenty-seven, he was
the youngest legislator but one in the history of New York
until that time.

Because Hill was already a firm believer in the virtue of
party regularity, his record in the assembly was neither
better nor worse than his party's. In 1871, Boss Tweed still
controlled the New York Democracy, and voting the straight
party line meant supporting him in many of his scheming
jobs. On the other hand, after Tweed's exposure, the reformer Samuel Tilden became the recognized leader of the
Democrats in the legislature, and Hill's participation in the
impeachment proceedings against the corrupt Tweed judge,
Barnard, was both able and honorable.[10]

The two years in Albany were important for Hill's future because of the opportunity they afforded, not only to gain valuable experience, but also to meet Democrats from all over the state. By far the most important of the men thus encountered was Samuel J. Tilden. Hill and Tilden worked side by side on the Judiciary Committee of the 1872 Reform Legislature, and they were instrumental in securing Barnard's impeachment. The fact that there were only twenty-seven Democrats in the assembly led them to work together more closely and to consult with each other more often than might otherwise have been the case. Tilden befriended Hill, and came to have a high regard for his young colleague's ability.[11]

Upon completion of these two terms in the legislature, Hill decided to return to private life and tend to his law practice and newspaper. Although he did not again run for office for a decade, he intensified his political activities and expanded his contacts. He continued to serve as his county's delegate to the annual state party conventions, and wielded a large influence in local party councils.[12]

Hill took a giant stride upward in state party circles in 1875, when he seized the party leadership in Chemung County. Tilden was then governor, and had opened his war on the Canal Ring. Someone was needed in the southern tier to help the Governor in this fight and also to break the iron grip in which the Arnot-Walker-McGee clique, now hostile to Tilden, held the local party organization.[13] For this job, Tilden turned to Hill and his newspaper, the *Elmira Gazette,* which were already supporting him. E. K. Apgar, a Tilden lieutenant, sent Hill his charge: "If you can draw the line in your county between the supporters of the Governor's policy of lifting up high our party standard and the baser sort, between the friends of Canal Reform and the friends of the Canal Ring, you will be doing a public service." [14]

The choice was squarely put to Hill: stand firm with his erstwhile local leaders and allies, or join forces with the Governor in his fight against them. The young attorney accepted the challenge and split with the Arnot forces. Hill was ready for the struggle. Although only thirty-two years old, he already had a carefully husbanded political organization in Chemung, with friendly leaders in every ward and township in the county. With Tilden's prestige behind him, Hill conducted a successful canvass to secure friendly delegates in the county convention. The Tilden men gained complete control of the convention,[15] and Hill jubilantly notified the Governor:

> We have met the enemy and routed them, "horse, foot, and dragoons. . . ." They sent money into the country towns, and money was poured out like water. Of course we did not leave a stone unturned and fought them with their own weapons.[16]

The Governor's forces were triumphant, and Hill, under the Tilden banner, had moved to the front of the local party.

While Hill's friendship with Tilden was an important factor in his advance to the head of the party in Chemung, his greatest asset in his rise through the ranks was Hill himself. He reached the top, not through influential friendship alone nor by reason of an overwhelming personality, but on his talent for organization and his meticulous attention to detail. Very early he had come to appreciate the elementary lesson that in politics, victories are won by votes cast. Getting out the vote might be menial, and it might be muddy, but it was as vital to success as the map-

ping of strategy, whether grand or petty; and Hill directed
his energies to getting out the vote. The social station of the
voter was immaterial: before that great leveller, the ballot
box, the vote garnered in the saloon was the equal of the
vote won in a fashionable residential district.[17]

David Hill seemed to enjoy thoroughly this side of political life. On election day he was a familiar figure at
the Thorn Coal Company office on Baldwin Street, which
served as the election booth in the old Third Ward. From
the opening of the polls to closing time, Hill could be seen
greeting friends and acquaintances, chatting with them,
inviting them to take Democratic ballots or pasters which
he drew from his black, double-breasted Prince Albert
coat, and helping them to complete their ballots.[18] And, as
his letter notifying Tilden of the Chemung victory illus-
trates, he knew how to use money to its best advantage in a
campaign.

Hill continued to support the state administration and his
editorial columns spread the Tilden gospel. A genuine
fondness grew up between the two, based on a mutual respect for ability. The young attorney was frequently called
to Albany by Tilden, though often, as Hill in later years
recounted with amusement, the Governor would keep him
waiting for hours and then utter some sententious remark
like, "Hill, we must keep the bad men to the rear," or "We
must elevate the standard. Thank you for coming. Good-
bye." [19]

Yet Hill frequently consulted with the Sage of Greystone
on party matters, and probably learned a good deal from
that master of political organization. Young Hill had influence with the Governor on matters of patronage and
the disposal of local legislation.[20] Tilden also thought
enough of Hill's abilities to appoint him to a commission
with such distinguished men as William Evarts and Judge

Hand to provide uniform charters for the cities of the
Empire State, but Hill declined to serve because of professional commitments.[21]

Only once did it seem that this confidence in Hill's political skill and maturity might have been misplaced. As
part of the Tilden program for controlling the 1877 state
Democratic convention, Hill was made temporary chairman.
He was expected to use his position to keep the convention
in line for the Tilden-Robinson slate by smothering any
challenges from the disgruntled, disaffected Boss John
Kelly and his Tammany cohorts. Hill, however, was tricked
by a Kelly ruse, blundered, and handed down a ruling
which placed the Kelly men in the saddle, allowing their
slate to capture the nominations. The ruling ultimately
cost Tilden and his friends control of the party machinery
for the next two years.[22]

Fortunately, despite this humiliating experience, Tilden's
confidence in Hill was not forfeited. Hill remained high
in party circles, retained his seat on the Democratic State
Committee, and chaired the 1881 convention, this time
without incident.

Hill's growing political prominence undoubtedly aided
his law practice, for it grew apace. When in 1875 his partner, Judge Smith, decided to abandon law in favor of an
industrial venture, Hill formed a new partnership with
William Muller, an old friend who was later to serve as a
trusted political aide. Several years later, the firm was
enlarged to include John Stanchfield, afterwards mayor of
Elmira and a Democratic candidate for governor. The new
firm counted many clients, and from its earnings the partners
derived comfortable incomes.[23] Hill's standing in the pro-
fession was attested when he was retained as counsel in the
McGraw-Fiske Will case, a contest over the legality of a
bequest of several million dollars to Cornell University. The

energetic young attorney also continued to devote a good deal of time to his newspaper enterprise, attending the up-state Associated Press meetings, where he met and befriended many Democratic editors.[24]

In 1881 Hill decided to run for public office once more, and secured the nomination and election for alderman from Elmira's Third Ward. The ward had a large Negro population, and in later years the tale was told that Hill had won the election by paying off the mortgage on the Negro church.[25] The story is probably apocryphal; it is far more likely that careful planning and effective organization—already Hill hallmarks—were responsible for his election.

Encouraged by this small victory, Hill decided to play for bigger stakes. In the spring of 1882, he sought and received his party's nomination for mayor of Elmira. Significantly, the nomination was presented to Hill as the representative of a partisan Democracy, a man whose strict devotion to party could unite all factions. Despite a number of unfavorable factors—the popularity of the Republican incumbent, the embarrassment of a printer's strike in the *Gazette* office, and an eleventh-hour denunciation by an influential local priest—Hill won by 352 votes, out of 3,650 cast. Perhaps as important as the victory itself was the fact that the election marked the healing of the split with the Arnots, and unified the local Democracy.[26]

During his few months in office, Hill established a reputation as a reform mayor. The reputation was built not on concrete accomplishments, but rather on Hill's unrealized program and his successful thwarting of raids on the city treasury. Improvement of sewage disposal, paving of sidewalks, and construction of a new city hall and jail were all badly needed in Elmira, and Hill fought vigorously for them. His proposals were doomed to failure, however, for it was clear that the Republican council would ignore them.

The battle between the Mayor and the council was a stand-off, the Republicans pushing aside Hill's programs, and Hill blocking a Republican attempt to oil their political machine with street repair and construction appropriations.[27]

Since Hill's proposals were probably foredoomed to failure, it is possible, in the light of his subsequent career, to question his sincerity in advocating them. In all probability, his program as mayor of Elmira was at least in part a sincere attempt at improvement and reform. But whether or not this was real reform, it was certainly good politics. The advocacy of just such measures as these—measures from which political capital could be made regardless of their enactment—was to be a thoroughly exploited technique in Hill's governorship.

The office of mayor was apparently meant only to be a steppingstone, for less than six months after he took office, Hill was sending out feelers for a place on the state ticket. The time seemed ripe for such a move. To his reputation as a reform mayor, Hill could add a record of faithful party service, friendship with Tilden, and a wide range of political acquaintances who were already under obligation to him for his previous support of their ambitions.[28]

Realistically, Hill decided not to aim too high. In the belief that lesser aspirations would encounter fewer obstacles, he modestly set his sights on the lieutenant-governorship. His campaign was launched quietly in August, 1882, with letters to influential Democrats all over the state, asking their support for the nomination. From many he received promises of such support.[29]

The chief claim which Hill put forward on his own behalf was that of service to the party, and especially to the Tilden-Manning wing. "My Dist.," he wrote to Daniel S. Lamont, an influential Democrat, "has never been wrong since Mr.

Tilden asked me to take hold and make it right, which was years ago. . . ." [30] In asking Tilden for his support, Hill recalled the many struggles he had waged on behalf of the former governor. "I have had to fight strong men," he wrote, "such men as Arnot, McGuire, Walker, and McGee, who have all been combined agst. me and who started a newspaper to crush me out and I have come out ahead every time. It has however, been a hard struggle for many years." [31]

The only other serious candidate for the lieutenant-governorship at the convention was George Raines of Rochester. Hill received unwitting aid in his campaign from the men who supported Grover Cleveland for governor. Realizing the necessity for geographical balance of the ticket, backers of the Buffalo bachelor prevailed upon Raines, another western New Yorker, to retire from the race in order to further Cleveland's chances. Thus the way was clear for Hill, a southern tier man. After Cleveland had won in the main contest of the convention—during which the cautious Hill split Chemung's three-man delegation among the three leading candidates—Hill received the nomination for lieutenant governor by acclamation.[32]

As to the outcome of the campaign there was never any doubt. The Republicans had settled that question in their own convention when, bowing to orders from Washington, they denied Governor Cornell a deserved renomination and entered instead Charles J. Folger, President Arthur's Secretary of the Treasury. The result was a stinging rebuke to this dictation from above. The final tabulation gave the Democratic ticket, headed by the two bachelor mayors, the greatest plurality ever achieved up to then in the state's history. Cleveland's margin was 192,000, Hill's 197,000.[33]

For the next two years Hill was buried in the relative

obscurity of the lieutenant-governorship. He did manage once to lift himself from this constitutionally imposed anonymity with a startling parliamentary ruling as president of the senate. On a bill aimed at allowing the Democrats to squeeze more patronage out of the construction of the new capitol building, the Republican minority refused to answer a rollcall, hoping thereby to defeat the bill on a no-quorum technicality. Hill thereupon ordered the clerk to record the silent Republicans as present but not voting, and declared the bill passed. This ruling stirred the press to immediate comment, although party affiliation rather than objective appraisal determined whether the tone was one of commendation or condemnation.[34] The incident was not without irony, for seven years later in Congress "Czar" Reed, Republican Speaker of the House, cited Hill's ruling as a precedent for his own arbitrary quorum counts.[35]

Although his term as lieutenant governor was, with this one exception, uneventful and inconspicuous, Hill continued to be very active in party circles. During these years in Albany he spent a great deal of time with several other young rising Democrats, of whom he was the acknowledged leader. Known as Hill's "kitchen cabinet," this group met informally in a State Street house maintained by the party and discussed politics and party strategy.[36] To Hill these meetings must have brought back vivid recollections of similar late-hour get-togethers in his old Elmira law offices.

With the coming of the national Democratic convention in 1884, Hill was among the first to urge Grover Cleveland's candidacy for the Presidency. At the convention itself, Hill arrived with a large group from the southern tier to lend vocal support to Cleveland's campaign. In the corridors and rooms of the hotel he labored through the night along with William C. Whitney, Smith M. Weed,

and others who were in Cleveland's camp.[37] No one could
have been more satisfied with Cleveland's nomination and
subsequent election than the calculating Elmiran, for Cleveland's elevation to the Presidency cleared the way for Hill
to the governorship.

Since 1882, when the main scene of Hill's political activity had shifted from the tiny theater of the Catherine
Valley to the much larger stage at Albany, the ties with
the area in which he had spent his early years were being
gradually broken. Family bonds were severed completely
with the death of both his mother and father, the latter
succumbing while en route to witness his son's inauguration as lieutenant governor. With larger demands being
made by his new position, more cords were loosened. Although he retained his ownership of the *Elmira Gazette,*
the actual job of publishing and editing was placed in
other hands. The law firm continued, but Hill withdrew
from an active role in it. Old friendships remained firm,
but new ones nurtured elsewhere took up more of Hill's
attention. For, by this time, Hill had made the decision
to devote all his energies to the furtherance of his political
career.

Yet, while Hill had now been elevated to the governorship by virtue of Cleveland's narrow presidential victory,
his political future was by no means secured. Had Reverend
Burchard of "Rum, Romanism, and Rebellion" fame not
succumbed to his unfortunate flair for alliteration; had the
notorious "Belshazzar's Feast"—the money-raising dinner
for Republican millionaires at fashionable Delmonico's—
yielded less publicity and more Republican campaign funds;
had election day, 1884, dawned bright and clear in rural
New York instead of overcast and wet; had the Prohibitionists drawn some eleven hundred fewer votes away from
the Republican presidential candidate; had any or all of

these things occurred, David B. Hill's anonymity as second-
in-command to a defeated presidential hopeful would, for
the time being at least, have been assured. As long as he
was governor by accident of history, Hill could never command a complete measure of respect and confidence from
party and state. The task of earning both, and more, still
lay before him.

*   *   *

New York State in the latter nineteenth century was in
many ways America, writ small. The era was one of almost
unbounded growth and expansion. New and larger indus-
tries mushroomed to meet the demands of a multiplying
population. The improvement and expansion of vast net-
works of transport and communication facilities bound the
nation more closely together, and stimulated the growth
of cities. The building of spectacular fortunes was all but
commonplace, encouraged as it was by the dominant social
and political philosophy of the period. Under the aegis
of this philosophy, and blessed by a naturally endowed
material wealth, America flourished.

But this material growth was only the gilding of the age.
There was another side, a seamier and sometimes sordid
side, stemming in large part from this unhindered and
unplanned expansion. With the sprawling growth of industry came the development of monopolies and trusts,
defying and circumventing all attempts at governmental
regulation. Problem as well as promise was inherent in the
rising population, especially in the mounting tide of immigrants. If railroads and canals contributed to rapid
urbanization, this very growth of metropolitan centers—
bedeviled by difficulties of their own—heightened the traditional antagonisms between the rural and urban areas.
Accumulation of huge fortunes was too often achieved

with the aid of questionable practices, devoid of ethical
and moral considerations; and the gaudy, flamboyant display of wealth emphasized to thoughtful persons the dis-
parity between productive might and distributive justice.
A few cracks began to appear in the exterior of exuberant
self-confidence which America presented to the world. The
age had its Algers; it had also its Lloyds, its Garlands, and
its Georges.

Both state and nation shared in this era of expansion,
and in the growing pains which accompanied it. Since
many of the problems of growth were increasingly invested
with political overtones, an ambitious young man bent
upon furthering his political career would do well to ap-
praise them as they were manifested in his state and as
they applied to his own future.

New York State was easily the most precious jewel in
Columbia's glittering crown. Measured by almost any standard, the Empire State was the leading industrial and manufacturing state in the nation. No one could question the
productive might and potential of the state; what was being
called more and more into question was the inequitable distribution of its wealth. Great fortunes were being amassed,
yet poverty could be seen on all sides. With the increasing
obviousness of this paradox, critics of the social order became more vocal, proposing solutions to the distributive
problem which ranged from the conservative to the violent,
from the feasible to the ludicrous.

The most practicable of the suggested remedies was that
of labor organization, which sought to achieve labor's demands through political as well as economic action. At
times, labor formed or supported third parties. More often,
they turned to the more effective course of supporting
candidates or parties in exchange for promises of a sympathetic consideration of labor's demands.

A large part of New York's laboring force was derived
from recently arrived immigrants. These new Americans
brought about peculiar social problems of their own. New
York City was the chief port of entry, and it was the
metropolis which had to cope with the major headaches
involved in the influx. Although some immigrants moved
on, many remained to tax the city's facilities. The phe-
nomenal rise in the city's population led to overcrowding
and the breeding of tenement slums.

These immigrant groups clung fondly to their national
customs, neither a difficult nor an especially objectionable
phenomenon in polyglot New York City. They retained
a fierce pride in their nationality and in their church, and
acted as one whenever these were concerned. In voting as
a bloc to advance the interests of their national group or
church or to defend them from actual or imagined attack,
these immigrants became influential pressure groups to be
reckoned with in politics. But these pathetically ignorant
newcomers were frequently duped. Their voting strength
was easily enlisted in support of almost any cause, as long
as the banners of Church and Homeland were prominently
displayed at the head of the parade.

The steady flow of immigrants swelled the population
of the state, but it was the cities, especially Brooklyn and
New York, that experienced the greatest rate of growth.
In New York City alone the population leaped from 800,000
in 1860 to 1,500,000 in 1890, 4,000,000 in 1910.[38] At the
turn of the century there were almost as many New Yorkers
living in the tiny area encompassing New York City and
Brooklyn as inhabited the rest of the Empire State.

The disproportionate growth experienced by the cities
accelerated the already strong trend toward urbanization,
and heightened the traditional rural-urban antagonism.
This antagonism, as old as the city itself, was based in part

upon conflicting economic interests, in part on different modes and philosophies of life, and was characterized by distrust on one side and disdain on the other. The farmer, imbued with simple values and homely virtues, and accustomed to pre-dawn-to-dusk labor, had a profound distrust for the city slicker, perpetrator of sharp practices, gaudy, prone to vice, wallowing in sin and obviously enjoying it. This distrust was accentuated by the religious differences between the Protestant farmer—usually native born—and the large Catholic population of the Big City, daily reinforced by new arrivals from Europe. The immigrants' national customs of drinking beer or spirits and of observing the Sabbath with gaiety further offended the temperate and more puritan residents.

On the other hand, resentment of rural influence ran high in the cities. City dwellers complained that their demands for greater representation in the legislature to correspond with their increased population went unheeded, as the apportionment continued to favor the rural districts. The thought of hayseeds running their affairs infuriated sophisticated New Yorkers. Especially objectionable were the attempts of rural legislators to foist upon urbanites their own rigid views of when, where, and how often—if, indeed, ever—alcoholic beverages might be consumed.

This question of liquor traffic restriction was another important factor in the politics of the period. During the latter half of the nineteenth century, the movement for prohibition had found political expression in the formation of a militant organized party. While it did not attract nearly enough supporters to be considered a major party, its influence in New York was far out of proportion to its numbers, for in a close election the Prohibition party could hold the balance. Its demands were therefore a central issue in state politics.

Since most of the adherents to prohibitionism were re-
cruited from temperate rural Republicans, prohibition was
in a sense a peculiarly Republican problem. But the Democracy was not without its own neat problem. Because the
Democratic party's main support came from heavily pop-
ulated New York City, and because Tammany Hall normally controlled the party in the metropolis, the Tammany
Tiger occupied a dominant position in state party councils.
This situation was anathema to many upstate Democrats
who resented Tammany's swaggering, bullying, threatening,
and sometimes treacherous ways. To these people and to
many potential Democratic voters, Tammany meant "the
draft riots, the Tweed Ring, the political gangsterism of
an ignorant, venal Irish element that was deeply repugnant
to their own Anglo-Saxon traditions." [39] Because of this
hostility within the party, in the normal course of events
a Democratic candidate could assure his success only by
delicately handling the task of gaining Tammany support
while at the same time avoiding the impression of accepting
its suzerainty. The one was as necessary to win downstate
votes as the other was to prevent the alienation of upstaters.

These, then, were some of the realities in the complex
pattern of New York politics. Each was capable of breaking any man who failed to grasp its significance, or who,
understanding it, lacked the imagination and political dex-
terity to cope with it. But while this Chinese puzzle had
its frustrations, it also had its fascination. The mastery of
this puzzle was the key to a dazzling political future, not
only in the state, but—given the importance of New York
in the national politics of the era—perhaps in the nation
as well.

CHAPTER II

The First Battle

AFTER serving two years of his three-year gubernatorial
term, Grover Cleveland resigned in January, 1885 to prepare for his presidential duties, and the governorship passed
into the hands of David Bennett Hill. There was a general
feeling of guarded optimism concerning the future of party
and state under the new Governor. Most Cleveland supporters were kindly disposed toward Hill, although few
expected him to be cut from the same cloth as his predecessor. Indeed, Hill found warm and cordial support in
a number of influential journals, while other editorial
columns, aside from the Republican press and an occasional
Mugwump organ like the *New York Times,* adopted no
worse than a wait-and-see attitude.

The prevailing atmosphere of friendliness was reinforced
by Hill's first annual message to the legislature.[1] After
lauding the retiring administration, Hill struck a concili-
atory note by urging the Republican legislature to "sink
partisan differences in behalf of good government." For
legislative action, Hill urged a consideration of the knotty
prison labor problem, the introduction of more flexibility
in the registration laws for voting by naturalized citizens,
the implementation and extension of the principle of freedom of worship, and the enactment of several measures

19

in the interests of labor. If there was politics in each of
these recommendations, reformers could take comfort in
Hill's sympathetic remarks about the civil service system,
as well as his advocacy of spring elections and home rule
for New York City. In addition, Hill pressed for action
on canal improvement and forest preservation, and urged
the establishment of a commission to aid the legislators
in drafting accurate laws.

For a first effort, it was a sound and suggestive message.
It was cordially received by much of the independent press,
and criticisms were for the most part few and gentle.
Harper's Weekly expressed its complete satisfaction with
the document, and to one Mugwump organ, the New York
Evening Post, the Governor's message breathed "from beginning to end the spirit of simple, honest government.
. . ." [2] Partisan sheets, as might be expected, went all out
in either irate condemnation or lyrical praise. If the message was too lavishly lauded in Democratic organs, it hardly
merited the epitaphs of "vapid" and "jejune" bestowed
upon it by the *New York Times* in its summary editorial
burial.[3]

The legislative session which followed was devoted chiefly
to partisan maneuvering, a not unnatural occurrence during an election year. The stakes were high. The party
that controlled the governorship and the legislature the
following term would reapportion the representation of
the state. Partisan politics were uppermost; proposals for
municipal reforms and a host of other worthwhile bills fell
by the wayside, and the cause of civil service reform only
narrowly averted a crippling setback. Jockeying for political position seemed at times to be the sole *raison d'être*
of the Republican legislature.

But the legislature was not alone in playing the game
of politics. Other eyes were also focused on the fall elec-

tions. Hill fully realized that, as a back-door governor, he still faced a struggle to be accepted on his own. His entire energies were therefore devoted to formulating and carrying out a political program that would secure him nomination and victory in the fall. To insure this eventuality, a three-pronged offensive seems to have been decided upon: certain large voting groups would have to be won over, issues would have to be made upon which the party could stand behind him, and a personal following must be molded out of uncommitted political elements—machines and organizations, prominent leaders, and the rank and file.

One large bloc of votes for which Hill set his cap was the Irish vote. Contemporary observers estimated that about one hundred thousand Irish had strayed from the state Democratic party in the 1884 elections.[4] Irish support had for decades been an important factor in Democratic successes, and the prospects for achieving victory without it were dim. Hill therefore moved to bring this vote back into the fold. In view of the strong religious loyalty of the Irish, the Governor hoped that a demonstration of friendship for the Catholic Church would be reciprocated by her grateful sons. A convenient opportunity to express this friendliness presented itself in the "freedom of worship" question.

For many years the Church had vainly demanded that the state permit the celebration of the Mass in state corrective and mental institutions in which Catholics were committed. One institution in particular, the New York House of Refuge on Randall's Island, drew the wrath of Catholics. This home, which received state aid, had been established originally by charitable citizens as a non-sectarian institution to train youthful offenders in the habits of regular industry. The board of managers, recognizing the near impossibility of holding religious observances ac-

cording to the several faiths of all the inmates, had decided
upon the policy of non-sectarian services. While this policy
did not exclude clergymen of any faith, and while it permitted each inmate to worship in his own way and to
keep his own prayerbook, it did insist that all teaching
and religious services held in the house must be non-sectarian. To Catholics, of course, this prohibition of the Mass
was intolerable. Between 1875 and 1885 a half-dozen bills
had been introduced to permit sectarian teaching and religious observances in institutions which were state-operated
or state-subsidized, but none became law.[5]

Hill now dusted off this old issue and introduced it in
his first message to the legislature. The introduction of
three different freedom of worship bills by Democratic
legislators in the next few weeks touched off a storm of
controversy. Mugwump journals leveled charges of dema-
goguery at Hill. Bishop McQuaid of Rochester, on the
other hand, expressed the conviction of many Catholics
when he stated that the "freedom of worship" clause in
the New York constitution obligated the state to provide
facilities for worship in its public institutions for any group
that wanted them.[6]

The Republican majority in the legislature found itself
in an awkward position. If a bill were enacted, even with
Republican support, credit would certainly go to Hill and
the Democrats. Yet opposing the bill could alienate the
Irish, and Republicans were most eager to keep their re-
cently-won political converts and to offset the ill effects of
Reverend Burchard's "Rum, Romanism, and Rebellion"
blunder of the previous year. Republican newspapers which
blasted Hill for raising the issue must have been somewhat
embarrassed by the affirmative vote of two-fifths of the
Republican senators on a freedom of worship bill. For a
time, it seemed that despite all criticism, the bill would

be enacted, as Republicans and Democrats stumbled over
each other in their fear of running second in the race to
curry Irish favor.

In the end the measure did not become law. Opposition
stiffened in the assembly, and the bill failed to reach a
vote before adjournment.[7] Yet Hill's revival of the issue was
a shrewd stroke. For the enactment of the bill was second-
ary; it was the stirring of the issue, with the opportunity
it afforded to pose as a champion of the Church, that was
primary. And this had clearly been accomplished.

Hill employed the same technique in his attempt to
capture the large labor vote. This so-called labor vote,
perhaps more than any other, was an unknown quantity.[8]
A direct approach to the working class as such was by no
means certain to bring support at the polls. Moreover,
inherent in such an appeal was the danger of alienating
the "better" elements of society. Yet if the risks involved
were great, so were the potential rewards. The workingmen's vote constituted a large reservoir of virtually un-
tapped strength which might be a deciding factor in an
election. To Hill, it seemed a gamble well worth taking.

Hill made his pitch for the labor vote beginning with
his very first official act as governor. In his January message,
he called for a number of measures in the interest of labor:
one to facilitate labor organization, another to put an end
to the importation of "pauper contract labor"; and a third
to establish a system of arbitration to settle labor dispute.
Hill also hinted that the government had an obligation to
the unemployed, although as yet he made no attempt to
spell out this idea.[9]

It was on the delicate prison labor question, however,
that Hill concentrated in his attempt to corral the workingmen's vote. This question had for decades defied political
solution. The decision of the electorate in 1883 to eliminate

contract labor—the hiring of prison labor by private contractors to manufacture products within the prison walls—
had done nothing to resolve the knotty issue. Manufacture
of goods by convicts and their subsequent sale in the open
market was regarded by labor as unfair competition. Yet
it was recognized that prisoners had to be kept at work
and, if possible, rehabilitated through learning a trade.
The headache for the politicians was to keep them at constructive work and at the same time minimize, if not completely eliminate, the competition between prison-made
goods and those made by free labor.

Hill was no stranger to the issue. As a young legislator
many years earlier, he had introduced a bill to abolish
the contract labor system in state prisons.[10] Now, as governor, he fully realized the delicate nature of the problem.
He had been warned that labor would be discontented no
matter how the issue was treated. As an astute politician,
he well knew that "it behooves us to make no moves calculated to drive any of the laboring classes away from
us." [11] The situation called for a political tight-rope act,
and Hill performed it admirably. In his message to the
legislature he urged prompt and positive action on the subject, but at the same time carefully avoided suggesting any
plausible solutions. He was content to make only the pious
pronouncement that the interests of labor ought to be pro-
tected.[12] Since no solution would win labor votes, and
almost any proposal would lose them, he craftily threw
this political hot potato into the laps of the Republican
legislators.

A number of bills were introduced, but the only one
which reached a vote was defeated. No prison labor bill,
in fact, was to be enacted for three years.[13] But here again,
as with the freedom of worship bill, the success or failure
of the measure was only incidental in Hill's plans. He had

succeeded in showing his concern for labor's welfare and his sympathy with its cause. For the moment, this was enough.

Hill hoped to garner support by establishing a reputation as an economy-minded governor as well as by appealing to vested interest groups. The scheduled state decennial census upon which legislative reapportionment was to be based gave Hill an opportunity to do just this. In a special message, the Governor recommended that the legislature make certain changes in the procedure of census-taking. He urged that the census be limited to enumeration only, that it be taken in the spring or fall rather than the summer, that its supervision be placed in the hands of the county clerks, and that the enumerators be brought within the jurisdiction of the civil service law.[14]

There was much to be commended in these suggestions, as even Hill's opponents admitted. A simple enumeration would cost the state and counties about $300,000 less than a census which included the gathering of numerous other statistics. Moreover, recently created state bureaus and departments collected much of this additional data, and their records, along with those of the federal census, rendered such a state effort redundant.

The adoption of Hill's proposals would also result in a more equitable count in the census. Changing the time of the enumeration from summer to fall or spring would enable a more accurate count in urban districts, where the July and August exodus make a correct count impossible. Accuracy would be further assured if supervision were turned over to the county clerks who were familiar with their respective counties, rather than to a state official sitting in remote Albany. In any event, an enumerator chosen under civil service rules would be less likely to take a partisan count than one appointed by a political leader.

Characteristically, while there was good sense in Hill's suggestions, there was also shrewd politics. He was not unaware that his proposal to save the state a large sum of money cast him in the role of a watchful and frugal guardian of state funds. A fall or spring census, while manifestly fair, was certain to benefit the Governor's party, for it would enable the urban areas, usually Democratic, to be counted at full strength.

The proposed changes for appointing census-taking personnel were also politically loaded. By giving the county clerks the responsibility of census-taking, the Republican secretary of state, previously invested with the job, would be stripped of the power to appoint the enumerators. Because the secretary of state, General Joseph B. Carr, loomed as Hill's most likely opponent in the fall, it was important to keep these 3,000 to 3,500 jobs out of his hands. Bringing the enumerators within the scope of the civil service law was a further step in this direction. This last proposal also served to head off Mugwump criticism, for civil service extension was always a Trojan horse that dispelled the suspicions of uneasy Independents.

The Republican legislators, of course, had no intention of aiding the Governor in his schemes. After smothering an administration census bill, they proceeded to make their own plans for the census. The battle was joined from this point on. Hill countered with a ruling from the Civil Service Commission bringing enumerators within the civil service regulations. Armed with this ruling, Hill again demanded that the legislature enact his proposals. The Republicans, with party prestige at stake, once more refused, and defied the Governor by passing a census bill which failed to incorporate a single one of his proposals. A cleverly devised veto followed. In it, Hill offered to concede to the Republicans any patronage and political ad-

vantage they could squeeze from a census bill, if only they
would agree to save the people's money by limiting the
census to enumeration only. The Republicans were enraged, and the session adjourned with no further action
on the issue.[15]

The wily Governor, however, did not intend to let a
good thing die. Calling the legislature into special session,
he demanded action on his census proposals. The Republicans were faced with a dilemma. To give in to Hill now
would convey the impression of weakness and seem an
admission of error; to enact their own measure would confirm Hill as the sole champion of economy. Their first
move was to crowd onto the economy bandwagon by re-
leasing all but a skeleton staff of employees for the special
session.[16] Party leaders then decided to defy Hill, and after
quickly pushing through their own bill, they adjourned.
Hill left little doubt as to what his action would be when
he immediately characterized the measure as "more odious
than the one I vetoed." [17] Hill's rejection of the bill meant
that there would be no census and reapportionment. But
it also meant that Hill had another issue with which he
could go before the electorate.

While Hill recognized the importance of creating issues
and attracting voting groups to support the ticket in the
fall elections, he also realized that he would have to work
to assure himself first place on that ticket. The Governor
knew that other Democrats also coveted the nomination.
He had been cautioned as early as January that Mayor
William R. Grace of New York "has the Gubernatorial
bee damned big in his bonnet." [18] Roswell P. Flower, a
wealthy New York merchant who had received some support for the presidential nomination in 1884, was also
expected to join in the race for state honors.[19] With the
threat of strong competition, Hill devoted much time and

energy during the legislative session and especially during
the summer months to nailing down the nomination.

The chief stronghold of the Democratic party was, of
course, New York City. Although the endorsement of Big
City Democrats was not always essential for the nomination, their support was often a determining factor. Hill
was therefore anxious to receive their blessing, not only
to increase his own following but also to head off any support that might develop for other candidates like Flower
and Grace, whose chances of victory depended almost entirely on a strong New York showing.

Control of the Democratic party in the downstate metropolis was lodged in the hands of three rival organizations: the County Democracy, Tammany Hall, and Irving
Hall. Of the three, the most prominent in 1885 was
the youngest, the County Democracy. Originally a reform
organization which had backed Cleveland, the County
Democracy was now led by Hubert O. Thompson, a young,
energetic, and imperious politician. Close behind was the
omnipresent Tammany Hall and its beady-eyed chieftain,
Richard Croker. Tammany's fortunes had been gradually
rebuilt after the malodorous Tweed era, until by the mid-
eighties the sachems were prepared to challenge the County
Democracy for supremacy. The foundering Irving Hall
trailed far behind its rivals, but still controlled enough
votes to be a factor in a close election. Across the river
a fourth organization, Boss Hughie McLaughlin's Kings
County Democracy, held sway in Brooklyn. All four groups
harbored mutual distrust and envy; each waited for the
opportunity to humble the others and achieve pre-eminence
for itself.

The task facing Hill was to wring or coax an endorsement from as many of these factions as possible. It was

not an easy one. To flirt with any one group was almost
sure to alienate the others. An attempt to appeal to all,
in view of their mutual jealousies and hatreds, might well
result in getting the backing of none. The course which
Hill seems to have decided upon was to spread a net of
kind words and deeds wide enough to accommodate all,
and hope that enough could be gathered in to secure the
nomination.

The first move in this direction was made early in 1885,
when Hill considered charges of official misconduct brought
against an Irving Hall leader, Alexander Davidson. Davidson, Sheriff of the County of New York, had padded his
expenses and grossly overcharged the city for maintenance
of prisoners, even to the point of requesting reimbursement
for the care of several thousand who did not exist. Hill,
probably influenced more by political prospects than by
Christian charity, dismissed the charges, stating his belief
that the overcharges had been made without intent.[20] The
Governor undoubtedly felt that Davidson's gratitude would
find a suitable channel for expression in the fall.

Tammany received its share of favors. State patronage
was fairly tight throughout 1885, but with the aid of Hill's
endorsements, several federal appointments were secured
for Tammany men. The official countenance shone also
upon the County Democracy and its leader, Hubert Thompson. Thompson's wishes on several pieces of legislation
were accepted as fiat by the Governor, and relations between
the two men were cordial.[21]

The organization which bid fair to be the most difficult
of persuasion was McLaughlin's Brooklyn machine. Eight
years before, an inexperienced Hill had made a decision
as chairman of the state convention which had hurt the
Kings County boss. Hill knew well that the "soreness, grow-

ing out of that *damned* Albany Convention of 1877," had still not been completely healed.[22] Boss Hughie had to be handled with great care.

There was one important fact working in Hill's favor. McLaughlin had, with the exception of a brief windfall at the Brooklyn Navy Yard, received almost nothing from the national administration. The Kings County leader might well be receptive to a reconciliation with Hill, if the Governor were able to give concrete expression to his professions of friendship. Two opportunities to do just this presented themselves in June in the form of the Kings County clerk and register bills. If approved, these measures would have dealt a serious blow to McLaughlin's prestige and his machine. Hughie hastened to Albany for an evening conference with Hill. The following day both bills were vetoed.[23]

Thus through favors and friendship, Hill attempted to bind to himself the Big City factions. But the Elmira politician was far too astute to put all his political eggs in the downstate basket. He was fully aware that local jealousies might well ruin his candidacy if there were no convincing support outside the metropolitan area. Therefore Hill early set to work to cultivate the upstate urban and rural areas.

Born, raised, and still residing in the southern tier, Hill had a natural appeal for upstate Democrats, whose resentment of the Big City's domination of the party ever welcomed expression. The shrewd Hill had determined to take advantage of this potential. His emphasis on economy and the appeal to the "little man" throughout the legislative session were undoubtedly aimed in part at the upstate vote.[24] During the summer he devoted a great deal of time to the northern, central, and southern tiers of New York, making numerous appearances in the small villages of the state on "inspection tours." He attended county fairs, where

he made "non-political speeches" about agriculture and
the farmer's problems.[25] Opponents endowed him with the
nickname "Farmer Hill"; but belittling sobriquets could
not offset the gains resulting from the flattering attentions
showered upon the rural element by the Democratic Governor.

Hill also set into motion the extremely efficient personal
organization which he had built over the years. The Governor's executive office was the general headquarters of the
organization, and Hill was in every sense the commander.
In his notebook was registered every leader of importance.
From his office were issued hundreds of letters to politicians in all corners of the state inquiring about local situ-
ations. Friends and confidants periodically reported to him
on the outlook in their areas. Not a county or district was
overlooked. Where there was a delegate to be won over,
there was a Hill man on the scene, coaxing, convincing,
promising, cajoling. Field reports poured in to Hill, suggesting that a friendly letter here or a complimentary note
there might swing some important local Democrat into
the Hill column. William L. Muller and Charles Bacon,
both former law partners of the Elmira politician, traveled
around the state in his interest, and State Treasurer Robert
Maxwell also toiled diligently for him.

Hill himself traveled widely during the summer, rounding up support for his candidacy. On these "pipe-laying"
trips the Governor might work out acceptable combinations
for the state and local tickets with local leaders; he might
promise not to interfere with an ambitious politician's
desire to seek a higher office; he might attempt to restore
harmony between warring factions.[26] Whatever the immediate purpose of any journey, however, the ultimate aim
was to bring all hands into the Hill fold.

Every opportunity for garnering new supporters was
utilized. On the one-day trip to Niagara, where he was to
officiate at the ceremonies turning the park over to the
state, Hill managed to address large crowds at the Utica,
Syracuse, and Rochester railroad stations, and another huge
throng at Buffalo in the evening. The time not consumed
by public speaking was assiduously devoted to the cultivation of local Democratic leaders.[27]

The task of fashioning a solid political following from
the diverse elements and factions in the state was one which
involved constant exertion and exhortation. There was one
source of potential support, however, which required little
effort to tap. This was the substantial group of Democrats
who were dissatisfied with the patronage policies of the
national administration. The coolness of these men toward
Cleveland's civil service policy was understandable. After
twenty-four years in the wilderness, the Democrats had
finally been delivered, only to find that their leader—a man
they regarded as at best a political amateur—was withholding from them the fruits of victory. There were "kickers"
of all sorts: men who had been removed from office by
Cleveland as governor or president, and those who were
disappointed office-seekers; those who had quarreled with
the pugnacious President, and those who merely disliked
or distrusted him personally.

These opponents of the President were eager to express
their discontent, and many of them now chose as the most
convenient vehicle for doing this the candidacy of David
Bennett Hill. It was not that Hill was the complete antithesis of Cleveland; but there was no doubt that he was a
more traditional party man than the President. The attitude of the kickers was perhaps best set forth by a correspondent who wrote to Hill concerning the "decided and
growing dissatisfaction with the Federal Administration."

This feeling [he continued] is not by any means confined
to the place-seekers, but extends to those who have been
and are democrats from principle alone. . . . The temper of our people . . . is to have as the Gubernatorial
candidate a man who is "all Democrat"—and win or
lose with him at the head of the ticket. Our people look
upon you as filling and as more than filling the bill. Your
administration has been most satisfactory to them. . . .[28]

Thus a number of anti-Cleveland Democrats eagerly
boarded the Hill train with pledges to support the Governor "with a vim." [29] Others were gradually drawn aboard
by what Hill's opponents called his "disposition to coddle
the kickers and rally the riff-raff by beating a partisan
drum." [30] The lure for many, of course, was the promise of
office or reward. Although Hill had little patronage to
dispense at the moment, it seems clear that he mortgaged a
considerable number of future offices in exchange for
pledges of support. As one critic put it, "he has devoted
himself to cutting bait, as well as angling for the renomination. Wherever a Democrat exists who is disaffected . . .
there the Governor drops his baited hook, and patiently
waits a bite." [31]

Hill had good reason to campaign vigorously, for new
challengers were appearing almost daily. In speculating
about possible candidates, newspapers combed public statements for clues, and read double meanings into even the
most innocent remarks of Democratic leaders. Secretary of
the Treasury Manning innocently remarked that he preferred Albany's weather to that of Washington, and soon
found himself a leading candidate for the gubernatorial
nomination.[32] Of self-announced candidates there was an
abundance. By the end of August the *Times* could list some
twenty possibilities, most of them willing ones.[33]

Although Hill was steadily forging ahead upstate, there was still no clear indication, as late as mid-August, that any of the downstate factions would endorse him. Despite two trips to Brooklyn, the Governor had been unable to extract any promises from McLaughlin.[34] If the Democratic State Committee meeting of August 18 shed any light at all on the situation, it served to point up the fact that the leading politicians were still shopping.

Only one of the New York City organizations, the County Democracy, had taken a stand, and that was one of opposition to Hill. The ambitious Hubert Thompson saw in the nominations an opportunity to catapult himself into Manning's old position of state leadership in the party. Were Thompson able to hand-pick a candidate and guide him to victory, his recognition as a state boss was practically assured. The time seemed ripe for such a move. The influence and prestige of the County Democracy were never higher, the party was dependent upon it for the bulk of the campaign funds, and there was within the organization an abundance of gubernatorial timber.[35]

Thompson made his move early in July when he entered as his candidate Edward Cooper, son of the philanthropist Peter Cooper and a former mayor of New York. Cooper posed a serious threat to Hill. He was well known throughout the state, and was likely to command strong support. Even if Cooper did not walk off with the laurels, a strong showing on his part might mean a bitter convention struggle, in which event a compromise candidate could be presented with the prize. The wealthy Roswell Flower was, as everyone knew, waiting expectantly in the wings for just such a situation to develop.[36]

But the factional rivalry which at times threatened to be a curse to Hill's hopes now became a blessing. For what the County Democracy supported, Tammany as a matter of course opposed. In mid-July, Joseph J. O'Donahue, a New York businessman with Tammany ties, denounced Cooper as a "bigot," and declared that he would be an independent candidate for governor, should the ex-mayor receive the Democratic nomination.[37] Kings County Democrats were also adamantly opposed to Cooper's candidacy, for they nursed the memory of Thompson's swallowing "the Custom House whole without so much as throwing a bone to them." Moreover, Boss Hughie intended to do nothing which might help Thompson to become the overlord of the state. Thompson journeyed across the river many times during that summer with penitent offers to disgorge a share of the port patronage, but McLaughlin would not yield.[38]

The refusal of local rivals to support Thompson's choice, and even the threat of a third ticket in the field, did not immediately deter him from continuing his campaign for Cooper. But the nightmare of 1879[39] must have soured other Democrats on Cooper's candidacy. And while the downstate Democrats quarreled, Hill's efficient machine continued to swell his following.

The Governor's chances were brightened still further when Samuel Tilden announced that he would support David B. Hill for the nomination. Although out of public office since 1877, the Sage of Greystone still cut a large figure in state and national politics, and his declaration promised to bring in its wake many loyal Tildenites. The announcement also dealt a severe blow to Cooper's candidacy, for it shattered all hopes of getting behind himself the old Tilden organization, still strong in the Hudson Valley and upstate region.[40]

One big question mark still remained in the race for Democratic honors. If the national administration wished to exercise its power and influence, it could have a very large say in the shaping of the ticket. Several rumors con-

cerning the administration's position had from time to time
gained currency: now Cleveland was setting up his own
slate for the New York elections, now he favored this candidate, now that one. The President steadfastly refused to
confirm or deny these stories. As a result of the continued
silence on Cleveland's part, adherents of almost all the candidates were claiming his support. The Hill camp pointed
to both the August visit of the President with the Governor and to Hill's subsequent conference with Cleveland's
secretary, Daniel Lamont, as a sure sign of endorsement.
Cooper's followers countered with the observation that the
County Democracy's association with the White House had
borne fruit several times, and could logically be expected
to do so again. Even Roswell P. Flower's small band announced that Cleveland was in its camp, although it took
some labored and circuitous reasoning to get him there.[41]

Actually the Cooper forces were fairly close to the truth
in their assessment of the situation. Whitney and Manning,
both in Cleveland's cabinet and both powers in state politics, favored the nomination of Cooper. Cleveland was also
sympathetic to the candidacy of a County Democracy man,
although his personal choice seems to have been Mayor
William R. Grace.[42] Yet if Grace was his personal choice,
it was never made public, for Cleveland maintained his
reticence. The President had not forgotten how popular
resentment at Washington's dictation of the Republican
candidate had swelled his own margin of victory in 1882.
Since then he had determined upon a hands-off policy in
local party contests, and he held firmly to this policy now.[43]

Several aspiring candidates were, of course, sorely disappointed when Cleveland failed to rally to their support,
but Hill was quite satisfied with the administration's abstention. There was every reason to believe that had the
President spoken out, it would not have been for one whose

following was now so clearly tinged with an anti-Cleveland hue. Since an endorsement was unlikely, a continued neutrality was highly desirable, for it enabled the Hill bandwagon to roll on without an embarrassing hitch.

During the four weeks prior to the convention, the fruits of Hill's eight-month effort began to manifest themselves. When Chemung and Schuyler, the first counties to hold their conventions, met on August 29, they both pledged their delegates to Hill. This action by the southern tier counties was a signal for an advance all along the line. The Batavia convention also elected Hill delegates, and the Governor received private assurances that Delaware County would stand with him. Thus the upstate area had demonstrated its strong support. Within a week, an additional twelve county conventions pledged their support to Hill. Over a dozen more fell into line the following week. The State Labor Assembly, carefully managed by Hill's ally George Blair, joined with a resolution amounting to endorsement. The whirlwind drive was leaving the other candidates far behind, and only a handful of delegates outside the Big City organizations were still not committed to the Governor.[44]

From the New York area came reports of widespread enthusiasm for Hill in both the Tammany and Kings County organizations. Their support was now practically assured. Irving Hall, too, was sympathetic to the Governor, but in view of the Davidson case it refrained from an endorsement to avoid embarrassing Hill.[45]

There were sound reasons for these organizations to fall in now behind Hill. None of them had a strong candidate of its own to support. Each counted among its members a large number of kickers who were already favorably inclined toward the Governor. Furthermore, the indications of overwhelming upstate support encouraged the machines to join the ranks of one whose chances of winning were daily becoming brighter. Thompson's insistence upon opposing Hill presented all three rivals with a golden opportunity to humble the imperious County Democracy ruler and cripple his influence in the state and city.

Thus fully two weeks before the convention, Hill could feel quite sure that his nomination was assured. The *Times* might bravely insist that Hill could not possibly garner more than 78 votes, but the newspaper was clearly whistling in the dark. On the eve of the convention, even the *Times* conceded that the day would be won by Hill.[46]

The Democratic state convention met at Saratoga on September 24. If Hubert O. Thompson still nursed his naive notions about Hill's inability to win without him, he was jolted out of them as Hill delegates streamed into the convention hall. From the outset it was apparent that the conclave would be little more than a ratification meeting for Hill. The only hopeful sign to which opponents of the Governor might point was the widespread publication on that morning of a letter from the President to Dorman B. Eaton, a retiring civil service commissioner. In this letter accepting Eaton's resignation, Cleveland made a number of vigorous remarks about the reform movement which were construed by some to be a slap at Hill. Both the contents of the letter and the timing of its publication enraged Hill's anti-civil service friends, who characterized it as a "shot in the back." Whether it was written with any such intent is doubtful; but it did seem more than a coincidence that the letter, dated September 11, was not released for publication until the morning of the Democratic convention.[47]

Letter or no, Hill's strength was too much for the opposition. With the slogan, "short speeches, and vote for Hill every time" as their watchword,[48] Hill delegates con-

trolled the convention. Anti-Hill men fought desperately
for adjournment in the hope of effecting some workable
combination, but they were beaten down by the Governor's
supporters under the able floor leadership of D-Cady Herrick of Albany and Alton B. Parker, later to be a presidential candidate, but then a surrogate in Ulster County.
Delaying motions were quickly disposed of, and by evening
the nominations began.

Hill was placed in nomination by Jeremiah J. O'Connor,
an Elmira liquor dealer blessed with an unfettered imagination. In his nominating speech, O'Connor extolled Hill's
virtues and compared him favorably to Thomas Jefferson.
Cleveland-haters got in their licks as they shouted their
approval and boasted defiantly, "We love him for the
friends he has made." The County Democracy, seeing no
hope for Cooper, nominated instead Abram S. Hewitt, but
Thompson might just as well have gracefully surrendered.
All attempts to delay the balloting were crushed, and the
Hill forces jammed through, by an almost three-to-one
majority, a motion to poll the delegations.

By midnight it was all over. As one delegation after
another fell into line, the completeness of Hill's victory
became apparent. Hill had amassed 338 votes, while Hewitt
had received 33 and General Slocum of Brooklyn, 8. Roswell
Flower managed to get a lone vote. Thompson made no
attempt to make the nomination unanimous.[49]

The following day the rest of the slate was selected. In a
move to catch the German vote, Frederick Cook of Monroe
County was nominated for secretary of state. Flower was
chosen for lieutenant governor in the hope that he would
finance the campaign. This Democratic millionaire was
"expected to prove irresistibly magnetic by the use of
boundless wealth, scattered like chaff over the hills and
valleys of the entire state." [50]

The party platform was confined for the most part to straddling generalities. One plank advocated a tariff revision "in the spirit of fairness to all interests." Another endorsed the principle of civil service reform, though at the same time declaring the veteran's preference under the civil service regulations. The platform stood squarely behind Hill in his appeal to the laboring class, opposing contract labor and the employment of children under fourteen. Opposition to laws restricting the sale of liquor was implied in the denunciation of all legislation "that interferes with the constitutional right of personal liberty." [51]

Newspapers announced the results of the convention in headlines that reflected their partisan spirit. The New York *World* and New York *Sun* exulted in Hill's nomination, and Republican organs damned both Hill and his party. The *Times,* regarding the Governor's victory as "The Spoilsmen's Triumph," urged its readers to support the Republican ticket of Ira Davenport and Joseph B. Carr for governor and lieutenant governor, and let the Democrats "go sledding down Hill." [52]

The Democrats got off on the left foot almost immediately. Hopes of digging into "Flower's Bar'l" were dashed when, on the day after the convention, Flower declined the nomination for lieutenant governor. The loss of the millionaire's expected financial support dimmed hopes for success. Moreover, the refusal of Flower, a political perennial, to run for the second highest state office was a black eye to the rest of the ticket.

The state committee was hastily called together to fill the vacant spot with some prominent Democrat. With an eye to the soldier vote and as a counter to General Carr, the Republican nominee for lieutenant governor, campaign chairman Alton B. Parker hurried to Brooklyn to feel out General Slocum. Slocum's response was biting: "The idea

that I, who was once second in command under General
Grant, in the Union army, should play second fiddle to
David B. Hill, is preposterous." Warned that a nomination
of the General would bring "a letter of declination that
will make their hair stand on end," [53] the state committee
quickly dropped the idea. Prodded by Hill, the committee
then selected General Edward F. Jones of Binghamton, a
Colonel in the Civil War and now a wealthy manufacturer
of scales, to fill out the ticket.

At the outset, Hill's prospects for financing his campaign
were anything but rosy. One of his chief problems was the
aloofness of Thompson and his County Democracy. Although they insisted that their failure to make Hill's nomination unanimous was merely "an oversight," [54] and though
they now pledged to support Hill fully, there was little
question that the County Democrats were sulking. Their
organization had been a major source of funds in previous
years, but during this campaign only token contributions
were forthcoming. The tightening of the County Democracy's purse strings and the virtual sealing of Flower's
"barrel" now left the party coffers in a depleted state.
Faced with a shortage of funds, the state committee resorted
to loans. Paradoxically, the money borrowed to help win
the election of 1885 was to bring Hill's career nearly to
ruin three years later.[55]

The coolness of the County Democracy led to other
headaches. A number of municipal posts as well as state
offices were to be filled in the November elections, and the
County Democracy, still smarting from its defeat at Saratoga, saw in these contests an opportunity to regain prestige. If it could elect its own candidates in a contest with
Tammany, the organization could continue to rule the
party roost in New York City. Hill, on the other hand,
was anxious to avoid an intra-party struggle, and urged the

several metropolitan factions to arrange a harmony ticket
which all could support. The Governor probably feared a
Republican victory over a divided New York City Democracy far less than he did the likelihood of "trades" in such
a factional struggle, for he realized that he was expendable
to each organization.

Hill made strenuous efforts to effect a united front, but
the County Democracy would have none of it. His hurried
trips to New York in early October, his dinners with
Thompson and Cooper, his own pleadings and those of
Parker, availed him nothing. The County Democracy remained adamant in its determination to run its own slate,
because "the life of the organization is involved." Parker
salvaged what he could from the situation by pointing out
to Thompson and several other leaders that if their defection caused the defeat of Hill, their organization might
expect to get the same treatment that Tammany had
received after knifing the ticket in 1879. Parker came away
from this meeting convinced "that they dare not do anything less than fight for their lives for the ticket." [56]

Hill's troubles did not begin and end with the County
Democracy. Many reform Democrats and Independents who
had supported Cleveland announced their opposition to the
Governor. The Committee of One Hundred of Brooklyn
declared that those who supported reform and Cleveland
"should refuse to vote for David B. Hill." The national
committee which led the campaign for the Independents
in 1884 also called on its followers to defeat Hill.[57] Similar
sentiments were voiced in many reform journals. The
Nation worked itself up to a fever pitch in denouncing
David Hill as the "chosen captain" of the machine politicians who were not only the enemies of good government
but "of civilization itself, the apostles of disorder, corruption, and violence. . . ." [58]

Hill's anti-reform followers did little to dispel the assertion that a vote for Hill was a vote against Cleveland.
Thomas Grady, a Tammany bigwig and bitter foe of Cleveland, congratulated Hill on his fight for the Democratic
"faith," and sneered that "recent converts can find accom-
odations [sic] in the rear pews." More direct was Mark
"Brick" Pomeroy, the editor of a small pro-Hill newspaper
in New York City, who advertised his sheet with handbills
reading "KICK OUT CIVIL SERVICE—ALWAYS READ-
ABLE—POMEROY'S DEMOCRAT." [59]

President Cleveland did little to aid the Democratic campaign in New York. Hill was privately assured that all in
Washington "are anxious for our ticket," but Cleveland's
reluctance to speak out publicly for Hill encouraged the
belief, already fostered by the independent press, that the
President hoped for Hill's defeat. The most Cleveland could
be persuaded to do was to authorize a general statement of
his desire for the party's success in New York.[60]

This was in line, of course, with Cleveland's determination not to interfere with local elections. While not enthusiastic about Hill, he undoubtedly wished to see him
elected rather than Davenport, for a Republican victory
in his own state would weaken the President's prestige.
Cleveland did contribute $1,000 to Hill's campaign, and
expressed the belief that he was doing all he legitimately
could to help.[61] To the public, the press, and the Democrats,
however, that did not seem like very much.

What threatened to blast Hill's hopes more than anything
else were the widely circulated charges of wrongdoing in
his earlier private and public career. From the first days of
the campaign to the last, the anti-Hill press carried allegations of corruption in the Governor's past. One of the
earliest assertions was that Hill had purchased votes in the
old Third Ward of Elmira, a charge which, according to

one paper, could be proven "to the satisfaction of any reasonable mind." The *New York Times* pictured Hill as a "standard bearer with a banner in one hand inscribed 'Reform Democracy' and in the other a wad of greenbacks for the depraved voter." [62] Although the accusation of vote-buying was a grave one, it was difficult of substantiation, and as such might be dismissed by many as a mudslinging tactic.

More serious were charges that Hill had instigated and participated in allegedly fraudulent canal claims. In 1869 Hill and his partner Gabriel Smith had been attorneys for several Chemung County residents in a damage suit against the state charging negligence in canal floods some twelve years earlier. The cases were duly heard and awards totaling $61,000 were made, of which the attorneys received about one-third in fees. In a senate investigation of canal claims in 1875, these cases were dug up and reviewed. This investigation revealed that Hill and Smith had suggested to the farmers that they might collect substantial amounts for the damage caused by the floods of a dozen years before; that the lawyers had instituted proceedings and handled all arrangements in return for one-third of the awards; that the state had not been adequately represented by an attorney; and that no witnesses had even been called by the state.[63]

From the testimony taken by the senate committee, it would appear that while his solicitation of business may have been a breach of professional ethics, Hill had otherwise merely performed the usual duties of an attorney. He had prepared the best possible case for his clients, and the state, not Hill, had been at fault for failing to challenge any questionable claims properly.[64] Nonetheless, the fact that Hill had been involved in an investigation of alleged canal frauds was enough for some newspapers. The

New York Tribune ran carefully selected columns of the testimony to support its charges that Hill had milked the state with bogus damage claims. Other papers followed suit.[65] These charges dogged Hill for the duration of the campaign.

The most damaging revelations of all were those linking Hill with Boss Tweed in the ownership of the *Elmira Gazette*. In the summer of 1870 Hill and several other Elmirans had purchased a half-interest in the Gazette Company. The other half, amounting to $10,000 worth of stock, was sold secretly to William Marcy Tweed. About a year later, Tweed sold these shares back to Hill and his associates at fifty cents on the dollar. During their year of financial partnership, Hill and Tweed both sat in the state legislature, and the resale of the stock to Hill at a $5,000 profit, so the charges ran, constituted Hill's reward for doing Tweed's bidding in Albany.[66]

That Hill was merely Tweed's tool in the legislature is doubtful. Neither his election to the assembly, nor for that matter even his nomination as the Democratic candidate for the assembly seat, had occurred at the time the original purchase was made. Given his partisan philosophy, it is more than likely that when Hill supported Tweed-sponsored bills, he was doing so chiefly from a desire to hew to the party line. Moreover, the Tweed Ring was not exposed until the fall of 1871, and until that time support of the Tammany chieftain was not wholly unrespectable. The *Times* itself, which later exposed Tweed, had hailed his new city charter, one of the most corrupt pieces of jobbery ever enacted, as a "reform charter." [67]

Still, Hill had been associated with Tweed in the newspaper venture, and the revelations of this association with one of the most unsavory characters of nineteenth-century America threatened to smash all hopes for election. Hill's plight was pointed up by the incomparable Thomas Nast in a cartoon depicting Hill trying to jam shut the door of a closet, inside which was Tweed's skeleton.[68]

Hill fought back desperately. An affidavit was hastily procured from Horton Tidd, one of the participants in the 1870 purchase of the *Gazette*, describing the entire transaction as an "open, straightforward business matter, without concealment or wrong of any kind." William L. Muller immediately went to the offices of the important Democratic newspapers in New York to see that they prominently displayed the affidavit in their columns.[69] The Democratic State Committee issued a statement explaining that Tweed's resale of stock at half the original price was quite legitimate; that Tweed had tried to unload the *Gazette* stock on other Elmirans but that none were interested; and that as a result he sold to Hill, who offered him the best price.[70] Explanations, however, seldom catch up with allegations, and there can be little doubt that the Tweed story was a severe blow to Hill's campaign.

Hill's reaction to these charges of fraud and corruption was to ignore them. There was nothing to be gained by personally issuing public denials and explanations for past actions; his friends could do that. Instead, he attempted to offset whatever damage had been done by devoting his time and talent to more positive work. Throughout the winter and spring he had cultivated the friendship of several large voting blocs. Now he set out to reap his November harvest.

Great effort was expended in gathering in the support of the Irish. Democratic campaign literature stressed Hill's friendship to the naturalized citizen. The portions of his January message dealing with naturalized citizens and the registration laws concerning them were contrasted with the "vexatious" enactments of the Republicans. The Irish were

also reminded of Hill's advocacy of the freedom of worship
bill, and of his sympathy with the Irish Nationalists in the
United Kingdom.[71] These reminders of friendship for the
adopted citizen were not lost on the Irish. The *Irish American* endorsed the Governor, and the *Irish World,* which
for a year had been urging its readers to vote Republican,
now did an about-face and supported Hill.[72]

Labor, too, came to Hill's support. The Political Branch
of the State Trades' Assembly had sent out questionnaires
to both Hill and Davenport asking their position on a
number of measures affecting labor. Davenport hedged on
most of the issues. Hill by contrast adopted a pro-labor
stand on all of them. These replies were published in a
broadside, which urged labor to support the Governor.
Hill's record as a friend of labor was given wide circulation
in campaign literature.[73]

Aware that an appeal to the working class might alienate
some, Hill took great pains to balance his labor following
with endorsements from the business community. Wide
publicity was given to an editorial from the nonpolitical
Journal of Commerce which commended Hill's administration and saw "no good reason why he should not be re-
elected." A document signed by over a thousand prominent
New York businessmen in September urging Hill's nomination also was pressed into service as a campaign document.[74]

Hill used to good advantage another group that was
rapidly becoming an important, if unwilling, ally of the
Democratic party. The Prohibition party had been growing
in strength in New York, and in both 1882 and 1884 had
polled some 25,000 votes. Most of these votes were drawn
from the strong temperance wing of the Republican party,
especially from the rural areas. While a vote for the Prohibition candidate was not a vote for Hill, it was one vote
less for Davenport.

The Democrats expended great amounts of effort and money to increase the vote of the Prohibitionists. Brass bands and special excursion trains for Prohibition rallies were made possible through the generosity of the Democratic State Committee. The Democrats worked both sides of the street. From the "whiskey headquarters" of the Democrats in New York City's Westminster Hotel went literature to proliquor people, playing up the temperance or prohibition records of some Republican candidates. At the same time, the main Democratic headquarters in the Hoffman House mailed out temperance literature to rural Republicans.[75]

Davenport's association with a wine company several years back was also publicized in the attempt to discredit him in prohibitionist eyes. Although Davenport had served as an officer in the company only as an administrator of a friend's estate, and although he himself was a temperance man, the Democratic press gleefully seized the opportunity to make political capital. Typical of attempts to exploit this weak point in the Republican candidate's moral armor was a bogus conversation between Carr and Davenport printed in the *Sun:*

> Mr. Carr: Er—Mr. Davenport, are you related in any way to the celebrated Davenport Brothers whose spiritualistic seances a few years ago created such excitement?
> Mr. Davenport: Certainly not.
> Mr. Carr: Thanks. I didn't know but what there might be some relationship. The similarity of your businesses—dealing in spirits—prompted the question. How are you feeling today, Mr. Davenport? [76]

There were few major speeches by either of the candidates during the campaign, but the few times that Hill did speak he scored heavily. Although not a brilliant orator, he presented the issues precisely and skillfully, and delighted his partisan audiences with his biting attacks upon the enemy. It was in the course of one such attack that Hill hit upon the simple yet proud declaration, "I am a Democrat," the slogan with which he was to be identified throughout his political career. It was a peculiarly fortunate phrase, for it meant all things to all Democrats. To some it was simply an affirmation of faith, linking the Governor to the glorious traditions of Jefferson and Jackson; to others it meant steadfast opposition to the Republican party and every distasteful position or issue associated with it. Still others interpreted it either as a slap at the Johnny-come-lately President and his Mugwump friends, or as an endorsement of the spoils system.

The election results attested to the skill and political judgment of Hill. Although betting men in New York were quoting seven-to-ten odds on Davenport's election,[77] Hill and the entire Democratic slate were victorious. Hill's plurality, although only 11,134 out of a total of over one million votes cast, was 10,000 better than Cleveland's margin in 1884. The Prohibition party, in drawing over 30,000 votes, contributed materially to Hill's victory.

The small plurality led to many post-mortems on the Republican defeat. Among the many causes assigned were apathy, overconfidence, mismanagement, and the introduction of the "bloody shirt." [78] Most contemporaries seem to have missed the mark by laying the blame at the Republicans' doorstep. Had they been more perceptive, they would have given Hill credit for an astute campaign. It required considerable political skill to conduct a successful campaign in the face of damaging charges, as Hill had done. He had been throughout a master.

The election of 1885 was a turning point for Hill. The

revelations of his early career had been so thoroughly exploited that a defeat now would consign him to political oblivion. For other defeated candidates there might be a second chance; for Hill there could be none. But none was needed; for Hill had won, and the way had been cleared for even greater political triumphs.

CHAPTER III

Principles and Politics

DAVID BENNETT HILL's triumph in the 1885 election marked the beginning of a new phase of his political career. Until this achievement his prestige as a chief executive had been limited by the fact that he was a back-door governor. With the victory of 1885, Hill emerged as governor in his own right, entitled to enjoy a power and stature fully commensurate with his high position.

Prestige alone, however, does not win battles, and Hill's term of office promised to be filled with battles. Although the entire Democratic state ticket had been elected, the Republicans maintained firm control of the outrageously gerrymandered legislature. The natural hostility between a highly partisan governor and an equally partisan legislature of different political allegiance made the transaction of state business difficult. At times it manifested itself in a ludicrous and shameful tug-of-war.

These battles between Hill and the legislature were not always motivated by intrigue and petty partisanship, however. Quite often they occurred because of Hill's insistence on maintaining certain principles of legislation which he deemed essential to sound government. While he was not above using these avowed principles as an excuse for disapproving distasteful legislation, on the whole Hill consistently supported them, and his governorship soon became identified with them.

One of these principles which immediately became evident grew from Hill's aversion, as a lawyer, to defective legislation. All too often, the lawmakers would rush through a poorly drawn measure containing vague, ambiguous, or contradictory provisions. Hill was determined to keep such legislation off the statute books. If a defective bill came to his desk while the legislature was still in session, the Governor would send for its author, point out its defects, and have it recalled for correction. If, on the other hand, the bill came to him after adjournment, he would refuse to approve it, no matter how laudable its purpose. Hill's fetish of keeping the books unmarred by slipshod legislation led him more than once to recommend the creation of a commission of legal experts to help frame bills properly. The legislators, however, consistently ignored the suggestion.[1]

Hill also took a keen interest in checking what he termed "special legislation." The legislature had in recent years succumbed with increasing frequency to the requests of certain interests and localities for special laws relating to these groups alone. There was nothing sinister or underhanded about this practice, for these acts usually dealt with such matters as granting a group authority to incorporate, or authorizing a town to build a new public building. Hill's objection to such legislation did not concern its purpose, which frequently commanded his sympathy, but its character. Many of these measures were unnecessary since the authority granted in these acts could be derived from enabling legislation within existing statutes. Hill repeatedly returned such bills to the legislature with a reference to the statute from which the desired power could be derived.[2]

Another type of special legislation which Hill opposed was the enactment of bills for specific groups or interests, public or private, made in the absence of a general statute. Hill's position was simple and sound: if the purposes of the bill were not legitimate, they should not be enacted; if they had merit, then they should be incorporated, not in a special law for one specific interest, but in a general statute from which authority to achieve the objectives could be derived by other interests as well.[3]

Governor Hill cautioned the lawmakers in a special message in 1887 that the amount of special legislation had increased at a disturbing rate over the previous five years. These special acts cluttered up the statute books with unnecessary laws and occupied time which the legislators might otherwise have devoted to the consideration of more important matters. To obviate this special legislation, Hill urged the enactment of more general laws, and recommended the establishment of a commission to help in the task of drafting them.[4]

This suggestion was not acted upon, and the legislature continued to pass special bills. Hill did not budge an inch, and he just as regularly rejected these bills. In the end, it was Hill who won. Toward the end of his term the legislature, tired of encountering rebuffs, began to enact more general laws.[5]

Hill took a firm stand on still another legislative principle, that of home rule for cities. During his administration this issue was related chiefly to the management—or mismanagement—of New York City. Debate over home rule was not new. The problem stemmed from the original relationship of the city to the state. Since cities were the creatures of the state legislature which granted them charters, all power to govern them derived from that body. That power might be delegated or retained by the legislature in any degree. Proponents of complete home rule claimed that as a matter of right, laws relating specifically to, and affecting only, a given city should be made by local officials; and that rule of a city by a remote legislature made for irresponsible, inefficient, and, not infrequently, dishonest government. Opponents of home rule, on the other hand, could quickly point to Boss Tweed, Oakey Hall, and Fernando Wood as examples of similar irresponsibility and corruption by local officials.

As long as those who ruled were men and not angels, neither system—rule by legislature or home rule—could absolutely ensure pure government. Each could be perverted by mean and corrupt schemers. Yet it was equally true that one system was sounder in fundamental democratic principle than the other.

To Hill, the answer—insofar as there was one—lay in greater home rule for cities. Throughout his governorship he admonished the legislature to respect the principle of home rule. "All matters of discretion, . . ." he insisted, "taxes, . . . public improvements, . . . selection of officials, . . . and all other questions of purely local cognizance should . . . be remitted to the local authorities for their sole action. . . ." [6] Hill urged a sweeping revision of New York's charter to grant the mayor greater powers, and recommended further that New York's municipal elections be divorced from the state and national contests so that only local issues would be factors in its elections. [7]

The legislature grudgingly met Hill halfway on his recommendations. While refusing to grant a charter revision, it did pass a spring elections bill for New York City. The bill provided also for a two-year term for both the mayor and the president of the board of aldermen. The board itself was to be composed of fourteen aldermen with four-year terms, half of whom would be up for election every two years.

This much was satisfactory to Hill. But Republicans, in an attempt to shake the Democratic hold on the city's government, tied to the bill a provision for cumulative voting. According to this plan the candidates for the seven aldermanic seats would run on a citywide ticket rather than from individual districts. Each voter could cast as many votes as there were seats to be filled. These seven votes might all be cast for one man, or they might be divided in any manner the voter wished. In this way, the Republicans hoped to secure larger representation on the board by concentrating their votes on a few of their candidates. In its effect the system would approximate proportional representation.[8]

The bill as it stood was unacceptable to Hill. If enacted it would have loosened his party's grip on New York's governmental machinery. Although he wanted a spring elections bill as much as before, the price the Republicans demanded was too steep. Hill vetoed the measure.[9]

Despite this action, Governor Hill upheld the principle of home rule fairly consistently. If a bill "directed" rather than "authorized" a local official to perform a duty purely local, he vetoed the measure, no matter how laudable its purpose. When a bill which concerned the interests of a local area came before him, he consulted the appropriate local authorities.[10] But despite Hill's efforts on behalf of home rule, no substantial relief from the legislature's interference was to be secured for cities until the constitutional revision of 1894.

Hill also took the initiative in bringing about some minor reforms. As a lawyer he was disturbed by the cumbersome machinery of appeals in first degree murder cases,

and brought about a change to expedite these cases. He
was also instrumental in having enacted a statute for preventing the adulteration of food, which, while not affording
complete protection, was a vast improvement over the
earlier chaos. In addition, Hill made a number of recommendations, all eventually adopted, for the abolition of
vestigial state boards and offices, for canal improvements,
and for the reform of a taxation system which overbur-
dened real estate. The Governor demonstrated an intel-
ligent concern with the problems of his age in his request
for laws preventing stock-watering by corporations, establishing a state commission with supervisory powers over
the gas companies, and reforming municipal governments.
His reputation as a jealous guardian of the state's treasury
was also amply justified by his actions.[11]

But the true business of a politician is, after all, politics;
and David Bennett Hill was above all else a politician.
While he was concerned with the problems of governing,
he was more concerned with the political strategy and
maneuvering which perpetuated party—and personal—
supremacy. Not infrequently the two interests could be
harmoniously reconciled with no sacrifice of one to the
other. When the two conflicted, however, the former concern was made subordinate to the latter.

One of the major factors involved in maintaining such
supremacy was the patronage, and much of Hill's efforts
were involved in a struggle for control of it with the hostile
Republican legislature. Hill's position was aptly summed
up in his slogan, "I am a Democrat." Of the many thousands of state jobs, less than four thousand came under
the civil service laws,[12] and Hill made it abundantly clear
that most of the others would go to deserving Democrats.
"I do not think," he remarked wryly in a postelection interview, "it is necessary for the Democratic party to ask

the advice and consent of the Republicans in making removals from office. . . ." [13]

Republican reaction was immediate and predictable. For twenty-four years they had controlled the federal patronage, and during much of that period the state patronage as well. Now within the space of ten months, control of both had been lost. Fearful of the onslaught upon their entrenched positions, the Republicans took steps to defend what jobs they held.

The weapon relied upon was the confirming power of the senate. By withholding senate approval of a Hill nominee, the Republicans hoped to bludgeon the Governor into turning over a share of the state patronage. Moreover, refusal to confirm a new Democratic appointee allowed the Republican incumbent to remain in office, even though his term had expired. Thus Republicans could be frozen in their jobs by a sympathetic legislature.

Frequent use of this device spurred Hill to countermeasures. At one point he advocated stripping the senate of its power of confirmation.[14] This was probably as much a political maneuver as a reflection of frustration, however. By pointing up the fact that the legislature was abusing its constitutional privileges, Hill hoped to lay the blame for the failure to fill expired terms at the Republican's doorstep.

Hill also turned the nominating process to political advantage whenever it became clear that the senate planned to keep in office an incumbent of questionable honesty or competence. The clever Elmiran would nominate for the position an eminent public figure of acknowledged ability to replace the entrenched machine politician. The contrast between the rectitude of the Governor in his nominee and the devious course of the legislature in keeping in office a misfit was invariably favorable to the Governor.

This technique was used to greatest advantage in Hill's struggle to oust Thomas C. Platt, the Republican state boss, from his post as quarantine commissioner. The quarantine commission was composed of three members, who, with the health officer of the Port of New York, were charged with the duty of preventing diseased cargoes from entering the state. All three commissioners were Republicans who had remained in office—although their terms had expired in 1883—through the senate's refusal to confirm the nominees of a Democratic executive. Membership on the commission was a valuable plum for, although each commissioner received only a small salary, his income was handsomely augmented by the fees exacted for the performance of duties. These fees netted the health officer alone, by his own admission, some $27,000 a year, after expenses. The commissioners also had a financial interest in the disinfecting company at the port, and by forcing all rag importers to disinfect their cargoes before unloading, they added still more to their income. Even after all this had been revealed in testimony to a senate committee, the senate refused either to displace the commissioners or correct the abuses.[15]

Such an opportunity to make political capital was made to order for Hill. Early in 1886 he nominated two eminent Republicans and two equally competent Democrats to replace the commissioners and the health officer. When, as Hill had expected, the senate "hung up" the nominations for two months, the Governor rebuked that body for its dereliction of constitutional duties in refusing either to reject or confirm the appointees.[16]

The reason why the senate had taken no action was obvious. Tom Platt controlled a large number of Republican senators, and it was hardly likely that he would permit them to acquiesce in his own removal from this lucrative

post. Realizing this, Hill had put the Republicans further
in a hole by making his nominees as unexceptionable as
possible.

The year passed with no further action taken, but after
a private court suit in 1887 produced evidence of mal-
administration by the health officer,[17] Hill once more
launched a righteous attack on the Quarantine Ring. Again,
he nominated four able men, this time including Colonel
Fred Grant, son of the recently deceased President. Again,
the legislature ignored the nominations, and the Governor
withdrew them.

Newspaper opinion was on Hill's side in this dispute,
and as pressure to displace the Quarantine Ring mounted,
Boss Platt made one of his rare strategic errors. Aware
that Hill was piling up political points, Platt attempted
to outmaneuver him by calling his bluff. In a dramatic
open letter to Hill, the Easy Boss graciously offered to
resign his post, if the Governor would make a "deal" and
renominate Fred Grant. The letter was a blunder, for it
gave Hill still another opportunity to assume a role of
uprightness. "I must decline," stated the Governor indig-
nantly in his public reply, "to give any 'assurance' or en-
gage in any 'dicker' in reference to this or any other office."
The position was an absolutely correct one, and the press
applauded the Governor.[18]

Hill was winning the battle of words, but he was unable
to budge the senate. It was clear that some other way would
have to be found to oust Platt. During the summer of
1887 Hill watched and waited patiently for Platt to make
a mistake; then, catlike, he pounced. In late July the Republican boss rigged the county convention in his native
Tioga and had himself selected as a delegate to the Republican state convention in the fall. Hill and his attorney
general immediately trotted out the law establishing the

quarantine commission, and pointed to the requirement
that the commissioners must reside in metropolitan New
York. Platt, they said, could not reside in both Tioga and
New York. Since he himself seemed to have fixed his resi-
dence through his selection as a Tioga County delegate,
proceedings were instituted to remove Platt on the resi-
dence requirement.[19] Pressure for Platt's ouster was increased by further shocking revelations of dereliction of
duty.[20]

Platt fought back vigorously, but Hill won, and the Easy
Boss was forced out. Incidentally or otherwise, the people
of New York shared the fruits of Hill's victory, for with
Platt's removal, the quarantine commission was reorganized, its duties redefined, its efficiency increased, and its
corruption eliminated.[21]

While Hill made opportune use of the nominating power
to turn the legislature's hostility to political gain, he used
other devices as well. One was the repeated demand for
measures which he well knew Republicans would not pass,
a device he had used to advantage previously as mayor of
Elmira and as interim governor. It was not important that
he could not wring a freedom of worship bill or a simple
enumeration law from the legislature. The simple act
of yearly demanding their passage gained him as much
support from the interested groups as actual enactment
would.[22]

In this game of peanut politics there seemed, at times,
almost a public-be-damned attitude to which both the
legislature and the Governor contributed. On the census
question, it mattered not that enumeration of the state's
inhabitants was due in 1885; neither side would defer
to the wishes of the other as to what information should
be collected and by whom, and the census, although constitutionally required, was not conducted.

An even more flagrant abuse of public trust followed the overwhelming vote of the electorate in 1886 in favor of holding a convention to revise the state constitution. Despite this mandate, the Democratic executive and the Republican legislature deadlocked over the method of selecting delegates. Each desired to gain for its party the dominant position in such a convention. The Democratic plan, though hardly unpartisan in motive, had at least some degree of fairness and equity to commend it over the transparent Republican scheme. Nonetheless the Republican majority pushed through its measure, one of them declaring that he would sooner give control of the convention to the condemned Chicago anarchists than to the Democratic party. Hill, of course, vetoed the bill, and there the matter rested, with the public will frustrated once more.[23]

Struggling with the opposition for control of the patronage; squeezing advantage out of nominations which would never be confirmed; enticing support by championing measures which would never be enacted—all of these had a role to play in Hill's quest for party and personal supremacy. But more important than any of these in achieving this goal was Hill's astute handling of two major issues which arose during his first term as governor. These issues were liquor and labor.

Each of these issues assumed a magnified importance in 1886 and 1887 because of the presence of two new political parties, Prohibition and Labor. The one posed a serious threat to the Republican party; the other, to the Democrats. Both of the major parties maneuvered feverishly to prevent large losses to these splinter groups.

To Hill, the rise of these new parties presented both an opportunity and a challenge. His role was to preserve, in so far as it was in his power to do so, an atmosphere in which the Prohibition party, steadily sapping Republican strength, could continue to grow. At the same time he would have to parry the Labor party's threat to Democratic voting strength by undercutting its appeal to the Democratic workingman.

The Prohibition party had grown rapidly in the Empire State. Able to draw only 1,517 voters to its banners in 1880, the party within five years had attracted enough supporters to affect decisively both a presidential and a gubernatorial election.[24]

Voting support for the Prohibition party came chiefly from upstate rural Republican strongholds, and thus it posed a grave threat to the Republican party. In an attempt to hold the allegiance of rural temperates, the New York Republican party in the 1880's adopted a position of relatively rigid restriction of the liquor traffic. But its failure to enact a law in consonance with its platform professions cost the party dearly, for impatient temperance Republicans abandoned their old ties and enlisted in the new crusade. After the Prohibition candidate for governor in 1882 polled over 25,000 votes, frightened Republicans attempted to take the liquor question out of politics. They pledged to submit to the voters a constitutional amendment dealing with the liquor traffic. They reneged, however, and the exodus from the party continued. By 1885, over 30,000 New Yorkers were voting the Prohibition ticket.[25]

Democrats, of course, were not disposed to come to the rescue by neutralizing the issue. Theodore Roosevelt was not far from the mark when he disgustedly implied that the Prohibition party was the Democrats' strongest ally.[26] Democratic delight with their opposition's plight was unmasked. Moreover, a great part of Democratic support came from immigrant stock to whom drink was part of a national custom. Party leaders had no desire to antagonize this large voting bloc.

Spurred by the desire to halt the increasing defections which had already cost them a presidency and a governorship, the Republican party finally resolved to grapple with the problem of regulating the liquor traffic. Early in the 1887 session Assemblyman Howard Crosby introduced an excise bill which, in its final form, raised to $1,000 the license fees for all places in New York City and Brooklyn selling distilled spirits and any other kind of alcoholic beverage to be drunk on the premises. The license fee for selling wine and beer only was set at $100. To prevent dealers from selling liquor surreptitiously while paying only for the beer and wine license, a provision was added making even the possession of liquor on the premises of a beer and wine licensee a misdemeanor. The bill applied only to New York and Brooklyn.[27]

The aim of this bill, other than the clearly political one of keeping Republican ranks intact, was to reduce the number of saloons by raising their operating costs, thereby reducing the amount of liquor consumed. Opposition to the bill produced strange bedfellows: prohibitionists and liquor dealers. The fact that the measure permitted any drink at all was enough for the prohibitionists, who insisted that "no evil can be exterminated by selling it the right to exist." [28] Liquor dealers opposed the bill for precisely opposite reasons. A dealers' association sent out circulars calling for recruits in the battle against the Crosby bill. The circular offered Hill electoral support in exchange for a veto. "We have one friend left, and this is H. D. [sic] Hill, the Governor of our State. We must show him that if he is our friend, we will carry the banner with him next elec-

tion." [29] Protest meetings were also held throughout the
bill's progress by German and Irish groups in New York
City.[30]

The events of the same week left little doubt as to Hill's
action on the bill. The day before the Crosby bill passed
the senate, Hill vetoed a measure which would have prohibited the sale of intoxicating liquors within half a mile
of a certain mental home on the grounds that the bill
constituted "special legislation." "The excise laws should
be substantially uniform in all parts of the State," asserted
the Governor, "and special laws should not be passed dis-
criminating for or against particular localities." [31] Hill
seemed to be whetting his knife for the Crosby bill, which
increased the license rates for New York and Brooklyn
only. On the following day, Hill sent a special message to
the lawmakers professing concern about the increasing
amount of special legislation on the law books.[32]

It was a surprise to no one, then, when Hill vetoed the
Crosby high license bill. As expected, the burden of the
veto rested on the assertion that the bill was special legislation, applying only to Brooklyn and New York.[33] "If the
measure be a benefit," the Governor commented wryly,
"New York and Brooklyn should not monopolize its advantages." The singling out of the two downstate cities was
especially unfair, Hill continued, since each ranked in the
lowest quarter of the state's cities on the basis of drinking
establishments per capita. Boldly extending the comparison
to thirty-three upstate villages—supposedly the dry areas—
Hill noted that New York had fewer establishments per
capita than nearly half, while Brooklyn had the fewest
of all. In their commendable desire to relieve Brooklyn
and New York from the evils of drink, Hill remarked with
drollery, the rural Republican legislators "must have overlooked the greater danger at their own homes, and will

appreciate the opportunity now afforded for further and more careful consideration of the subject."

While Hill pledged his "earnest and sincere co-operation" to further any impartially framed measure aimed at checking intemperance, he cautioned that "temperance, like other virtues, is not produced by law-makers, but by the influence of education, morality, and religion."

The Republicans were furious, and angry words flew across the floor of the legislature; but they could not override the veto. Another excise measure, the Vedder bill, was introduced and pushed through the legislature. This bill would levy a state tax on liquor licenses. The unfair and unsound provisions in this bill, however, were so numerous that Hill merely toyed with it in his veto message.[34] The year ended with neither a change in the excise laws, nor a halt in the defection of temperates from Republican ranks.

The real challenge to Hill's skill, however—and perhaps even to his political career—lay in the sudden rise of the Labor party. On the excise issue, Hill's role was a relatively passive one, merely turning back Republican attempts to solve their dilemma, and keeping them in a disadvantageous position. With the appearance of a Labor party, Hill was faced with a much more difficult task, one of trying to stunt this party's growth by successfully competing with it for the vote of the laboring man.

The Labor party had risen abruptly in New York in 1886. In Henry George, author of *Progress and Poverty* and prophet of a new social order, many poor and oppressed had found an idol. When a labor committee in New York City offered him its nomination for mayor in 1886, George accepted and drew a remarkable 68,000 votes. Although the crusty steelmaker Abram S. Hewitt won the election with 90,000 votes, George ran a respectable second, almost

8,000 votes better than the Republican candidate, young
Theodore Roosevelt.

Politicians differed as to the significance of the vote.
Some thought it heralded the arrival of a new political
party. Others, like Roosevelt, believed that it did not mean
a new party, but merely "a new element to be bid for by
the old parties." [35]

The strong showing of George was a subject of grave
concern to Hill. He had devoted great effort to the cultivation of the labor vote, and its support had been more
than an incidental factor in his 1885 victory. He had hoped
to bind labor firmly to him after this triumph for all
future contests. The sudden rise of the Labor party behind
the radical single-taxer threatened not only to upset Hill's
plans by siphoning off his labor support, but also to damage seriously the Democratic party in state and nation. In
order to prevent this loss, the Governor struck out on a
course calculated to undercut the new party's appeal to
the workingman.

This course was not wholly politically inspired, for Hill
was sympathetic to the cause of labor, and he was sincerely
interested in its welfare. It was fortunate, then, that a
political objective could now be subserved by this friendship for labor. Nor did this course require a sudden shift
in direction, for Hill had already been at work cementing
this friendship with labor, and his relations with state
labor leaders were extremely cordial.

Moreover, Hill had already demonstrated a concern for
labor's problems during his first two years in office. He
had urged in his message to the 1886 legislature that
"facilities . . . be afforded for the organization of labor,"
just as the law afforded industry an opportunity to
incorporate and combine, through the enactment of "a
general law specially providing for the incorporation of

trade unions." He had also advocated the abolition of
child labor, and insisted that the employment of minors
should be strictly regulated. Too, he had recommended
that wage disputes be submitted to arbitration, for
"properly understood, there is no conflict between capital
and labor." [36]

Some of these recommendations had been enacted into
law in the legislative session which followed. While the
Governor's suggestion of a law to facilitate unionization
was ignored, an act was passed prohibiting the employment of children under thirteen years of age in manufacturing establishments, and limiting the hours of employment
in such enterprises for women under twenty-one and
minors under eighteen to sixty hours in any one week.
To enforce the provisions of this act, the Governor was
authorized to appoint a factory inspector and an assistant.[37]

At the same time an arbitration measure was also
enacted. Based on the principle of voluntary submission,
this act provided for local boards of arbitrators to hear and
resolve disputes between employers and employees. It
also created a three-man board of arbitration, to which
appeals from the decision of the local boards might be
taken.[38]

In his appointments, too, Hill had demonstrated his
friendship for labor. One of his three appointees for the
board of arbitration was the secretary of the State Trades
Assembly's political branch, and his appointment of James
Connolly and John Franey, both labor leaders, as factory
inspectors were "labor appointment[s], pure and simple." [39]

When the size of the defection to Henry George became
clear in the November election returns, Hill redoubled his
efforts to keep labor within the fold. Whereas little more
than a page was devoted to labor's interests in his annual
message in 1885, and less than three pages in 1886, fully

one-third of the thirty-page message in January following
the George uprising concerned labor directly.[40] Expressing
concern over the "growing discontent among the industrial
classes . . . especially in our large cities," Hill urged that
measures be taken to alleviate the workingman's plight.
In an obvious swipe at the George single-taxers, Hill
expressed his belief that most workingmen recognized that
their true interest lay in the preservation of existing
institutions. Correction of labor's wrongs, he said, are
sought through modification, rather than "by violence,
anarchy, agrarianism, or communism, . . . nor do they
demand in their behalf any vague and incomprehensible
schemes of Utopian progress."

More specifically, Hill urged the adoption of a maximum
hours statute. If the legislature doubted the practicability
or enforcibility of such a law, Hill observed that the work
week could be shortened simply by declaring legal holi-
days. Every other Saturday or every Saturday afternoon,
he suggested, could be made a legal holiday, thus extending
to all businesses and occupations what was already the
custom in some. Moreover, Hill recommended that the
first Monday in September be set aside each year as a
legal holiday, designated "Labor Day," to be observed as
a day of "festivity and recreation, and devoted especially
to the interests of labor."

Hill also took a sympathetic position toward labor
unions and their methods. He recommended the elimination or modification of any sections of the Penal Code
which "by a fair or even a strained or harsh construction"
might permit to be construed as "conspiracies" any assemblage or combination of workingmen, strikes, boycotts,
or other action "illustrating the power of union. . . ."
Peripherally Hill recommended "a more generous recognition of [labor's] claim to public position."

The Governor urged that still more be done. Manual training, he suggested, should be introduced into the public schools to teach boys a trade. Pointing to the wretched living conditions of the workingmen in the state, he asked for "measures looking to the greater safety and better regulations of the tenement-houses in our large cities." Hill also asked for a bill extending the life of the state arbitration board. In case he had left any gaps, Hill made a catchall proposal that a special labor commission be established to examine the whole subject of labor grievances and to recommend measures for adoption.

A number of these recommendations became law, and other labor laws were amended during the 1887 legislative session. The state arbitration board was granted another three years to operate, and a tenement house bill was approved. The enforcement of the previous year's act regulating the employment of women and children was facilitated by a law permitting appointment of more deputy factory inspectors. The installation of safety devices in many factories was made mandatory by law. "Yellow dog" contracts, either written or verbal, were outlawed. The first Monday in September did become a legal holiday, known as Labor Day, and Saturday afternoon became a half-holiday for state offices and a number of businesses.[41]

These measures were not, of course, enacted by a Republican legislature through Hill's influence and power alone. While he was able to whip the Democrats into line, there was no pressure which Hill might exert on the Republicans to secure their votes. Pressure came from another source, however—the state's labor organizations. One organization in particular, the State Trades Assembly, was especially effective. Acting on the "reward or punish" philosophy later exploited by Gompers, the State Trades

Assembly exerted a substantial influence on many legislators in behalf of Hill's labor bills.[42]

Hill also courted labor favor by nominating laboring men to positions of public trust. The creation of more factory inspectorships enabled the appointment of additional officials from the workingmen's ranks. Others were nominated to long-established state posts.[43] The Republican legislators were placed in an awkward position by labor nominations. To confirm them would mark Hill as a friend of labor; to reject them would mark the Republicans as enemies of labor. The senators usually chose a third course, ignoring the nominations and eventually forcing their withdrawal.

One of these labor appointments followed a year-long wrangle with the legislature over confirmation. The term of one of the three railroad commissioners having expired in 1886, Hill nominated to fill the vacancy Michael Rickard, a Utica locomotive engineer and a leader in the Brotherhood of Locomotive Engineers. When the senate hung up the nomination, Hill withdrew it, and after a lengthy conference with a Knights of Labor leader, nominated one James A. Buckbee, a machine shop worker and a Knight. To fill a second vacancy on the commission, Hill sent the name of William A. Armstrong, the Master of the State Grange. These nominations were again ignored by the senate. After a few weeks, the Governor withdrew them in favor of two businessmen, who were confirmed.[44]

Before the confirmation, however, Republican senators tried to distract attention from their own failure to confirm laboring men by charging Hill with "peanut politics." They insisted that Hill had never wanted Buckbee and Armstrong confirmed, but was simply playing his old game of making nominations solely for political effect and then withdrawing them. Hill quickly took up the challenge. In a message to the senate, the Governor traced its course of inaction on his nominations, and announced that if the senate felt that Buckbee's and Armstrong's names had been withdrawn before it had had time to consider them, he would gladly submit them again. He did so, and the Republicans found themselves embarrassed. Having charged Hill with a desire for inaction, they could no longer follow their course of procrastination, but now had to go on record for or against the nominations. Following a caucus, they rejected the men on a party vote, then confirmed Hill's two businessmen appointees.[45] Hill had once more turned the senate's obstinacy to good advantage, managing to nominate two laboring men and one farmer for the vacancies in addition to the two men who were finally confirmed.

If there was any doubt that Hill actually would appoint a laboring man to a position of responsibility, it was dispelled when a resignation left another vacancy on the Railroad Commission in the fall. The senate was not in session, and Hill had the power to appoint without confirmation. For several weeks, Hill took no action. The Republican *Evening Journal* of Albany, mistaking the delay for weakness, thought to call Hill's bluff by challenging him to appoint a laboring man. Other Republican sheets took up the cry. When the clamor was at its loudest, Hill calmly announced the appointment of Rickard, the locomotive engineer, to fill the unexpired term. The mousetrapped newspapers tried to hide their embarrassment with criticisms of the appointment, but their fumbling attempts were pathetically inadequate.[46]

In a newspaper interview, Rickard proclaimed that his appointment was "a recognition of the workingmen of the State, coming from a sincere friend of their cause." He then added significantly that his appointment "will be a source of great satisfaction to the one hundred thousand railway men of the state who pressed me for the place." [47] Presumably, this thought was not a new one to Hill.

The final test of the effectiveness of Hill's efforts to thwart an independent labor party and at the same time to stimulate the Prohibition party's growth was provided in the 1887 elections. A full slate of state officers, headed by the secretary of state, were to be elected.

If Hill looked on with smugness in August as the Prohibition party entered its slate of nominees, his satisfaction with this event must have been offset by news from the labor camp. Henry George had decided to channel the enthusiasm shown for him in 1886 into the formation of a permanent labor party. In this undertaking he was aided by the remarkable Father McGlynn, an eloquent priest who could not content himself with an exclusively spiritual remedy for the widespread poverty he saw around him. With that high moral tone so often found in third-party movements, George proclaimed that this would be one political convention "from which professional politicians will be conspicuously absent, and in which there will be no struggle for the loaves and fishes." [48]

The convention, meeting in Syracuse on August 19, created the United Labor party, and selected a full ticket with George at its head. *Harper's Weekly* caught the ominous importance of this event for Hill and the Democratic party, "even if it [the Labor party] signify no more than a passing gust in the political atmosphere. A passing gust has been known to capsize a great many craft." [49] The Republican press did what it could to help along the Labor party, commending the whole ticket as "personally worthy and proper." [50]

Still another labor faction appeared in the field briefly when the Union Labor party, a newly formed group grow-

ing out of a February conclave in Cincinnati, convened in
Elmira on June 15. This infant party, still in its swaddling
clothes, was not very robust, and managed to sit up only with
outside help. Boss Platt was widely suspected of being a
"wet nurse" to the party in the hope of still further harassing
Hill.[51] The Union Labor party, however, failing in an
attempt to combine with George's United Labor, faded
away before election day.

While he had been unable to prevent a labor ticket from
entering the field, Hill had succeeded in binding to himself
one of the most important labor groups, the State Trades
Assembly. Meeting in Rochester, this politically inclined
yet nonpartisan labor group showed its gratitude to Hill
for his championing of its measures and appointments of its
members. They passed resolutions commending Hill, and denounced the George party for its recent censures of the
Governor.[52] Although the Republicans tried to pass off this
convention as "Hill's labor side show," [53] there was no
gainsaying the importance of its support.

During September the two major parties selected their
candidates and issues. The Republicans hoped to capitalize
on an honored name by nominating Fred Grant, the late
President's son, for secretary of state. Their platform artfully
dodged a clear stand on the liquor question, demanding only
"restriction by taxation in such localities as do not by their
option exclude absolutely the traffic." [54] "Restriction by
taxation" meant anything its reader wanted it to mean.
"High license" was nowhere to be found in the plank; for
as its author, Senator Evarts, explained: "We did not choose
to commit the convention to the word 'license,' to which
many sensible people object; nor to the phrase 'high,' which
means to many minds higher than it ought to be." [55] The
Crosby bill was not endorsed as such, but only "the purpose
of the Republican majority of the Legislature in passing

the bill. . . ." [56] In short, by straddling the issue the Republicans hoped to keep all their factions satisfied.

The Democrats, on the other hand, put in their bid for labor support by reminding the workingman of past legislation and declaring in favor of still further concessions to labor's interests, including a ten-hour day. The liquor plank, from which the Democrats had little to fear, favored a uniform revision of the excise laws, but opposed "all sumptuary laws grievously interfering with the personal liberties and reasonable habits and customs of any portion of our citizens." The candidates, while able men, were not especially distinguished. [57]

The campaign which followed was an active one. McGlynn and George toured the state expounding their theories, and Democratic and Republican orators each extolled the virtues of their respective candidates and parties. While most of his work was done behind the scenes, Hill made a number of public appearances during the campaign, attacking the confiscatory aspects of the George program on the one hand, and the "inconsistent, deceptive, and hypocritical" excise stand of the Republicans on the other. [58]

It was the excise question around which Hill centered his campaign, as he tried to drive the wedge between the Republicans and the Prohibitionists deeper. He reminded the voters that the Republicans had reneged on their promise to submit to the electorate a prohibition amendment, and were postponing it in an attempt to keep the prohibition vote for the presidential election. He also noted that the high license stand in the Crosby bill was directly contradictory to the Prohibition party's stand, since by taxing the traffic the Republicans tolerated it. [59]

While Hill was trying to draw off Republican votes from one end of the party, he was being aided in drawing off votes from the other end as well. The liquor interests, for the first time openly if tentatively engaging in a political contest, sponsored large rallies and spent money freely to increase the Democratic vote.[60] Many German Republicans also placed beer above party and deserted to the Democrats.[61]

The election results vindicated Hill's course. The Democratic candidates triumphed by margins ranging from 11,000 to 17,000. The Prohibitionists had once again cost the Republicans the election, polling over 41,000 votes, their highest total yet and an increase of 11,000 over 1885. While Henry George managed to garner 70,000 votes, this total was decidedly disappointing; his support from New York City voters was only little more than half of what it had been the year before, when he was a mayoralty candidate.[62]

The Democratic victory added to the luster of Hill's reputation. He had demonstrated once again his mastery of New York politics, and had shown himself a winner. But Hill's ambition kept pace with his achievements. Even before this triumph, he had begun to look beyond the borders of the Empire State for newer and more rewarding fields to conquer.

CHAPTER IV

Hoisting the Flag

THE SHREWDNESS of David B. Hill, his political sagacity, and
his ability to carry his party to victory at the polls did not
go unnoticed outside New York State. The record of his
early years in office had marked him as a rising figure in
national Democratic circles. In part, of course, the recognition that Hill received was accorded to him not as an
individual, but as the chief executive of the state with the
largest electoral vote in the nation. Of the five Democratic
presidential nominees since the Civil War, three—Seymour,
Tilden, and Cleveland—had been New York governors, and
any occupant of New York's executive mansion automatically received national attention.

But Hill's strength in the national party did not stem
from his position as governor alone. There were many men
in the Democratic party who were strongly opposed to
Grover Cleveland, and who were anxious to dump him.
Hill's record as a straight party man, and his reputation as
in many ways the antithesis of Cleveland, made him attractive to many of these men. Just as anti-Cleveland forces in
his own state had expressed their discontent through support
of Hill, so many Democratic foes of Cleveland in other states
now looked to Hill as a rallying point.

The fundamental and irreconcilable difference between

Hill and Cleveland lay in their approach to politics and their conception of the nature of political parties. Although Cleveland believed in the efficacy of the party system and was himself a good party man, there was for him little room for partisanship. To Hill, however, there was room for little else. A vigorous, aggressive partisanship was a healthy and natural part of political life which needed neither defense nor apology, but rather commanded deep pride. When Hill began a political address with his familiar "I am a Democrat," he was not striving for oratorical effect but exulting in his association with the party. "The Democratic banner," proclaimed the Governor, "should be nailed to the outer wall, that all may see our colors and know under which flag we fight. I believe that the best interests of the country are to be subserved by Democratic rule, and we should not be ashamed to say so. We have no apologies to make, because we believe in the principles of our party." [1] To the Mugwumps whom the President befriended, Hill would present an unblushing partisan Democracy on a take-it-or-leave-it, no-compromise basis.

This difference in outlook manifested itself most sharply on the issue of civil service. Cleveland sincerely believed in the efficacy and justness of the merit system, and strove to expand its scope. Hill, on the other hand, narrowly circumscribed his acceptance of civil service reform. The merit system should apply only to "mere subordinate places, involving only the possession of clerical or other expert qualifications that can properly be tested by examination." [2] Even then, Hill would not completely remove these posts from politics, for he would permit the appointing officer "a reasonable discretion in selection" from the list of eligibles.[3] Thus, the merit system would assure the state of capable servants for routine work by eliminating from the list of job-seekers those who could not meet minimum standards of competence. But that was all. Beyond this, the old rules of patronage should continue to reign, the party in power retaining the right to appoint its own adherents from the list of eligibles.

Hill was "not in favor of mere sentimental appointments." [4] When civil service reform conflicted with the business of rewarding deserving Democrats, the system and its adherents would have to bow. Utilizing the discretionary power authorized in the state's civil service law, Hill had a number of jobs in the Department of State declassified for the edification of hungry Democrats. He also attempted to remove from the competitive category certain positions in the Department of Public Works; when the civil service commissioners balked, and then proceeded to fill the chief examiner's position with a civil service zealot, Hill simply removed the commissioners and appointed others more amenable to his desires.[5]

The difference in outlook between the Governor and the President on political appointments led Hill to regard certain of Cleveland's actions as indefensible. The removal of Republicans from federal offices on the grounds of "offensive partisanship" was to Hill an hypocrisy which implied apology. "I would remove republicans [sic] from office, in proper cases," he declared, "not upon technical or trumped up charges or false grounds, but because they are republicans [sic]. . . ." [6]

These were the views of an unabashed partisan, and as such, Hill attracted many orthodox Democrats who were increasingly alienated by the President's course. Following the 1886 elections, in which the loss of twenty-four seats almost cost the Democrats control of the House of Representatives, the discontented became more vocal and bold. The results of the election were regarded by them as a rebuke to the President and his policy, and as proof that

Cleveland had hurt the party. With their opposition to
Cleveland now justified on grounds of party welfare, some
of the President's foes began to feel out Hill. The editor
of a leading Democratic daily in Kansas, noting that many
regarded Hill as "the coming man" in 1888, expressed his
desire to open a "confidential correspondence with close
friends of Governor Hill with the view of securing concert
of action for the next presidential campaign." [7] From
W. S. Ray, president of the Democratic Editorial Association of Indiana, came letters and editorial clippings showing
"how Indiana Democrats view the situation." Ray had
already put forward his ticket for 1888: Hill and William
S. Holman, Indiana Congressman for more than two
decades.[8] Pictures of Hill and copies of his speeches turned
up as far away as Florida, and a pro-Cleveland newspaper
in distant Galveston, Texas, took note of the rising Hill
movement. A newly formed Democratic club in Denver,
Colorado, asked the New York Governor's permission to
name itself after him.[9]

While this support was scattered and as yet hardly substantial enough to make Hill a serious threat in 1888, it
did indicate that a movement was underway to overthrow
Cleveland, and that David B. Hill was considered by many
to be the most formidable challenger. The extent of Hill's
growing popularity with Democratic politicians throughout
the nation was revealed in a poll of Colorado Democrats
taken in the fall of 1886. Of one hundred twenty who expressed an opinion, sixty-eight preferred Hill to Cleveland
for the Democratic candidate in 1888, while only thirty
favored a second term for the President. The Hill tide
in the west was rising rapidly, wrote a correspondent, and
added suggestively, "it will not be less two years hence." [10]

In response to soundings about 1888, Hill was noncom-
mittal, steadily refusing either to confirm or deny "any

gossip relating to the matter of the next Presidency." [11]
This course was probably a wise one, for the time was not
yet ripe for an open declaration against the President.
Furthermore, Hill had probably not anticipated these invitations to rebellion, and wanted to be sure of his ground
before accepting them.

Meanwhile, Hill continued to maintain superficially
cordial relations with Cleveland, and went out of his way
in his speeches to warn that "those who expect me to
antagonize the national administration will . . . be disappointed." [12] Yet it could not be gainsaid that despite these
protestations, there was, in Hill's official actions and in his
public declarations, implicit criticism of the President.

Hill's boldest sally against President Cleveland was made
in an address to the Young Men's Democratic Club of
Brooklyn in February, 1887. In a slap at the reforming
element in the Democratic party, led by Cleveland, Hill
repudiated "the suggestion that there have been or are
Democrats who are not responsible for any faults of their
party, or in other words, Democrats who are better than
their party. . . ." The party's greatness has ever been in
measures, not in men, and the party is, as always, greater
than any person in it. "'. . . We pin our faith upon no
man's sleeve.'" [13]

Hill also took a sly dig at Cleveland, noting that New
York was normally Democratic with majorities ranging from
1,100 to 197,000. The contrast between Cleveland's meager
plurality in 1884 and Hill's thumping majority in 1882 was
hardly calculated to be unfavorable to the wily Elmiran.

This speech drew wide attention, and was adjudged by a
considerable portion of the press to be a declaration of
intention by the Governor. "It is addressed to the Democratic party of the nation . . . ," proclaimed the *Albany
Express*, and it announces "that Governor Hill is willing to

be the presidential candidate of that party. . . ." The pro-
Hill *World* regarded the speech as a great rallying call to
the confused and demoralized forces of Democracy: "It
rings the air with the boldness, clearness, and penetrative
force of a bugle call. . . ." [14] A more cautious party organ
was content simply to remark that it was "sound Democratic
doctrine." [15]

That Hill intended to throw his hat in the ring at this
time is doubtful, for there were still too many fluid and
undecided factors. Moreover, the Governor had been
cautioned by Daniel Manning, Cleveland's Secretary of the
Treasury and one-time state party boss, to avoid rivalry with
the President, for "we have got to stick to Cleveland. It
won't do for the New York delegation to go to the convention split on Cleveland's renomination," said Manning,
"and then have him crowded down our throat by other
delegations." [16] Nevertheless, despite Manning's warning
that "there is no sense in riding for a fall," Hill was
becoming more outspoken and explicit in his criticism of
the President; and the flattering unsolicited offers of
support from anti-Cleveland men the nation over would
have given wings to the ambitions of lesser men.

To a great extent Hill's chances to overthrow Cleveland
in 1888 hinged on his ability to demonstrate control of the
party organization in his own state. With such control, the
nomination was within the realm of possibility; without
it, there was not one chance in a thousand. Even an out-
of-state editor who was chafing to raise the banner of revolt
tempered his offer of support with a large reservation:
"We want to *know just how the land lies in New York.*" [17]

Despite Cleveland's prestige and the influence which as
President he wielded in his state's party councils, the outlook for Hill's control of the party was bright. Three of
the major organizations in New York—Tammany, Irving

Hall, and the Kings County Democracy—were in conflict
with the President as a result of his civil service policies,
which had thus far netted a poor return on their invest-
ment of votes in 1884. The fourth, the County Democracy,
continued to support the President, but its stature had been
lowered by revelations of a scandalous nature concerning
some of its leaders.[18]

The three discontented groups showed the extent of their
ill feelings at their meetings. When letters from both
Hill and Cleveland were read to the Tammany braves in the
annual Independence Day celebration at the wigwam, the
contrast in the reception of the two was marked. While
Cleveland's note got a cool-to-lukewarm response, deafening
applause and cries of "He's no Mugwump!" and "He's our
man for President!" greeted Hill's message.[19] At a convention of Brooklyn Democrats this scene was repeated as "delegates and spectators cheered until they were tired and then
stamped on the floor and clapped their hands for a minute."
An astonished observer declared that in thirty years of both
stormy and sedate conventions, he had never seen anything
like it.[20] Irving Hall Democrats, soon to endorse Henry
George for mayor in a fit of pique, denounced Cleveland's
course as "the rule of an ingrate" and cheered the prema-
ture references to "President Hill." [21]

Hill did not delude himself, however, into equating these
demonstrations for him with iron-bound support. The
shrewd Elmiran realized that this feeling was in large
measure anti-Cleveland rather than pro-Hill, and that he
was being cheered chiefly because he was the most convenient vehicle of protest. Each of these organizations was
still interested in its own future first and in Hill only
insofar as he contributed to its own well-being. Hill's task,
therefore, was to convince each faction that its welfare was
to be enhanced by Hill's future success. This was to be

achieved through a continuing policy of kind words and kind deeds. Patronage grants to the leading members of the New York City factions continued, and their wishes on the disposal of legislation were followed whenever Hill could consistently do so.[22]

The downstate organizations, however, were only one part of the Democratic party in the state, albeit an important part. In addition to singing the siren song to these factions, Hill continued to strengthen his own personal organization. One step in this direction was the replacement of Democrats who had loyalties to other leaders with men who would owe allegiance to David Bennett Hill. The process was gradual but constant; in at least one instance, Republicans were allowed to continue in their jobs unmolested while Manning Democrats were replaced by Hill men.[23] The old guard was gradually replaced by more trustworthy sentries.

Further, Hill continued to cultivate the upstate Democrats who had scored so handsomely for him both at the 1885 nominating convention and in the election which followed. A southern tier man and a staunch supporter of the Governor, C. C. B. Walker, was selected as the new chairman of the Democratic State Committee.[24] Moreover, Hill had long enjoyed the support of a large part of the old Tilden organization, as had Cleveland. In the months following Cleveland's accession to the presidency, it became increasingly difficult for these Tildenites to support both the President and the Governor. Many of them, whose views on party were more orthodox than Cleveland's, cast their lot with Hill.[25]

There was ample newspaper support, too. Upstate editors like William Purcell of the *Rochester Post-Union*, who had once called Cleveland a "social leper," beat the Hill drums loudly. Support ranged from the timid to the pugnacious. The temper of many was caricatured by one newspaper, a

little more uncritical than others, which fell only slightly
short of deifying Hill. "Not one error has he made,"
trumpeted the editor. "He has not boasted of his admira-
tion for bastard Civil Service Reform, but has struggled
for the legitimate heir of a well-intentioned Democracy." [26]
In New York City, Hill had the backing of two influential
journals. Pulitzer's *World* was outspoken in championing
a vigorous Democracy and looked to Hill as its leading
exponent. Hill's personal relations with Pulitzer were
extremely cordial,[27] as they were with Charles Dana, the
embittered and venomous editor of the New York *Sun*.
Dana had already suggested in mid-1886 that "Hill and
Carlisle" would make "a rather attractive ticket." [28]

All in all, there was good reason for guarded optimism
regarding Hill's chances. The sources of support, actual
and potential, were substantial. Hill's strength among the
Democratic politicians in the state was revealed in a
canvass of the Democratic state legislators: a majority of
those who expressed an opinion favored Hill as the party's
presidential nominee in 1888.[29]

The situation in the state was alarming enough to swing
the national administration into action. Whitney and
Lamont, neither of them political amateurs, maneuvered to
stall the Hill offensive by heading off his support. Insiders
were now treated to the spectacle of a reform administration
feeding and petting the rapacious Tammany Tiger. Boss
Croker, with whom Whitney had remained on friendly
terms, became even friendlier after his brother was given
a federal office, and other Tammany bigwigs suddenly found
themselves in official favor. The other organizations came
in for their share, too. Higher wages were granted to
employees of the Brooklyn Navy Yard, McLaughlin's
bailiwick, in the hope of weaning Boss Hughie from the
Governor.[30] The County Democracy was kept in line by

promising to give to it the ten delegates formerly assigned
to Irving Hall. The latter faction was now to be ruthlessly
excluded from the 1887 convention for its treachery in the
previous year's mayoralty race.[31]

Moreover, some opposition to the President had been
dissolved by a marked change in the heretofore rigidly
ethical tone of his patronage policies. Following Hill's
triumph in New York and the sweeping victory of Senator
Arthur Pue Gorman's Maryland machine in 1885, the
politicians found the administration more amenable to their
demands. One by one barriers were lowered, and quietly
but steadily Republicans were being replaced by Democrats
as "offensive partisanship" was interpreted more broadly.
To many it was becoming apparent that while the turnover
had not resembled a tidal wave, it was only slightly less
sweeping in its result.[32]

The test of strength between the two Democratic factions
was precipitated somewhat unexpectedly at the meeting of
the Democratic State Committee on August 30, 1887. The
resignation of an Erie County member almost two months
before had left a vacancy which had still not been filled at
the time of this meeting. Under these circumstances the
remaining thirty-one committee members had the right to
elect a successor, upon the nomination of the local organization. A committee of Buffalo Democrats selected William
F. Sheehan, a bright young politician who had been Hill's
lieutenant in the assembly for the last two years, to fill the
post. The matter seemed settled. In the last few days before
the meetings, however, a number of Cleveland supporters
from Erie County, realizing Sheehan's avowed hostility to
the President and his friendship for Hill, determined to
block Sheehan. Fearing that his appointment to the committee might be construed by the Democratic party and the
nation as a rebuke to the President from his home county

and state, these Erie County Democrats challenged the
authority of the group that had chosen Sheehan, and trotted
out as their candidate for the seat General Peter C. Doyle.

Since there were now two candidates, the selection by the
state committee could no longer take the form of a mere
ratification, but involved an expression of preference.
Judge William L. Muller, Hill's close friend and adviser,
decided to fight for the seat, and canvassed the committeemen on their arrival in Saratoga for the support of Sheehan.
When this canvass revealed that Sheehan could not be
elected, Muller tried to table the motion to fill the vacancy
until the forthcoming convention. This motion was lost,
eighteen to thirteen, the four Tammany members voting
with the pro-Cleveland majority. Sheehan then withdrew
from the contest as gracefully as possible and urged the
unanimous approval of Doyle.[33]

The newspapers the following day told the whole story.
The Independent and pro-Cleveland press gleefully reported that Hill had been thrashed by administration
forces, and that his boom was over before it had begun.[34]
Dana's *Sun* frankly admitted that Hill had come off second-
best in a test of strength, but cloaked itself in an ill-fitting
robe of political purity, observing that Cleveland had won
only through the support of the unsavory Tammany Hall.[35]
Others also tried to assuage their disappointment with
thrusts at this Achilles heel in the President's moral armor.
An upstate editor revived John Randolph's "Blifl and Black
George" allusion to express his contempt for Tammany's
support of Cleveland.[36] All this venom, however, did not
change the results of the meeting. Less candid Democratic
sheets tried to pass off the whole affair as a "harmonious"
meeting devoid of any political significance. The *New York
Herald* assumed the role of the great pacificator, insisting
that there was no rivalry between Cleveland and Hill, and

imploring the party not to waste its energies on factional
struggles. To Hill's supporters the newspaper urged modera-
tion and patience: "Governor Hill's time will come, but it
has not yet arrived. He has a future, will doubtless occupy
the Governor's chair for another term, and then—well, then
we shall see what we shall see." [37]

There could be no denying, of course, that the defeat at
Saratoga was a severe blow to Hill's ambitions. Actually,
the whole contest had been a blunder. The entire incident
had occurred over one vacant seat. Yet whoever was chosen
to fill that seat would hold it for only one month, when at
the state convention an entirely new Democratic State Committee was to be chosen. If a contest was necessary at any
time, it most certainly should have been deferred until then,
when the stakes were commensurate with the risks involved.
When the Cleveland men decided to enter Doyle, it would
have been a simple matter to withdraw Sheehan before any
vote was taken, and the contest would have been avoided.
Muller, however, had misjudged Hill's strength and decided
upon a show of hands. By the time he realized his miscalculation it was too late, and the debacle followed.

The Saratoga defeat ended for the time being the incipi-
ent Hill boom. Although Hill was still the power in the state
convention, dictating nominations and much of the platform, the new Democratic State Committee had a pro-
Cleveland tinge, with more than two out of every three
members leaning toward the President. Edward Murphy of
Troy and Judge Muller, both friends of Hill, were given
executive posts on the committee, but this was merely a sop
to the Governor.[38] For the time being, at least, the party
machinery was in the administration's hands. Hill's brilliant
handling of the 1887 campaign—shrewdly building up the
Prohibition party at the expense of the Republicans and at
the same time checking the threat of the Labor party by

undercutting its appeal to the laboring man—restored some of the luster to his reputation, but it could not completely eradicate the tarnish of the summer defeat. Hill appeared to be through as a presidential hopeful; indeed, his friend and advisor, John O'Brien, announced that Hill would not be a candidate in 1888.[39]

Had the national convention been held that fall, no one could have doubted the finality of O'Brien's announcement. But it was not to be held until June, 1888. Before that time had arrived, Hill's hopes for the presidential nomination, fed by fuel from a wholly unexpected quarter, were kindled once again, and for a brief while flickered erratically before finally being snuffed out.

On December 6, 1887, Grover Cleveland sent his memorable tariff message to Congress, surprising his own party and the Republicans alike. Tariff revision was not a new position for the Democratic party, for a low tariff had been traditionally associated with the Democracy. Nor was this a completely new position for the Cleveland administration to take, for it had already spoken out strongly for a low tariff through Secretary of the Treasury Manning.[40] The novelty lay rather in the manner of its announcement. By devoting his entire message to the tariff, to the exclusion of all other topics, Cleveland spotlighted the issue as no one had done for two generations, and made it the major, if not the only, issue in the 1888 presidential election.

Republicans were overjoyed and Democratic professionals dismayed by Cleveland's treatment of the tariff issue, and his daring injection of it into the presidential canvass. The President's advisers felt that, in doing so, he had thrown away all his advantages. Instead of going before the people on a record of civil service reform, honesty, and efficiency, the Democrats would now have to campaign on an issue on which they had no advantage at all. The issue was bad enough, but the President's timing in introducing it was an even greater cause of gloom. If the issue had to be brought up at all, argued the professionals—Hill among them—either it should have been brought up six months earlier to allow sufficient time for the public to be educated, or it should have been postponed until after the election was secured.[41]

The misgivings in Democratic circles over Cleveland's tariff demands gave an unexpected renewal to Hill's presidential chances. Almost immediately he and his lieutenants began to manipulate and pull strings to round up support in the state committee. Sheehan in Buffalo and Purcell in Rochester made no effort to hide their enmity toward Cleveland and dangled lures in front of state committeemen.[42] How successful they were was demonstrated in an Albany meeting of the committee on January 26. Called to fill a vacancy of the national committee, this body, only the previous November aligned twenty-four to ten for the President, now deadlocked at seventeen votes each for a Cleveland and a Hill candidate.[43]

Cleveland was kept informed of these developments by his friends in New York State. Before the tie vote had illustrated the degree of Hill's success, Cleveland wrote to his friend Bissell of his conviction that ". . . schemes are on foot for an anti-administration control in New York. . . ."[44] Another friend wrote that the "political pirates" were conducting "a still hunt but one of the most industrious Hunts [sic] you have ever seen."[45]

When the success of Hill's "hunt" became clear, anti-Hill organs attempted to forestall any possible Hill boom. Stories about the Governor's alleged extravagance in repairing and refurnishing the executive mansion were widely circulated.[46] In repairing the mansion, Hill had exceeded the legislature's appropriation by some $37,000. The money was paid for necessary work. It was ridiculous to charge the bachelor Governor, whose reputation for unostentatious living was as widespread as his reputation for frugality, with squandering the state's money on luxuries. A piano and a billiard table were the central targets of the critics.

If these petty attacks were made out of fear that Hill was launching a great boom, they were not necessary. Although he had by no means relinquished all hopes for the presidency, it seems highly unlikely that Hill believed himself capable of winning the Democratic contest in a direct contest with Cleveland at this time. His actions rather indicate that his chief objective was to control the New York delegation and go to the convention as its head. There New York would probably cast its ballots for Grover Cleveland, but it would be plain to all that the party in New York State was a Hill party, which lent its support to Cleveland through the magnanimity of the Governor.

In such a setting lay his only hope for the nomination, and it is unlikely that even ambition blinded the cunning Elmiran to the political realities. If President Cleveland was in complete control of the convention, Hill had no look-in under any circumstances. If, however, something should go amiss in the President's plans—if enough opposition should arise to block a two-thirds majority for him and throw the convention into a deadlock—there would be Hill, his presence a reminder of his availability as an ideal compromise candidate, one who could carry the key state of New York and who would be acceptable to all sections of the country. It could happen. It had happened before. Horatio Seymour in 1868 and more recently Garfield had been nominated under similar circumstances. And each of them had been unwilling candidates. How much more likely was it that one who was eager to make known his availability would capture the prize! [47]

Both Whitney and Lamont were alive to the possibilities of the situation. There was the chance that opposition to the President might develop at the St. Louis convention. Since this was so, they deemed it unwise to allow Hill control of the New York delegation, or even to attend the conclave. Once more pressure was applied to Democratic leaders, on state and local levels.[48] By the time of the state committee meeting on April 6, everyone, even William Sheehan, conceded that the delegation would be pledged to Cleveland.[49] So effective was the work of Whitney and Lamont that one month later, at the assembling of the state convention which was to choose the New York delegation, Hill's friends were publicly saying that he did not desire to go to St. Louis. The delegation that was chosen was solidly for Cleveland, and Hill was left to stay in Albany during the convention.[50]

In retrospect, it appears that Whitney and Lamont were overcautious. The Democracy, for several reasons, had no choice but to renominate Cleveland, once it was known that he desired to run again. To refuse him the nomination would be a repudiation of the Democracy's only president in a generation. Moreover, the same tariff address which revived Hill's chances paradoxically made it impossible for the Democrats to run anyone but Cleveland. To nominate anyone else would be an invitation to defeat.

At St. Louis the nomination was presented to Cleveland by acclamation. Before the nomination, some of the more venomous Cleveland-haters from New York circulated a vicious pamphlet attacking the President's party and public record. It was regarded by some as a Hill move, since the pamphlet glorified the Governor as the ideal Democratic candidate.[51] There is no evidence, however, that Hill had anything to do with this intemperate attack, and it is almost certain that he knew nothing about it until its appearance.

Weeks before, Hill had reconciled himself to Cleveland's renomination, and in fact, within a week after the convention he addressed a great ratification rally at Tammany Hall, urging the support of the national ticket.[52]

The nomination of 1888 was now a closed book. Yet Hill's failure to wrest the presidential nomination from Grover Cleveland by no means ruled him out of future races. He was still the proud governor of the nation's greatest state, a man who had yet to taste defeat at the hands of the electorate. While his presidential ambitions had been frustrated for the present, there would be, as the *New York Herald* reminded him, another opportunity four years hence.

But that opportunity almost certainly depended upon Hill's election to another term at Albany, and by the summer of 1888, the outlook for re-election was bleak. On a major issue of the previous legislative session, Hill had taken a stand which promised to alienate a great many voters. Even more serious, during these same months, an angry storm had broken which threatened to bring his entire political career to an ignominious end.

CHAPTER V

Weathering the Storm

THE SAME months of 1888 which witnessed Hill's unsuccessful maneuvering for the presidential nomination also saw
him engaging in his annual tussle with the Republican
legislature of New York. It was more than ordinarily important for Hill to make a strong record in this session; for
this record would have not only a possible relationship to
the outcome of his immediate quest for the Presidency, but
also—should he fail in this quest—a strong bearing on his
bid for re-election to the governorship.

The legislative session of 1888 was dominated by two issues, the excise question and ballot reform. Other matters
of varying importance competed with these two concerns for
the time and attention of the legislature. The Governor renewed his recommendations for more favorable labor laws,
for revision of the taxation policy, and for increased home
rule. His frontal assault on the senate's power of appointment, in which he demanded its abolishment or at least cur-
tailment to prevent "hanging up" nominations, caused some
agitation and heated exchanges. A suggestion that the whole
problem of the commitment of insane persons be considered,
evoked a discussion which bore fruit in a humane statute
the following year. The quarantine establishment was re-
formed, work on the new state capitol was furthered, and

a new method of capital punishment—the electric chair—
was adopted.[1] Yet in a real sense, these subjects were
peripheral, merely sidelights to the main struggles over
excise revision and ballot reform. The story of the 1888
session is largely their story.

The liquor question was the first to come before the law-
makers. Chagrined at the increased Prohibition vote in the
previous elections, the Republicans determined to confront
Hill with a new excise measure that would offer no plausible
pretexts for rejection. A bill designed to meet all of Governor Hill's stated objections to the Crosby and Vedder bills
of 1887 was introduced early in the session. On every point
save the central one of high license the Republicans yielded.
The bill was stripped to its essentials. Maximum and minimum fees for all cities, towns, and villages in the state were
established, and power was vested in local authorities to set
the exact fees for their areas within the permissible limits.

In an effort to head off this bill, and also to get himself on
record as a friend of excise revision without committing
himself to any specific details, Hill sent a special message to
the legislature calling for a thorough revision of the state's
excise laws. As he did so often, Hill skillfully utilized a
sound public stand to subserve his political aims.

Hill pointed out[2] that conditions in the state had altered
radically since the enactment of the last general excise law
in 1857. The numerous efforts to remedy the inadequacies
and inequities of that law during the previous thirty-one
years had been sporadic and uneven, with the result that
the mass of excise legislation was now in a confused and
chaotic state. With interest in dealing with the liquor traffic
having increased in the last two years, Hill suggested that
the time for a thorough overhaul was now at hand. This
revision, he recommended, should be carried out by a commission of men "of recognized knowledge and high charac-

ter," who would consider in an unpartisan way the "rights, interests, privileges, wishes, and requirements of all the people."

The Republicans refused to be sidetracked. They immediately sent the message to committee, and proceeded to push their own bill through both the assembly and the senate. When it reached the Governor near the close of the session, this bill fared no better than its predecessor.[3]

While Hill conceded that the new bill "radically differs" from the 1887 measure, he insisted that it was "equally as unjust, defective, and objectionable." Actually Hill entered only two objections. The first was trivial, although he made much of its importance. The measure had been framed as an independent act rather than an amendment to the general excise law of the state. This alone, asserted Hill, rendered it "defective in form, and therefore objectionable." But the chief objection to the bill rested entirely upon the minimum and maximum fees which it established. Hill declared these fees to be unreasonable and excessive. Indeed, Hill asserted that even the minimum fees would be so high in some rural areas and small towns that they would in practice foist complete prohibition on areas which had indicated no desire for it. To this, Hill declared, he would not be a party.

Hill's fundamental position in this veto is worth noting. Any high license bill would meet with his disapproval. Usually, however, Hill managed to find enough inadvisable features in a bill he wished to veto for political reasons, so that the veto seemed wise on grounds of legislative principle or constitutional rights as well. Deprived of such pretexts for rejecting this bill, save the minor one already mentioned, Hill now retreated to the final unassailable position, impregnable to attacks of logic, principle, or precedent: his own judgment. The entire veto of this "unreasonable and extreme" measure rested upon what he himself considered to be reasonable. Moreover, Hill never gave any indication, either prior to this veto or after it, as to what he believed was a "just" and "reasonable" rate.

On the day following this veto, the committee which had held Hill's recommendation for an excise commission issued its report. The document was a slashing partisan attack upon the Governor. Its bitterness was tempered only by a pervading sense of pitiable futility. Although it recommended against the proposed commission, most Republicans realized that a commission offered the only hope of revision while Hill was governor. The committee was overruled, and the commission was established.[4]

The second problem which shared with the excise question the center of the legislative stage in 1888 was a new issue in state politics, but one which during the next few years was to dwarf all others in importance. This was the subject of ballot reform.

For years a major problem in American elections had been the actual achievement of a free and secret ballot.[5] An election without corruption or questionable practices had been more an ideal than a reality. The wholesale fraud of the Tweed era had led to a reform of election laws in New York State in the form of registration acts. In two important respects, however, the election laws were still deficient. While they prescribed the form and details of the ballots, they said nothing about who should print and distribute them; and they contained no safeguards for secrecy in voting. Through these loopholes poured abuses more subtle, and for that reason more dangerous, than the open violations of the previous decades.

Since the law was silent on the question of the printing and distribution of ballots, the task was willingly assumed by each political party. This system of privately printed ballots was an important factor in the continuing power of the machines. The ballots were distributed by the machine captain of each election district to the residents of his territory. These residents then chose between the Republican and the Democratic ballots, depositing the one of their choice on election day. This system enabled the machines to poll a large illiterate vote, for the nonwriter had merely to drop his prepared ballot in the box. Moreover, this simplicity in voting encouraged straight party voting, with the result that many inefficient men at the bottom of the ticket, if not at the top as well, were put into office.

The private ballot system also invited a number of abuses. Each district captain had it in his power to knife a candidate simply by covering his name with a "paster" of his opponent before distributing the ballots. When attached to a regularly printed ballot, this paster—a slip of gummed paper bearing the name of a candidate—resulted in a vote cast for the name appearing on the paster rather than for the regularly nominated candidate whose name had been covered over. Few indeed were those who took the trouble to examine their ballots or, for that matter, who would know that a change had been made, if they did examine it.

The method of ballot distribution led to another evil. Since "trading" and "knifing" were so easy, candidates were forced to take precautions against these acts of treachery. Each district leader and captain had to be paid for his services rendered in distributing the ballots. This payment was also regarded as a premium on an anti-knifing insurance policy. The payments were made to the machines, which then distributed the moneys to the workers. Thus, candidates were assessed anywhere from ten dollars up per election district, with the assessment for some offices, including judgeships, running as high as $15,000 to $20,000.[6] This practice was deplorable, but the more realistic acknowl-

edged that "so long as our election system remains as it
now is, money must be raised to get the vote out, *and those
who dance must be the ones to pay the piper*." [7] Moreover
the size of these assessments meant that only the wealthy or
those who were willing to milk their offices to offset campaign expenses could afford to run for office. It amounted
to little more than sale of office.

The lack of secrecy in voting also led to a number of
abuses. Machines could easily check on their members and
so maintain their grip on them. Bribery was also made
easier. The voter was in full view of everyone in the voting
room when he dropped his ballot into the box. Since each
party's ballots were distinguishable,[8] the briber could see
for himself that the vote was delivered as contracted for.
These circumstances also made easy the intimidation of
workers by employers who made continued employment
contingent upon casting ballots as instructed.

The unhealthy influence of the political machine and
the flagrance of these abuses led to widespread agitation
for ballot reform. In response to this agitation the Com-
monwealth Club, a reform group embracing members of all
political faiths, drew up a bill designed to plug the loopholes in the existing election laws. This bill was approved
by a number of other prominent reform organizations and
was introduced into the 1888 legislative session by Republican Senator Charles Saxton.

In its final form, the Saxton bill provided that all ballots
were to be printed at public expense, and distributed only
by the ballot clerks at the polls. Each party which polled
more than three per cent of the vote in the previous election would automatically qualify for a place on the printed
ballot. If a person were unaffiliated, or if a new party wished
to enter the field, a place on the ballot could be secured on
the presentation of a petition with one thousand signatures.

There was also to be a space left blank for write-in votes. As a safeguard against fraudulent ballots, it was provided that no ballot be valid unless it had the initials of the ballot clerk, in his own handwriting, on the back of it.

A number of other safeguards were set up to insure secrecy of the ballot. Each voter was required to make out his ballot in a private booth within a five-minute period. No one was to be allowed to see the ballot as it was dropped into the box. To prevent circumvention of this provision, it was made a misdemeanor for a voter even voluntarily to show his ballot to anyone else. Exception to this provision was to be made only for invalids, illiterates, or others who for some reason were not able to make out the ballots by themselves. In such cases, the ballot clerk was permitted to help in the voting process.[9]

The measure, while far from a perfect one, was a long step in the direction of a truly secret ballot, and its merits far outweighed its defects. When the bill came before Governor Hill, however, it was rejected.

Hill's veto message[10] consumed some fifteen pages, in which the Governor elaborately set forth his objections. These objections were directed chiefly at the official ballots, and fell into two broad categories: practicability and constitutionality. For one thing, the Governor declared, the public assumption of the cost of printing and distributing the ballots would impose an unnecessary burden upon the taxpayers. While it would increase taxes it would bring about no corresponding benefits, for the assessment of candidates would continue in order to meet other campaign expenses. Moreover, the Governor predicted, ballots printed at public expense would invite "adventurers" to gather a thousand names on a petition—or only one hundred for a local office—and thereby compel the state to print all of their ballots. The number of candidates at each election would thus increase manyfold, and would unnecessarily confuse the voters.

Hill's constitutional objections to the bill were based on the postulate that the legislature must not in any way impinge upon the citizens' suffrage beyond the restrictions set forth in the state constitution. Certain features of this bill, claimed the Governor, contained within them the seeds of possible infringement of suffrage rights, and were therefore unconstitutional. The voter might be deprived of his vote in any of a number of ways. A ballot clerk, either intentionally or unwittingly, might void a ballot simply by failing to initial it. Failure of the proper officials to deliver the ballots to the polling places would deprive citizens of their franchise. Since no changes or substitutions could be made on the ballots within fifteen days of the election, the death, declination, or disability of a candidate within that period would deprive the voter of a choice between candidates. The time limit of five minutes was inadequate for the slow, the aged, and the undecided, and would thus work a hardship on them. And the compulsory disclosure of his choices to the ballot clerk deprived the illiterate voter of his secret ballot. It did not matter that most of these contingencies were unlikely to occur; as long as they were remotely possible, held the Governor, the bill was unconstitutional.

Hill added many more minor defects in the bill to his list of objections, and stressed the fact that the proposed system had not as yet been tried anywhere in the United States. Its foreign origin—it was widely known as the Australian ballot—was the target for an attack by the Governor. He fulminated against this "mongrel foreign system" whose prohibition of even a voluntary disclosure of one's ballot would deprive the voter of the right to converse and "electioneer" at the polls, a right which he traced back to the new England town meetings.

Some of Hill's arguments were valid; others were specious. But it was plain that if excuses for a veto had not existed, Hill would have invented them, for he had no intention of signing this bill into law. The real objection to the bill was not to be found in the veto message, but in the character of the Democratic urban vote. A substantial part of this vote came from the organized efforts of the machine, especially among the illiterate. The official ballot would severely hamper the organization's ability to poll its full strength, and would cut into the Democratic column on election day. Insofar as the bill dealt with bribery, intimidation, and gross corruption, Hill was sympathetic to it. If a fair bill for their elimination under the existing system could have been devised, Hill would undoubtedly have supported it.[11] But as long as any such scheme was tied to an exclusively official ballot, Hill would reject it as an assault upon his party's interests.

At the end of this message, Hill delivered a ridiculing, demagogic attack on the reformers, "a class of well-meaning people who seem to hail with delight every new scheme which masquerades under the seductive name of 'reform,' especially if it comes from foreign shores and bears the approval of a monarchical government. . . ." The legislature having already adjourned, there the subject of ballot reform rested.

Hill's rejection of the Saxton ballot reform bill and his veto of another measure concerned with purifying elections, the so-called Fassett antibribery bill, promised to alienate a good deal of voting support in the November elections. But the impact of these vetoes, substantial as it threatened to be, was soon overshadowed by a far greater issue which brought into question not merely Hill's political judgment but his integrity as well.

On April 12, 1888 the *New York Times,* in its daily column recording the work of the legislature, reported that Senator Fassett's resolution to investigate the aqueduct project had been carried. This item, mixed with other news of the legislature's activities in a column which failed to make the front page, heralded the beginning of an investigation which threatened to bring to an abrupt close the charmed political career of David Bennett Hill.

The resolution to conduct this investigation had been instigated by Tom Platt. Already humiliated by his removal from the quarantine post, Platt was still further tormented by Hill's veto of a bill designed to aid a railroad company of which the Easy Boss was president.[12] Platt burned for revenge, and looked for an opportunity to humble Hill, as well as for campaign material for the coming election. He found both in the aqueduct investigation.

In June, 1883, the legislature had provided for the construction of a new aqueduct for New York City to carry water to the city from Croton Lake, some thirty miles north. A commission of six, composed of the mayor, commissioner of public works, and comptroller of New York City along with three private citizens, was to award the contracts and supervise the work. In 1886 the legislature had reorganized the commission, dropping the mayor and comptroller and adding three more private members, one a Republican, one a Democrat, and one a nonpartisan engineer. By 1888 rumors concerning some questionable contract awards by the commissioners were freely circulating.[13] The investigation by Fassett's committee, which got underway in June and continued through the summer, confirmed many of these rumors and brought before the public a shameful story of prostitution of public trust.

The earliest testimony revealed that the first contracts let in December, 1884 were divided between two firms, Brown, Howard, and Company, and O'Brien and Clark. Because these firms were not always the lowest bidders, the city paid more than $186,000 in excess of the minimum cost. Furthermore, on January 28, 1886 a contract for section 12 of the aqueduct was let to O'Brien and Clark for $430,-345, a bid which was $34,000 higher than the next lowest bidder, Beckwith and Quackenbush, and $54,000 more than the low bid of Rogers and Company.[14] The contract did not have to be granted to the lowest bidder, of course, if the awarding commission were satisfied that for one reason or another the city's interests would not best be subserved by such an award. What caused many eyebrows to be raised, however, was the fact that O'Brien and Clark immediately sublet the work on section 12 to Beckwith and Quackenbush at a $30,000 profit. Moreover, it developed that even the lowest bidder, Rogers and Company, was perfectly capable of doing this work, had offered to post bonds to that effect, and was in fact at the very time of the award working on the adjoining section of the aqueduct by virtue of a sublet contract from O'Brien and Clark. The revelations were especially damning since aqueduct rules forbade subletting contracts.[15]

All of this was shocking enough, but the stain of scandal and suspicion soon spread to a still higher public figure. The head of the firm O'Brien and Clark was John O'Brien, chairman of the Democratic State Committee during the 1885 gubernatorial campaign and a friend of David B. Hill. The Democrats that year were embarrassed for funds, and on October 29 Hill drew a promissory note for $10,000 to the order of his friend, William L. Muller, then secretary of the Democratic State Committee. The note was endorsed by Muller, O'Brien, and Heman Clark, O'Brien's partner and also a director of the bank in which the note was discounted. The proceeds of the note were paid to Muller and used to cover last-minute campaign expenses. When the note fell due four months later, it was replaced by another note, not bearing Hill's signature or endorsement. The debt was finally paid to the bank not by Hill but by John O'Brien, and it was charged to his account on the books of O'Brien and Clark.[16]

Testimony also showed that when the contract for section 12 was let, Judge Muller, who had no connection with the aqueduct commission, applied great pressure on the commissioner to award the contract to O'Brien and Clark, despite the fact that their bid was not the lowest one.[17] The inference was clear: Hill had exerted his influence, through Muller, on behalf of O'Brien and Clark; this firm received the contract, sublet the work at a profit of $30,000, and with his share of the money, O'Brien paid Hill's $10,000 note. When former Mayor Grace testified [18] that he had heard there had been $30,000 in unredeemed notes after the 1885 campaign—the precise amount of profit made by the subletting of the section 12 contracts—the circumstances attendant to the original award seemed more than coincidental.

Nor was this all. The act which reorganized the commission in 1886 had dropped the city's two chief watchdogs, the mayor and comptroller, and left only the commissioner of public works to guard the city's interests. These interests had been better left unguarded, for the commissioner of public works, Rollin Squire, was a slippery scoundrel with a questionable past.

Squire, fortunately, had been ousted before he could do much harm. In the summer of 1886 a remarkable document had come to light which resulted in his removal. Anxious to be appointed commissioner of public works, Squire had

written the following pledge in December, 1884 to Maurice
B. Flynn, a power in the County Democracy:[19]

> Dear Sir: In consideration of your securing not less than
> four County Democracy Aldermen who shall vote for my
> confirmation as Commissioner of Public Works, in the
> event that the Mayor shall send in my name for that office,
> I hereby agree to place my resignation as Commissioner
> in your hands whenever you may demand the same, and
> further to make no appointment in said office without
> your approval and to make such removal as you may
> suggest and request, and to transact the business of said
> office as you may direct.

Since Flynn had a large interest in a construction firm
which was bidding for aqueduct work, the impropriety of
this letter was even more obvious. Mayor Grace had immediately preferred charges against Squire, and after a
brief hearing, Governor Hill had sustained the charges and
approved his removal.[20]

All this, of course, had been known in 1886. What the
present investigation made clear was that the reorganization
bill which made Squire the key man on the aqueduct commission had been drawn up by Hamilton Fish, Jr., a Republican assemblyman; that Fish, as part of a prearranged
deal for splitting patronage, was immediately appointed by
Hill as one of the three new commissioners; that this bill
was bitterly opposed by Mayor Grace and Comptroller
Lowe, who appealed to Hill to veto it as a violation of home
rule; and that Hill promised Grace he would not sign it as
it stood, and then proceeded to break this promise.[21]

The only reason that the Democrats and Republicans
both would favor a bill so clearly opposed to the interests
of New York City was that each expected to dig deep into

the pork barrel which would now be guarded by more
friendly sentries. Squire, it was true, was removed from
his position within a few months. Yet in the months following the reorganization of the commission, construction
costs rose sharply above the estimates, as laxity in supervision permitted contractors to cut corners and still show
higher costs. One favorite device was the substitution of one
type of fill for another, which netted the contractor a profit
of $3.80 per cubic yard.[22]

All in all it was not a pretty picture. The opposition
press immediately centered its fire on Hill. The entire affair
was pictured as Hill's scheme to pay off a campaign debt
and reward his friends. For every matter that was called to
question, Hill was belabored for a direct or indirect responsibility.[23]

Many of these accusations were unjustified by the facts,
which were these: in the last week of the 1885 campaign,
the Democratic State Committee was embarassed for funds.
Because his signature on a note would quickly produce
this money, Governor Hill signed a promissory note for
$10,000 to the order of William L. Muller, who assured
the Governor that the state committee would assume responsibility for its payment. O'Brien, head of the state
committee, eventually did pay the note out of his own
pocket, just as he had already paid many thousands of
dollars to defray campaign expenses. When the contracts for
section 12 were being let, Judge Muller did intercede with
the commissioners on behalf of O'Brien and Clark, who
received the contact although their bid was $54,000 higher
than the lowest bidder. But the testimony also showed that
the commissioners had been advised by the chief engineer
of the aqueduct that in the interest of efficiency and good
work the contract should be given to O'Brien and Clark.[24]

There is no doubt that Muller improperly used his influence with the commissioners to get the section 12 contract awarded to his friends. It is not clear whether he acted with Hill's knowledge, though it is quite possible that he was entirely on his own. The pressure was undoubtedly exerted because O'Brien was a deserving Democrat, and it was felt that he should reap some benefit from the success of his party. To connect the award of the contract with the payment of a specific campaign note, however, is a far different matter than saying that O'Brien received favored treatment because of his political connections. It may well be that O'Brien regarded his large contributions to the campaign, including the $10,000 note, as an investment; and it may be that he expected to benefit by a Democratic victory wherever preference could legitimately be given to his firm. While not on the highest moral ground, this was condoned in practice even by many who condemned it in theory. To make a deal, however, for payment of a specific campaign note through a plot to milk the city's treasury would be to enter into a corrupt bargain. The assertion that this was done is unsubstantiated by the evidence. Moreover, it seems unlikely that O'Brien, whose firm already held over six million dollars worth of aqueduct contracts alone—all awarded before Hill was governor—would enter into a plot to regain a paltry $10,000 he had paid in a political campaign.

This much having been said for Hill, however, it must also be stated that the Governor's garments were far from spotless. He had approved the reorganization bill over the protests of the Mayor and with the evident intention of injecting politics into the aqueduct project. He had wittingly arranged to leave the shady Squire in a dominant position on the aqueduct commission, and probably had an

understanding with him on patronage matters.[25] While not
entering into a deal himself, he had created a situation
in which such deals could flourish.

The situation was grave. Hill called a special session of
the legislature to meet on July 17. To minimize his embarrassment, Hill declared that the main reasons for the
extra session was to deal with the prison labor problem.[26]
Within a day, however, he turned to the obvious subject of
concern. Declaring that all the aqueduct's ills stemmed from
the denial of home rule in both the 1883 and 1886 statutes,
Hill recommended that the present board be abolished and
a new one created, comprised of four city officials and three
private citizens to be chosen by the mayor, rather than by
the governor. This reversion to the principle of home rule,
he asserted, would assure proper handling of the aqueduct
project.[27]

Public pressure was intense, and the Republican legislature, which shared the blame for enacting the deal in 1886,
immediately passed a bill creating a new commission composed of New York's mayor, comptroller, and commissioner
of public works, and four private citizens to be appointed
by the mayor. Hill signed it with a flourish, proclaiming
that at last the principle of home rule, which he had so
long championed, was embodied into law by a reluctant
legislature.[28] It was a brazen attempt to convert censure to
credit, but it was as transparent as it was bold.

The disclosures of the aqueduct investigation threatened
to play havoc with Hill's political future. The senate probe
lasted until well into August, and public furor could not
be expected to die down in the short time that elapsed before the nominating convention. Hill's enemies, both without the party and within, seized the opportunity to move in
for the kill. The Governor's vetoes of the ballot act and
the several excise measures were raked over again, and

strong efforts were made to tie him firmly to the liquor and
saloon element.[29] The choice of the long-time temperance
advocate Warner Miller as the Republican candidate for
governor was made largely to emphasize by contrast Hill's
record on the excise question. So alarming was the situation that Dana's *Sun*, always staunchly pro-Hill, felt it wise
to open the door marked "exit" as gracefully as possible:
"a great number of respectable gentlemen of the Democratic
faith are looking to William C. Whitney as the man for
whom they expect to vote for governor, provided Governor
Hill should decide to retire." [30]

The most vigorous demonstration of the anti-Hill strength
was presented in a mass meeting at Cooper Union just
five days before the nominating convention.[31] An overflow
audience, predominantly Democratic, enthusiastically applauded addresses delivered by Wheeler H. Peckham, Henry
George, Louis F. Post, and other prominent reformers,
and greeted each mention of Hill's name with loud hisses.
Hill, it was asserted, had damaged the cause of reform
through his veto of the ballot act and his covert opposition
to the principle of home rule. Moreover, his mere presence
on the ticket threatened to repel so many voters from
supporting the national candidates that the success of tariff
revision was jeopardized. Not only was Hill an obstacle in
the path of reform and thus bad for the party in the long
run, but he had already done harm to the party in his
political maneuverings. It was charged that Hill's veto of
the 1885 census measure, by preventing a long overdue
reapportionment which would have followed, had cost his
party control of the legislature.

The opposition to Hill was strong and widespread, as it
had been in his first race for the governorship; as in 1885,
grave doubts about his personal and official integrity were
engendered and given weight by the disclosure of his con-

nection with corrupt persons. Yet as was the case three years before, existing political circumstances, artful utilization of these circumstances by the Governor, and clever political handling of his own forces combined to give the shrewd Elmiran a renomination.

One of the chief factors in Hill's success in 1888 was the failure of the opposition to unite upon any one candidate. At various times during the summer months Hewitt, Grace, and Smith M. Weed were mentioned as possible choices, but at no time were these suggestions followed up by a movement of any substance. Moreover, Grover Cleveland's refusal to lend his support to any candidate, in keeping with his "hands off" policy, was a severe blow to the forces trying to overturn the Governor.[32]

Any effective opposition to Hill would also require the backing of at least one downstate organization, and in 1888 there was little chance of that. McLaughlin was already in Hill's pocket, and Croker, under the constant prodding of Troy's Edward Murphy, was coming around once more after his display of independence in 1887. The treacherous Irving Hall faction was now defunct. That left only the County Democracy, and by 1888, this once proud organization was in decline, weakened by scandal and torn by internal strife.

The Flynn-Squire incident had shaken the County Democracy to its foundations, severely damaging its prestige as a reform organization. To many persons it now appeared that the organization was like any other political machine, its chief concern being the lining of its leaders' pockets. Disillusioned, these people drifted away from the erstwhile reform group.

Crusty old Hewitt, too, hurt the County Democracy with his dyspeptic attitude, cranky statements, and cantankerous actions. For reasons both personal and political, relations between Hewitt and President Cleveland had progressively deteriorated, until the Mayor openly refused to support Cleveland for renomination, because he "is no statesman, and I don't believe in his re-election." [33] The open break between one of their leaders and the national party's chieftain, whom they had in the past enthusiastically supported, confused and disheartened the members of the County Democracy.

Hewitt did still more damage to himself and his organization when he refused to review a Saint Patrick's Day parade. If this alienation of Irish voters was not guarantee enough of political suicide in New York, Hewitt proceeded to nail the lid on his coffin with several impolitic remarks about "hyphenated Americans" in general.[34] Many Irish-Americans in the County Democracy already hostile to Hewitt were tired of their association with the organization, and longed to return to their compatriots in the wigwam. Thus, when Henry D. Purroy, a County Democracy leader, accused Hewitt of fostering a revival of "Know-Nothingism," his charge struck a responsive chord in Gaelic breasts. A mass desertion from the ranks of the County Democracy ensued as Purroy bolted to join Croker, with whom he had been in close touch. These "Hoy Purroy" now worked actively with Tammany for the Tiger's control of the city government, and for the nomination of Hill.[35]

Meanwhile, Hill was not idling. Plans for securing the battle lines were laid in midsummer at a midnight conference in Saratoga's Grand Hotel where Sheehan, Edward Murphy of Troy, and the Governor huddled.[36] Murphy's friendship with Croker was utilized to bring the beady-eyed chieftain and his warriors back into the fold, and Sheehan continued his yeoman work upstate. As in 1885, the quiet roundup of delegates got underway. Three years of wielding the executive and appointing power made this task con-

siderably easier. Letters were again diligently sent out to
friends in each county requesting an appraisal of the local
situation. Where pressure or attention was needed, a Hill
man was on the spot to apply it.[37] The corralling of delegations continued so smoothly that Hill, a man not given to
complacency, made no effort to conceal his complete satisfaction with the canvass. "Everything," he wrote to a
friend, "seems to be all one way so far as delegates are
concerned." [38]

From the disorganized camp of the opposition there
emanated a continuous stream of denunciation during the
last weeks before the nomination, but Hill's machine rolled
on relentlessly. The futility of trying to stop it was strik-
ingly if unintentionally underscored when the *New York
Herald,* in the column adjoining the report of the anti-Hill
demonstration at Cooper Union, ran a story on the increasing momentum of the Hill juggernaut.[39] In the juxtaposi-
tion of these two reports there was also starkly presented the
reason for the Governor's success. Hill had oriented his
efforts around the basic political fact that, in the last
analysis, the withholding or bestowal of a nomination was
controlled not by public meetings nor editorials, important
as these might be in the molding of opinion, but by the
voting delegates. As a result, Hill was in firm command of
the situation almost from the outset. The convention which
met on September 11 was little more than a ratification
meeting. Hill was nominated by acclamation.

The platform, prepared by Hill himself, was a blanket
approval of his course over the past several years.[40] After
the usual pointing with pride to the record of the national
administration, the platform launched into what might best
be called "righteous straddling." It sought to justify the
Governor's excise vetoes by declaring that while it favored
the restriction of the liquor traffic "by just and equitable

excise laws," it opposed "all sumptuary laws heedlessly
interfering with the personal liberties and reasonable
habits and customs of any part of our citizens." Similarly,
the Democratic party was unequivocally in favor of the
purity of the ballot and honest elections, but it approved
the Governor's veto of the Saxton bill, which was unconstitutional, grossly ineffective, clearly impracticable, and
otherwise objectionable." As for the recent revelations
about Hill's connection with the aqueduct fraud, these
attempts by "Republican partisan investigating committees
. . . to discredit him . . . have only served to strengthen
him in the public confidence." Just how this happy result
had been effected the platform did not say.

Throughout the campaign that ensued, Governor Hill devoted a considerable portion of his efforts towards securing
success for the national ticket. In this respect the Governor
keynoted his campaign on the very night of his nomination. To a throng which had gathered to serenade him on
his triumph, Hill stated emphatically:[41]

Let me be clearly understood. It is my sincere wish and
desire that every Democrat in the State, and particularly
every friend of mine, shall vote for Cleveland and Thurman. I also trust that everyone who calls himself an
"Independent" and every conservative Republican who
believes with us upon the issue of tariff reform will like-
wise vote for our national ticket, whether he votes for
me or not; and while I should be gratified to receive his
suffrage, yet, if he thinks that he cannot consistently
give it, I hope that his objections to me or to any part
of our ticket will not prevent his loyal support to our
presidential standard-bearer. Our success in the nation is
of paramount importance. It overtowers all personal
considerations.

In his private correspondence, too, the Governor reiterated
to workers and friends his desire for the success of the national ticket and urged them all to get the voters to "pull
straight for the whole ticket." [42] Moreover, Hill practiced
his preachings, making numerous appearances on behalf of
the national slate. In nearly all his speeches he devoted
a great deal of attention to the tariff and extolled Cleveland's record as president.[43] Although he was himself engaged in a bitter struggle, Hill put his service at the disposal
of the national committee for speaking assignments. At the
request of the committee he stumped the key state of Indiana for two days, speaking several times a day, and campaigned also in the doubtful states of New York and
Connecticut. This he did at his own expense, refusing any
reimbursement from the national committee.[44]

Hill made these vigorous efforts on behalf of the national
ticket despite the knowledge that there would be no
reciprocation from Cleveland. Chairman Calvin S. Brice
of the national committee, dangling the bait of several
thousand liquor votes, had pleaded with Cleveland to write
an endorsement of Hill, but Cleveland had flatly refused.
When Brice persisted with the observation that Hill was,
after all, a Democratic nominee like himself, Cleveland
had replied heatedly: "I don't care a damn if he is—each
tub must stand on its own bottom." [45]

With or without Cleveland's endorsement, it was clear
that Hill had a fight on his hands. The aqueduct disclosure,
along with Hill's record on the ballot and excise legislation, precluded any possibility of Hill's gaining support
from Independents and reform Democrats. Now more than
ever opposed to the Governor, these reform circles denounced him almost daily. Cleveland's refusal to endorse
his former running-mate thus cost the Governor very little
support, for it merely hardened the determination of those

already pledged to defeat him. Hill fully realized this to be the case, but he also knew that the sword cut both ways: many who would support him on certain issues pertinent only to New York State would not back the party's candidate for national honors. "There are many persons, to be sure, who will vote for him [Cleveland] and not vote for me," the Governor stated in an interview, and then added cryptically, "but this loss will be compensated to me." [46]

Although he could accept this as a political fact, Hill nonetheless bitterly resented the continuous attacks upon him by the *New York Times* and Godkin's *Evening Post*, both Cleveland organs. "I'll speak plainly," said Hill to a newspaperman. "There are some people in the rank and file who don't think it is quite the right thing that these two papers should attack me so seriously when I'm doing all I can to win for Cleveland. They think that the national leaders ought to squelch these newspapers which are endeavoring to make their little circle and Mr. Cleveland believe that he is above the party." [47] Hill looked for no thanks for his efforts on Cleveland's behalf, but he was rankled by what he considered a base ingratitude.

Although the lack of support from certain elements of his own party was a serious matter, Hill's chief efforts had to be directed toward countering the vigorous campaign of the Republicans. Especially damaging was the wide circulation given to a three-by-nine inch handbill in the form of a promissory note, a facsimile of Hill's $10,000 note for 1885 campaign expenses. On the reverse side were suggestive excerpts from the testimony in the aqueduct investigation.[48]

A strong challenge was meanwhile being offered by Hill's opposite number, Warner Miller. Miller, a temperance man, concentrated almost exclusively on the liquor issue. Although his party's plank on liquor[49] contained

more water than spirit, Miller met the issue head on. In
daily speeches he forcefully expounded the arguments
against the liquor traffic to the residents of almost every
county in the state.[50]

While Miller hammered away at liquor, other Republicans directed their fire at Hill's veto of the ballot act.
The Governor had never wanted electoral reform, they
charged, and the reasons he gave for his veto were both
weak and spurious. The *Nation* asserted that electoral
reform would never be realized as long as the executive
chair was occupied by a man who characterized the secret
ballot as a "mongrel foreign system." [51]

The Republicans' concentration on these two issues appears to have been effective. By stressing Hill's opposition
to electoral reform, the Republicans weakened Hill's position with non-machine members, and cost him some support.[52] At the same time, Miller's forthright campaign
against liquor undercut the appeal of the Prohibition party
and brought to a halt its continuous siphoning of Republican rural votes.[53]

But if Hill's vetoes of the ballot act and excise measures
left him vulnerable to the oratorical and editorial thrusts
of Republicans and Independents, they also brought solidly
behind him two important blocs of votes. From the first
of these groups, the Democratic city machine, Hill would
normally expect support as the regularly nominated candidate of the party. His veto of the Saxton bill, however,
which was aimed primarily at political machines, preserved
the ability of these machines to deliver an undiminished
vote on election day. Moreover, the veto insured him against
any possible lukewarmness. These organizations now had
a vital interest in keeping in office the man who stood between them and this crippling act, and their efforts on
Hill's behalf were redoubled.

The largest bloc acquired by Hill was the liquor vote. This included all those concerned in the manufacture and sale of liquor and malt beverages, from the hop grower to the retailer in the saloon or liquor store. Although their economic interests had been challenged before, the present assault on the liquor element was the most serious threat in recent years. At just this critical time, the liquor interest was fortunate in having the governor's chair occupied by a man whose action, regardless of motive, had resulted in the preservation of its economic position.

With Warner Miller now singling out the regulation of the liquor traffic as the chief issue in his campaign, those interested in the perpetuation and expansion of that traffic found themselves faced with a show-down struggle. Cloaking their desperate fear with a militant spirit, these men now organized for the defense of their interests, and entered the electoral lists in support of the one candidate who had proven himself a friend, David Bennett Hill.

The Grocers of New York City and Brooklyn, a trade organization of those who retailed bottled liquor, lined itself up behind the Governor. Arrangements were made for some 17,000 copies of a Democratic campaign leaflet "of interest to the retail grocers of the State," to be included in the mailing of the trade newspaper, the *Retail Grocers Advocate,* to the dealers all over the state. The New York State Hotel Association, through its newspaper, the *Hotel Register,* urged all of its 3,500 members to support Hill and to get others to support him because of his favorable stand on the excise issue. Substantial sums were contributed to the campaign coffers by the brewers, and the full weight—votes, money, and influence—of some 35,000 to 40,000 saloon keepers, in addition to the powerful liquor manufacturers, wholesalers, and all others who had an economic interest in preventing restriction, was brought to bear on Hill's behalf.[54]

While privately welcoming this support, Hill strove to avoid too close identification with the liquor people, in order that their zealousness for him might not embarrass his campaign. To the State Liquor Dealers' Association meeting in Buffalo the week before the Democratic nominating convention, Hill sent his young lieutenant William Sheehan with instructions to urge discretion upon its leaders.

In the first place, I do not think that they should pass any resolution of thanks to me for my previous action. In the second place, I do not think they ought to endorse my candidacy for Governor, nor nominate me, nor in any manner refer to me by name or otherwise. They can aid my cause more at the present time by a discreet and wise silence. Their resolutions should be most carefully worded. . . . It should be a business convention and not a political one.[55]

Hill's vetoes of the excise legislation brought into his camp not only those engaged in the manufacture and sale of liquor, but also many of those who consumed it. Two national groups, the Irish and the Germans, were included in this category. Most of the Irish were already in the Democratic fold, and their full sympathy with Hill's vetoes probably did not bring the Governor many new votes. It was the normally Republican German vote from which Hill made substantial gains. To the Germans, especially, beer was a national beverage, and they could be counted upon to rally as they had in the past[56] against any move to restrict their right to drink it.

Here again, however, Hill had to tread carefully in gar-

nering this support, lest he frighten into the Republican
column those favoring a modest regulation of the liquor
traffic. This was a real danger in the upstate area, which
had always been counted as a Hill stronghold. The task
was a delicate one. Having already satisfied opponents of
regulation with deeds, he would now have to attempt to
keep the advocates of regulation with words.

A large part of Hill's speeches was devoted to the liquor
issue. Making much of the fact that he himself did not
drink, Hill declared that he deplored excessive drinking,
and would welcome an equitable law to curb the liquor
traffic. As evidence of this, he pointed to his approval of the
Five-Gallon Bill in 1887, a mild regulatory measure.[57] The
Governor also recalled his suggestion, adopted by the legislature, to establish a commission for the study and overhaul
of the state's excise statutes in a revision fair to all interests.
His vetoes of the Republicans' hypocritical excise legislation were necessary, he explained, in order to prevent inequitable, unconstitutional, and politically motivated bills
from becoming law.[58]

In this same spirit of "running with the hares and hunt-
ing with the hounds," Hill tried to keep the support of
proponents of ballot reform. The Governor declared con-
tinually that he favored electoral reform, and that he would
"cheerfully approve" a sound measure.[59] He insisted, however, that the Republican bill of 1888 was not such a
measure, but was defective, unfair, and unconstitutional.
Hill's veto message was also widely distributed as a campaign document to acquaint the electorate with his position.[60]

Hill, of course, did not base his campaign entirely on the
ballot and excise issues. As in previous campaigns, he again
made a play to win the labor vote. One great obstacle to the
attainment of this goal had already been removed. The dis-

appointing showing of the Labor party in the 1887 election
after its promising initial effort the year before had disheartened the leaders of the movement. Shortly afterward, the
party disintegrated as abruptly as it had first appeared.
The end was signalled when Henry George announced in
January that he would support Cleveland for the presidency. George refused to put up another ticket in 1888
because he feared it might draw enough votes away from
Cleveland to beat him, and he did not want that "Butler
business over again." [61] Father McGlynn split with the
single-tax prophet and attempted to keep the movement
alive, but it was an almost hopeless task.

Not only was Hill's chief threat for the labor vote gone,
but it had orphaned some 70,000 voters, now unattached.
Hill was more than willing to adopt them. His record of
friendship for labor during his first term was a good one:
an arbitration act, a factory inspector act, the Saturday
half-holiday bill, Labor Day, and many other measures in
the interest of labor had been enacted upon his recommendation. He had amply demonstrated his interest in the
laboring man and the union movement. He had rejected an
attempted repeal of the half-holiday law,[62] had urged
labor's interest in the prison labor question, and had appointed laboring men to responsible positions in the state
government.

This record was exploited to the full. Speeches and
pamphlets emphasized it. About one-half of the Democratic
campaign literature bore directly on Hill's friendship with
labor.[63] Theodore Roosevelt privately acknowledged the
success of Hill's program. In a letter to his friend Henry
Cabot Lodge, he tempered his optimism concerning the
forthcoming election with the grudging admission that "Hill
has a tremendous pull among the workingmen, however,
for some inexplicable reason. . . ." [64]

Moreover, Hill made use of his partisan appeal. The
phrase "I am a Democrat"—a call which rallied the state
Democracy to greater efforts—echoed throughout the campaign. Those Democrats who did not rush to answer the call
were gently reminded of their obligation to do so.[65]

The election returns demonstrated the effectiveness of
Hill's strategy and campaign. The Governor carried the
state by more than 19,000 votes over Warner Miller. The
Prohibitionists, their appeal effectively checked by Miller's
high license campaign, were held to 30,000, as compared to
41,000 in 1887. Although Cleveland had received some 100,-
000 votes more than Harrison, the electoral count was
233 to 168 in the general's favor. The loss of New York by
13,002 votes cost Cleveland the election.[66]

Almost immediately after the results were known, a
storm of abuse was showered upon Hill by the Mugwump,
independent, and reform Democratic press. Some openly
charged that Hill had knifed the ticket in order to insure
his own election. Other journals, more responsible, stopped
short of the knifing charge, but contended that the Elmiran's
candidacy on the Democratic ballot disgusted many independent voters who would otherwise have supported Cleveland, but who now turned instead to vote the straight Republican ticket.[67] This version of the loss of New York is
also accepted by Cleveland's biographer as an important
factor in Cleveland's defeat.[68]

These charges constituted a grave indictment. If the
first were true, it would be especially damning to this man
who preached that the highest virtue was party allegiance;
if the second were true, it would be equally damning in
view of his pronouncements on the necessity for personal
sacrifice for the sake of the party. In either case, Hill would
have been guilty of the basest hypocrisy and deception. A

scrutiny of the evidence and the logic of the situation, however, fails to substantiate either charge.

Hill's yeoman work on behalf of the national ticket; his constant reiteration in his private correspondence and public utterances that he desired to stand or fall with Cleveland, and that Cleveland's election was of paramount importance; and his speaking tours in other key states for the President have already been recounted. The value of the Governor's services both in and outside New York was gratefully acknowledged by Daniel Lamont, Cleveland's private secretary and political adviser. Although disheartened by the President's defeat, Lamont conceded that "but for the aid of your remarkable campaign [it] would have been much more staggering." [69] National Chairman Brice, in a note to Hill after the election, thanked the Governor for having done "your utmost," and added his personal testimony as to the unselfishness with which you carried on your campaign. You did everything that you could do, but it seems that the tide was running too strong." [70]

Grover Cleveland himself did not hold Hill responsible for his defeat. Years later he told a friend:[71]

I want you sometime to correct the false impression abroad that I either have, or had, any idea or impression that the Presidential ticket was the victim of treachery in New York in the election of 1888. Nobody could understand better than I how that seemingly contradictory result was reached. My campaign for reelection was, of necessity, made upon a single national issue so forced to the front that, as I had foreseen, there was no such thing as evading it, even if my party or myself had so desired.

On the other hand, the State campaign had issues peculiar to itself, with their own supporters, men to

whom the tariff had, from a business and political point
of view, only the remotest interest. The brewers had their
own organization for the purpose of protecting the
property under their management and jurisdiction. They
had the right to use their power for their own protection,
and that they exercised this right and power in their own
way, in no way constituted grievance so far as the presidential ticket was concerned. If they could attract votes
from a weak and unpopular Republican candidate—
supposed to be inimical to them—to his opponent who
would be fair because he was strong, they had a perfect
right to do so. I had had sufficient experience in state
politics to understand the whole situation and never permitted myself to reproach Governor Hill or his friends
for the untoward result so far as I was personally concerned.

Moreover, there was no reason for Hill to turn against
the national ticket. A motive of pique or vengeance would
hardly fit the character of a sly, calculating politician. While
his critics conceded this, they contended that Hill had committed this treacherous act for reasons of personal gain. Yet
in terms of his political future and ambitions for the presidency, Hill stood to gain much more from Cleveland's
election. The President's re-election would have effectively
removed him from the field in 1892 and left the path clear
for Hill; his defeat, instead, left him eligible to compete
for the next presidential nomination. Furthermore, a
Cleveland defeat coupled with a Hill triumph was sure to
result in raised eyebrows and a suspicion, if not actual
accusation, of treachery which would be almost impossible to
allay. The lingering doubt about Hill's loyalty could be an
obstacle in the realization of his ambitions. Thus while
winning the nomination in 1892 was not made impossible

by Cleveland's defeat, the task would have been rendered easier by his victory. Hill evidently realized this, for he himself remarked that the stories of his knifing Cleveland amounted to charging him "not with being a traitor but with being an idiot." [72]

A second arraignment against Hill was that his presence on the ticket caused many Independents and Mugwumps to turn from the Democrats in disgust and support the entire Republican slate. The desertion of this element led to Cleveland's defeat, according to the charge, but since Hill would not have received its support under any circumstances, he lost no votes, and won his race for the governorship.

On the surface, this implication of passive responsibility seems to be a plausible explanation of Cleveland's defeat. Certainly the reforming element was deeply chagrined at the designation of Hill as the Democratic candidate for governor. Yet one of the basic tenets underlying the Independent position, one which is implied in its name, is that votes are not automatically cast along straight party lines, but for the individual and the issue, each to be judged on its own merits. It therefore seems highly unlikely that this element would turn from Cleveland, who after all never endorsed Hill, simply because it was disgusted with his party's choice for governor. It would have been more consistent to vote for Cleveland and Miller, thus supporting those whom the Independents regarded as the best qualified candidates. They were faced with no dilemma of choosing either a good president or a good governor, for they were free to vote for both.

It seems grossly unfair to lay at Hill's feet the blame for the national ticket's failure to carry New York. Cleveland's defeat can be explained without resort to accusations of treachery and selfishness. The fortunate circumstances

which had contributed to Cleveland's meager plurality of
1134 votes in New York in 1884 were not present in 1888.
Moreover, the President's vetoes of pension bills, the feelings
aroused by the Confederate flag incident, the Murchison
letter, the collapse of vice-presidential candidate Thurman
during the campaign, the less-than-lukewarm management
of the national Democratic campaign, the unquestioned
integrity of Harrison as compared to Cleveland's opponent
in 1884, the success of Republicans in "frying the fat" out
of manufacturers, the effectiveness of Warner Miller's campaign in halting the loss of Republican votes to the Prohibitionists—all of these are quite sufficient to account for
Cleveland's defeat.[73]

Although he had no part in Cleveland's defeat, and had
labored earnestly and tirelessly to prevent it, Hill was
resigned to the near impossibility of dispelling all suspicion
of his responsibility. When the results of the election were
known, Hill said to his friend Alton B. Parker:[74]

> This ends me as a presidential candidate, whether for
> nomination or election. No explanation either by myself
> or my friends can make headway against the logic of
> events. Unjust as these inferences are, nothing will ever
> convince the party that I was not to blame in some way,
> either direct or mysterious, for the result in this State
> which showed my election and the defeat of the Presi-
> dential ticket with Mr. Cleveland at its head. It is one of
> the penalties of politics that no man must succeed at the
> expense of his associates on a party ticket—whether this
> success comes with or without his procurement or knowl-
> edge.

Hill, however, was not a fatalist. Having made this
gloomy prediction, he bent his every effort during the suc-
ceeding years to prove himself a false prophet.

CHAPTER VI

A Place in the Sun

DAVID BENNETT HILL was inaugurated to his second full term as governor of the Empire State in January, 1889, amid a dazzling display of color and splendor. The main streets of Albany leading to the Capitol were clogged with nattily uniformed bands and parading militiamen. Political supporters of the Governor marched with their clubs and organizations, carrying aloft their gaily colored placards.[1] This extravagant display heralding the latest popular triumph of the Elmira politician was in marked contrast, as perhaps it was intended to be, with the quiet preparations being made in Washington for the orderly transfer of government to the Republican party.

If Hill was not bearing his honors modestly, it was understandable. For almost a decade he had had to walk in the shadow of Grover Cleveland, first in state and then in national politics. Now, all at once, the bulky figure was gone from before him, and light could be seen ahead. Hill had at last elbowed his way to a place in the sun, and he was basking ostentatiously in its warm rays.

There were others, however, who were also eager to travel the road of political preferment. Power vacuums are not long maintained in politics, and many would soon rush to fill the void in the party's leadership occasioned by

126

Cleveland's defeat. Hill's prospects were as bright as any, and his record as a winner in a key state was an important factor in his favor. Yet the selection of a new standard bearer was still four years away, and if Hill were to press his claim at that time with any hope of success, he would have to demonstrate a continuing hold on his state. This in large measure depended upon his ability either to bring to a happy solution some of the unresolved problems before him, or at very least to turn them to political advantage.

When Hill returned to the legislative concerns of the state, he was confronted with two such problems, both of which he had been called upon to deal with before: excise legislation, and the demand for ballot reform. The first of these, the excise question, caused Hill no grave concern. It was the Republicans rather than Hill who were holding this tiger by the tail. After two unhappy electoral experiences, they were anxious to be done with it, and hoped finally to arrive at a solution. While Hill was not averse to a solution on his own terms, he was also content to leave the matter where it was, so long as political advantage still accrued to him.

A more compelling problem, and also the most recent to arrive on the scene, was the insistent demand for ballot reform. Governor Hill's veto of the Saxton bill in 1888, far from silencing this demand, had magnified it and stirred the adherents of this infant movement to even greater activity. It was evident that the increasing strength and prominence of ballot reform could not be ignored, nor could it be subdued by another veto. To station his political career directly in the path of ballot reform would be perilous; yet Hill had already shown his antipathy toward the movement. To dispose of the issue in a manner which would at the very least neutralize its political effect was the challenge facing Hill.

Hill treated each of these problems at some length in his message to the legislature. About two-fifths of the message was devoted to the subject of electoral reform. During the preceding half-year, Hill's thoughts on the merits, the political overtones, and the consequences of ballot reform had begun to crystallize. He had wisely decided that the adamant position he had taken on the Saxton bill was no longer tenable. Some measure of electoral reform would plainly have to be conceded; it would be better to bend with the movement and satisfy some of its demands than to oppose it inflexibly and court disaster.

In his message,² therefore, Hill spelled out just how far he would retreat. While New York's election laws "as a whole are not excelled by any in the country," declared the Governor, the incontrovertible evidence that "vast and unusual sums of money" were raised by high-tariff advocates "for the purpose of debauching the electors" in 1888 had pointed up the "imperative" need for some change in these laws. There were two major abuses which had occurred in 1888 and which the legislature should now seek to remedy: bribery and intimidation.

Bribery, continued the Governor, although forbidden and punishable by law, had continued to flourish because of the difficulty of detection. What was needed, therefore, was an amendment which would decrease the opportunities for its successful consummation at the polls. Hill offered such a proposal: a "reasonable distance from the polls [should] be set aside or reserved by ropes, or barriers of some kind," within which only peace officers and one elector at a time would be permitted to enter. In this roped-off area would be a private booth or compartment in which each voter would prepare his ballot alone; then, still alone, he would proceed to the ballot box and deposit his ballots. "The value of such a provision," stated the Governor, "consists not in *permitting* the elector to cast a secret ballot, but *compelling* him to do so." Since a briber is less likely to pay for a vote which he cannot be sure will be cast as promised, this form of corruption would be frustrated.

These proposals if adopted would also deal effectively with the second flagrant abuse of the election laws, intimidation. The enforced secrecy would serve to free the workingman from the scrutinizing gaze of his employer. To safeguard further the employee in his right to vote freely, Hill urged the legislature to punish as a crime the use of pay envelopes which threatened employees with loss of jobs if they should fail to vote as directed. The use of this device in the presidential elections of two months before had been widespread, the Governor noted, and only by taking drastic steps could it be stopped.

Hill had several other recommendations on the subject of electoral reform, which, while peripheral, were intended to counter the unfavorable impression left by his veto of the Saxton bill. The excessive use of money in elections could be checked, suggested Hill, by requiring each candidate for office at a general election to file with the secretary of state within ten days after his election a verified statement of all moneys expended by him to aid his election during the canvass. Failure to do so should be sufficient cause to forfeit his office. To make it easier for employees in manufacturing, mechanical, or mercantile establishments in the state to go to the polls and vote, he recommended a law setting aside a two hour period on election day when such employees could leave their work to vote, without suffering a loss of pay for the time away from work. Such a law had already been enacted in Massachusetts and had worked well, the Governor noted. Also, to prevent confusion at the polls, Hill urged that election districts be limited to three hundred inhabitants instead of including as many as one thousand, as was commonly the case.

This far Hill would willingly go, and indeed, he would gladly lead the way. On one point, however, he remained adamant. Under no circumstances would he countenance a law providing for an exclusively official ballot. He did modify slightly his absolute refusal of the previous year to allow any ballots to be furnished at public expense. While still doubting the wisdom of this innovation, he now conceded that it might be an experiment worth trying. The right of the state, county, or city to furnish ballots, however, must not be exclusive, but should be a right shared concurrently with parties, candidates, and individuals.

Thus Hill stated to the legislature the limit of his concessions. Anything beyond this he would regard as too radical, an attempt to overturn a system which had stood the test of years and replace it with "an entirely new and untried system." This he would never accept. His warning to the legislature was veiled but unmistakable. "If too much shall be attempted," he cautioned, "it is to be feared that nothing at all may be actually accomplished."

On the subject of liquor legislation, too, Hill laid down his minimum conditions and maximum concessions. The recommendations of the seven-month-old excise commission would soon be reported, but in the interim Hill made clear his intention to steer an even course between absolute prohibition on the one hand and unrestricted traffic on the other. Since illiberal and severe laws would not, he informed the legislature, be supported by public sentiment and could not be enforced, he would oppose them. Any excise laws, to meet his approval, must be "equitable," "uniform in their operation throughout the state, and reasonable in their provisions." Exorbitant rates which amounted to prohibition would not be approved, for "it is not good policy to attempt to do indirectly what the state is unwilling to do directly." License fees should go into the local treasuries, and local authorities should be empowered to fix the fee in their areas at any point between the minimum and the maximum, as local sentiment may determine. In this way, the cause of home rule would be served, and no one area of the state would have foisted upon it the will of another.

To those who clamored for high license, Hill had a devastating reply. For two months he had been gathering statistics on license rates throughout the Empire State,[3] and he now presented them to the legislature. These figures showed that in only one city—New York—out of all the cities, towns, and villages of the state was there being charged the maximum license fee permitted under existing laws. Hill noted caustically that those who advocated still higher license laws might better serve the cause of temperance and absolve themselves of charges of hypocrisy if they would devote a small part of their energies to seeing that the provisions of existing laws were fully exploited. In some of the state's so-called temperance areas, the fees were only about one-third of the permissible maximum. "It is hardly possible," chided the Governor with evident relish, "that the State as a whole is desirous of having that which each locality, acting separately, distinctly rejects."

In addition to these two major matters, Hill recommended other legislation. On the subject of prison labor, he trod as gingerly as he had in the past. The act of 1888 was, as he noted, only a temporary expedient, hastily and imperfectly drawn, and the legislature could no longer postpone a thorough consideration of the problem. The prisoners should not be idle, but their employment should be regulated so as to compete with free labor as little as possible. Once again, however, Hill carefully avoided making any specific proposals as to how this happy result was to be effected.

The Governor also renewed many of his earlier recommendations, still not enacted into law. Chief among these was the creation of a state commission with supervisory powers over gas, electric, telephone, and telegraph companies, and of a special labor commission to suggest measures in the interests of labor; provision for an enumeration and reapportionment as well as for a constitutional convention, abolition of the senate's confirming power, and a revision of the tax laws to end the favored treatment of personalty. There was also a suggestion that certain types of corporations should be required to pay their employees weekly wages.

Two recommendations of a novel nature rounded out the message. The first, a suggestion that voting be made compulsory, was based on the truism that "citizenship imposes obligations as well as confers privileges." The percentage of the electorate that did not vote was disturbingly large, but compulsory voting, under penalty of fine and imprisonment, would end this absenteeism at the polls. This proposal was clearly unrealistic and unfeasible, but Hill insisted that it had its practical side. For one thing, it would end a common practice that amounted to the sale of votes—the refusal by some voters to go to the polls unless reimbursed by a party or candidate for their travel expenses. More importantly, it would encourage an interest in civic affairs through participation. "Intense but honest partisanship," Hill declared, "is preferable to indifference in public affairs." [4]

The second novel proposal in the message dealt with the federal constitution. He suggested that the legislature declare itself in favor of a constitutional amendment limiting a president to a single six-year term, and providing that an outgoing president become a life member of the United States Senate.

It was obvious within a week of Hill's message that so far as electoral reform was concerned, the Republican legislature intended neither to heed his warnings nor to accept his recommendations. As soon as the senate was organized, Senator Saxton reintroduced his ballot bill which, with a few minor changes and one major innovation, was substantially the same measure Hill had vetoed the year before. The new feature in this bill was the so-called blanket ballot bearing the name of each party's candidates for office, it was proposed that one large ballot should contain the names of all the candidates for each office. Party affiliations of the candidates would be designated next to each name. The voter would cast his ballot by marking an "X" next to the name of his choice for each office.

Hill tried desperately to block this bill and prevent it from reaching his desk. Because of the growing appeal of the electoral reform movement, a veto would be unpopular, and Hill was committed to a veto. While the bill was in committee, Hill prevailed upon Judge Nelson Waterbury, a jurist who had agreed with Hill's veto on constitutional grounds the previous year, to journey to Albany and argue at the bill's hearing for an acceptable substitute.[5] The major move in Hill's counter-offensive was the introduction of his own bill in mid-March by Senator John Linson. Simultaneously letters went out to Democratic editors advising that the Linson bill was acceptable to the Governor, and inviting the united support of the Democratic press for this measure. The party was not going to drag its feet and maintain a negative position on the ballot reform:

"The Democratic members of the Legislature, instead of merely opposing the Saxton Bill, propose to make a fair fight for that of Senator Linson."[6]

Hill's lieutenants in the assembly and senate, especially Assemblyman William Sheehan, Senator James Pierce, and Senator Jacob Cantor, fought hard for his bill, using all the parliamentary devices at their command, but their efforts were of no avail. The Republicans had no intention of letting slip from their grasp this opportunity to make the Governor squirm. At least as desirous of reaping a political harvest from Hill's discomfort as of effecting a real reform, the Republican caucus took up the Saxton bill as a party measure, and in April pushed it through both houses on a straight party vote.[7]

The fact that no Democrat voted for the bill was a confirmation, if any were needed, of Hill's intentions. His veto came as a surprise to no one. The only thing which had not been predicted days before was the message's inordinate length. Most of the twenty-six printed pages[8] were consumed by a rehearsal of the Governor's objections to the Saxton bill of the previous year and a repetition of his recommendations to the legislature. Almost every feature of the new bill was the target of criticism. The Governor reserved his bitterest polemic for the exclusively official ballot and the "new-fangled" blanket ballot, which he denounced as "cumbersome, expensive, impractical, and unconstitutional."

The message was as labored as it was long, and much of the reasoning was neither cogent nor plausible. Some of the arguments which Hill recited against the exclusively official ballot betrayed his anxiety to find excuses for a veto. The argument that ballots printed and distributed at public expense might not be delivered to the polls on time was as specious this year as last. Hill seemed to be grasping at straws when he suggested that the official ballot, dependent for candidates on party nomination, could be the instrument for total disfranchisement: if parties should fail to nominate, no names would appear on the ballot, and the electorate would have no one to vote for. That this Alice-in-Wonderland situation was rather unlikely to occur in nineteenth century New York the Governor conceded; but the existence of the merest possibility that it might, he insisted, rendered the bill unconstitutional. Moreover, Hill indulged in an exercise in semantics, suggesting that the blanket ballot was not constitutional because it was not within the meaning of the word "ballot" at the time the voting provision in the constitution was written.

Hill vetoed this bill, of course, for the same reason that he had vetoed a ballot reform bill the year before. In some ways, in fact, that bill was less objectionable than the present measure, for the new blanket ballot was an additional obstacle to polling the full illiterate vote. Hill would accept reform, but there was always a higher desideratum: ". . . in framing a measure the rights of the Democratic party should be preserved," he wrote a friend. "I want a bill that is right, and that will protect our voters, or else I do not want any at all." [9] Although the veto was unpopular, Hill regarded it as vital to the interests of the Democratic party.

If the demand for electoral reform placed Hill in an awkward position, the scales were balanced by the Republican dilemma on the liquor question. In early January, the excise commission, appointed by the previous legislature to codify existing legislation and suggest equitable revisions, filed its report. Since the Republicans had carefully arranged for a Republican majority on the commission, they confidently expected a report favoring high license. They were not only disappointed, then, but embarrassed

by the commission's recommendation for only a mildly
higher license bill. The proposed increase in license fees
fell far short of the position adopted by the party under
Warner Miller's lead in 1888, and made his stand, and
previous Republican bills, seem excessive.[10]

For a time it seemed that while neither party found the
measure exactly to its liking, this compromise would be
enacted. Within the month, however, this hope was dashed
by the Republicans. Warner Miller, in a message to Republican law-makers, urged them not to support this bill because it would be a retreat from the high ground taken
in the 1888 campaign.[11] While Miller argued that retreat
was wrong as a matter of principle, other Republican
leaders believed that it was dangerous as a matter of
politics. From the strategist's point of view, such a move
entailed the greatest possible risks without the slightest
prospect of reward: compromising their position could not
win back the liquor vote, now beyond recall, and it would
be almost sure to alienate the strong temperance fringe
of the party. Republicans shuddered at the thought that
the trickle of deserters who daily crossed over the border
to Prohibitionism might be swelled into an army. Since
no course of action promised a net political gain, the Republicans chose that course which at least held some promise of mitigating the loss—an unchanged high license stand.

Thus the commission bill was doomed. While the measure was put aside, however, the Republicans attempted to
salvage what they could by making it appear that Hill
opposed even a moderate excise act. A new high license bill
was prepared and made a party measure. The majority
loudly proclaimed it as an acceptable substitute for the
excise commission's bill.[12] Hill promptly vetoed it, and
justified this action in a scorching message.[13] An exposure
of Republican intentions in passing this bill was accom-

panied by a chapter-and-verse recital of Republican hypocrisy in excise legislation over the years. The message, a
masterly philippic, was one of Hill's best efforts.

Aside from these session-long struggles over excise and
ballot reform and a minor improvement of the prison labor
law,[14] few matters of importance distinguished the 1889
legislative session. The only other major measure to be
considered, a rapid transit bill for New York City, was
blocked by patronage-seeking Republicans.[15] There was
also the usual large number of vetoes, mostly of bills which
Hill regarded either as special legislation, violations of
home rule, or simply defectively drawn.[16]

The paucity of important legislation was due in part
to the assembly's pre-occupation for almost half a session
with a ludicrous episode that became known as the assembly ceiling scandal. While awaiting the completion of the
new state capitol building, the legislature continued to
meet in its old chambers. Although repaired within the
year, the ceiling of the assembly room was in such bad condition during 1888 that pieces of it regularly crumbled and
dropped to the floor. It was frightening enough for an assemblyman to enter the chamber in the morning and find
a chunk of ceiling resting where he had sat only a few
hours before; but to this fright was added the indignity of
having the climax of an impassioned oratorical effort punc-
tuated by the resounding crash of a piece of ceiling. The
condition was altogether too intolerable to suffer, and the
lower house had its 128 seats moved into the small parlor
of the chamber, where the sessions were then conducted.
After several days of cramped discomfort, however, the
assemblymen decided to return and brave the perils of
plunging plaster.[17]

Early in 1889 it was decided to look into the cause of
the ceiling's deterioration. An investigation was undertaken

in January, and continued into March. It revealed that the contractors who had repaired the ceilings had not only used inferior materials in the very home of the state's lawmakers, but had had the brazen effrontery to overcharge the state $100,000. This situation was attributable to the incompetence of the state superintendent of this work, one Andrews, a pork-packer before his appointment. The sole result of the investigation was the removal of Andrews, although Comptroller Edward Wemple and Attorney General Charles Tabor came in for press censure for alleged laxity, the former for his approval of payments based upon the contractors' fraudulent vouchers, and the latter for a lack of zealousness in initiating prosecution.[18] The whole episode occasioned much mirthful comment about the occupational hazards of assemblymen, but few noted soberly that the months consumed by legislators in their amusing pursuit of the culprits might better have been spent on weightier matters.

When the legislature adjourned, Hill had already forged his major weapons for the fall contest. The alert Governor fashioned still another through a shrewd use of his itemized veto on the annual appropriations bill. In an extravagant mood, the legislature had appropriated some $12,000,000 for state expenses during the last days of the session, a sum considerably in excess of the previous year's expenditure. After a close scrutiny, Hill pruned away close to $2,000,000, about one-seventh of the total. The vetoes were unexceptionable, and the action was completely justified. Although opposition organs muddied Hill's motives, they had in the end to concede the rightness of his course.[19]

Armed with his arsenal of issues, Hill now cleared the field for the fall battle. For the Democrats, the campaign of 1889 was all Hill. For the first time since his rise to prominence, Hill was in complete control of the party in

the state, and he intended to use this power to enhance
his reputation. All Democrats conceded that Hill was to
master-mind the party's campaign. The watchword was
one of simple obeisance: "What Davy says goes." [20]

In an unusual move, Hill indicated in the formal call
for the convention his plan of attack for the next two
months. It was addressed to all citizens who "favor the
principles of taxation, economy, and retrenchment advocated by the Democratic party and who are opposed to
inequitable and oppressive sumptuary legislation." [21] Economy and excise policies—these were to be Hill's chief issues.
Supremely confident, Hill had shown his opponents his
high cards, and challenged them to trump them. Significantly, both of these issues were based upon his own executive vetoes of Republican measures. The Governor rested
his party's fate in November squarely on his own shoulders.

As he selected the issues, Hill also chose the slate. When
the Democrats convened, each of Hill's choices was selected
on the first ballot. All but two of the nominees were unop-
posed. A mild rebellion occurred when the County Democracy and Tammany Hall decided to oppose the re-election
of Comptroller Wemple and Attorney General Tabor. It
was feared that their connection with the assembly ceiling
scandal might put the party on the defensive and jeopardize the success of the entire ticket. This uprising was
snuffed out, however, as the convention obeyed Hill's demand that it honor the Democratic tradition of rewarding
faithful and capable officials with a second term.[22]

Only in New York City was Hill unable to make his
will prevail. There the traditional enmity between the
County Democracy and the Tammany Tiger boiled over
once more, and even Hill was unable to get the two to
unite on a local ticket. The County Democracy, steadily
losing prestige and supporters, decided to stake everything

on a fusion with the Republicans, and entered a Citizen ticket.[23]

Meanwhile Tom Platt's Republicans had already convened. Their strategy as outlined in their platform was to score Hill and the Democrats for their opposition to ballot reform. Wary after Miller's defeat on high license in 1888, the Republicans declined to pick up Hill's challenge on excise. Their innocuous excise plank promised only that "no steps backward will be taken," and pledged their determination "to persevere until salutary and adequate provisions of law are embodied in the statutes of the State." The words "salutary and adequate" were inspired, covering as they did the whole ground from high license to no license. The ticket, dictated by Platt, was as nondescript as was the party platform.[24]

The campaign itself was quiet on both sides, with most of the work being done behind the scenes. There were few speeches by the Democratic candidates, and the few rallies held were centered around addresses by Hill. The tax question was made the chief issue for the Democratic circulars, postal cards, and other literature bearing on this subject which were sent into every corner of the state.[25]

A concentrated effort was also made to bring out the votes of those who opposed high license. Especially sought was the German vote. Hill wrote to a prominent German-born citizen two weeks before the election:

> I think it best that our personal liberty friends among the Germans should be active again this fall, as they were in 1887, in favor of the Democratic State Ticket. The issues are the same now as then, and Republican Germans can be induced in large numbers to aid us. I think the "boom" among the personal liberty leagues and clubs should be started at once.[26]

The opposition, of course, was not inactive. Their attack was centered on Hill, and their mills received grist from independent groups like the Reform Club, which denounced the Governor as a "sham ballot reformer." [27]

The election was another triumph for Hill. With almost the entire campaign revolving around his actions and his issues, the full Democratic slate was swept into office by margins ranging from 10,000 to over 20,000. Although the Republicans continued to control both chambers of the legislature, the Democrats made substantial inroads in their majority in the Assembly.[28]

Even while Hill was directing his party to victory in the 1889 contest, he was engaged in another project of equal importance to him—that of remolding the state party in his own image. This was to be achieved through the capture and enfeoffment of the party organization. With the same thoroughness of planning, organization, and execution that was the hallmark of his electoral triumphs, Hill embarked on his mission of conquest.

The control of the state committee, as the policy-making organ of the party, was Hill's primary concern. Weeks before the convention at which the committeemen were to be selected, Hill had been making his quiet preparations, guarding against possible slip-ups. From his Albany headquarters went letters to friends in strategic local positions all over the state, declaring that this or that candidate would be acceptable, that here a contest should be avoided, and there one should be vigorously prosecuted. When a choice was left to a local leader, it was always with the understanding that the final selection would be made from "friendly" candidates.[29] The state committee in 1889 as finally selected reflected the thoroughness of the purge: ten Cleveland men had been replaced by more amenable Democrats, and the state committee was transformed into Hill's

rubber stamp. Only a few, notably D-Cady Herrick of
Albany County, successfully withstood the efforts to unseat
them, and remained on the committee to snipe at the
Governor.[30]

Wherever he could reach, Hill established himself more
firmly in control of the party. Cleveland men holding important appointive posts in the state government were
turned out to pasture, as the Governor replaced them with
his own followers or with members of friendly factions.[31]
One important Clevelandite to fall from a key office was
James Shanahan, who had controlled the vast patronage
of the Department of Public Works. The several state
boards underwent a thorough scrutiny and were overhauled
to get rid of "traitors." [32] The civil service commission was
again reorganized, with an eye not only to making it more
responsive to the Governor's wishes, but also to providing
offices for those whom Hill decided should be rewarded.
In a letter to his friend, General Daniel Sickles, requesting
his resignation as civil service commissioner, Hill conceded
that the General had discharged his duties satisfactorily,
but added frankly that ". . . in looking over the political
field and in 'repairing my fences' in some places, I think it is
desirable to place this office in the country districts. . . ." [33]

One of the new Commissioners appointed by Hill was the
Republican editor of _Leslie's Magazine_, John A. Sleicher.
Despite their political differences, Sleicher and Hill had
long been personal friends, but it hardly seems likely that
the calculating Governor had made his selection on the basis
of friendship alone. The appointment of editor Sleicher
appears to have been one move in a concerted effort to
strengthen Hill's press support.[34] Since few Cleveland partisans or Democratic editors of a reform persuasion could
be won over, Hill turned to the cultivation of certain editors with mildly Republican or strongly anti-Cleveland

leanings who had not been disposed toward personal un-
friendliness in the past.

Little more than a week after Sleicher's appointment
Hill made another move in the same vein when he trans-
ferred all of the public printing under his control from
the venerable *Albany Argus,* one of the most influential
Democratic sheets in the state, to its competitor, the *Evening Times.* The reason was transparent. The editor of the
Argus was James Manning, whose father had run both the
newspaper and the state Democracy before him. Young
Manning was an incorrigible Clevelandite who would be
sure to oppose Hill in a showdown between the two Democratic leaders. The transfer of the juicy state printing account was unquestionably intended to weaken Manning as
well as to court T. C. Callicot, the virulent anti-Cleveland-
ite who edited the *Evening Times.*[35]

At the same time, the relationship between Hill and the
machine groups, especially Tammany, was undergoing a
subtle change in 1889. On the surface, the situation seemed
similar to that in Hill's first years as governor. His election
had been made possible in part by the support of machines
which had been enlisted by acts of friendship and either
implicit or explicit promises of future co-operation. This
exchange of favors for support, this unwritten alliance between the organizations and the Governor, continued in
effect after the 1888 elections; but the political circumstances were such as to redefine the role of each in the
alliance.

Until now Hill had been in the position of having to
placate these groups with favors and offices in order to
assure himself of their support. The reason for this was
simple: while the machines could get along without Hill,
Hill could not get along without the machines. Although
Hill had not relied upon them exclusively, and had as-

siduously nursed and cultivated his own personal organization, he had been nonetheless responsive to the demands of these factions. The 1888 elections, however, had led to a shift in the balance of power in the state Democratic party. The loss of the Presidency meant an end to whatever federal patronage had been counted upon. Moreover, Cleveland's defeat had sufficiently weakened his position in the party councils of the state to allow Hill to elbow into a position of supremacy. By reason of these changes, Hill's bargaining position in dealing with the powerful factions within the party was considerably improved. Thus, while the alliance remained unchanged, by 1889 it had undergone an important shift in emphasis. Whereas Hill had earlier used his approvals and vetoes of measures vital to machine interests as an inducement for support, he could now use them for threats of reprisal as well.

Although circumstances had tilted the balance slightly in Hill's favor, the advantage was one not likely to be pressed. Hill was a man of ambitions, and to realize them, all possible support would have to be mustered. An indiscriminate exercise of advantage could goad erstwhile supporters to rebellion, and the shrewd Elmiran was not one to sacrifice future plans to present vanities. It was enough that all recognized him as the master of the party within the state.

While Hill was solidifying his control of the party in New York State, he was also active in acquainting party leaders in other sections of the nation with his record and his availability. Early in February, 1889, when Congress was in session, Hill made his first trip to Washington, at the invitation of Secretary Whitney. Hill had always wanted to visit Washington, but had been unable to accept any of President Cleveland's several invitations. His entrance in Washington, coinciding as it did with preparations for

Cleveland's departure, had a good deal more significance than a casual sightseeing tour. The Governor was in the capital for only twenty-four hours, but these hours were crammed with visits from Democratic senators and representatives anxious to meet and size up the potential presidential candidate. These visitors poured into Hill's hotel suite and later into Whitney's mansion, where Hill spent most of the day. Scores of prominent Democrats stopped in to greet the Governor and partake of Whitney's famed buffet table of terrapin stew and champagne.[36]

Hill made a very favorable impression on his visitors, who found him delightfully pleasant, affable, and clever. Far more significant than comments about his personal charm was the observation of one guest on his political availability. He seemed to be, according to this man, "what the old Latins called a man who went in the middle way—a safe man and a man of the people." [37]

Although too busy with the legislative session to travel for the next several months, Hill kept in touch with old friends and new acquaintances out-of-state, not only through an active correspondence but through personal visits of his political intimates. Hill's friends traveled around the nation singing the praises of the Governor, publicizing his electoral record, and closeting with local party leaders. Edward Murphy made the long trip to California "for his health," accompanied by Roswell P. Flower. During the course of their journey and two-month stay, these vacationers managed to visit and chat with prominent Democrats in Colorado, California, Washington, Dakota, Minnesota, and Illinois.[38] Later in the year another expedition, composed of State Treasurer Elliot Danforth and a Hill Republican named General James Woodward toured Virginia, acquainting local leaders with Hill's availability.[39]

In the fall of 1889 Hill made his first extensive tour.

The occasion was the opening of the Piedmont Exposition, the South's most important event, representing Georgia, Alabama, Florida, Tennessee, and the two Carolinas. Hill seized this opportunity to meet many of the most important Democrats in the South.

The Governor was received enthusiastically in Georgia. His train, although arriving in Atlanta hours late and well past midnight, was met by a huge crowd, including high state officials and prominent Georgians. All during the following day large excursions arrived in Atlanta to see and hear Hill speak. Throngs lined the streets from the Kimball Hotel to the Fair Grounds and cheered Hill all along the journey. At the Fair Grounds upwards of 50,000 persons overflowed the 8,000-seat grandstand to listen to the distinguished visitor from the North utter platitudes about the New South. Before leaving the next day, Hill was feted by the Irish-American Club of Atlanta, which boomed him for the Presidency in 1892. On the return trip northward, Hill also made speeches in Chattanooga and Knoxville, Tennessee. The trip was considered by many observers a significant success.[40]

The Governor and his emissaries worked tirelessly to promote his candidacy. To dismiss the sentiment for Hill, however, as a product entirely manufactured in and distributed from Albany would be to miss its character and significance. There were people from many states, of differing shades of opinion and station in life, who were genuinely anxious for Hill's success. Numbered among these people, as was to be expected, were the same congenital Cleveland-haters who had attempted to use Hill as a foil in 1888, as well as those who had backed other contenders in hopes of upsetting Cleveland. But there were other thoughtful Democrats who were now supporters of the Governor. Some of these felt that Cleveland's defeat,

no matter how regrettable, had made him unavailable in
1892, and now considered Hill to be the party's best hope.
Others believed that Cleveland's political ineptness, as evidenced by his handling of the patronage, had been responsible for his defeat in 1888 and disqualified him for another
nomination. There was also a feeling that, in his almost
exclusive emphasis on the tariff, the former President had
forsaken the full meaning of true Democracy. "Someone
must take up the old party flag, . . ." wrote a Missouri
Democrat to Hill. "If the tariff reform issue is all there
is of Democracy, when a satisfactory schedule is made,
Democracy expires." [41]

Thus in 1890 many Democrats were shopping for a new
standard-bearer, and by 1890, Democrats were being famil-
iarized with the name and record of David B. Hill. His
audience now far transcended his own state's boundaries—
watchful, waiting, some hopeful, some critical, all evalu-
ating. As he turned back to his state duties, Hill must have
been acutely aware of this audience, and he was eager to
impress it.

There was, however, one major state problem still be-
deviling Hill, a problem which threatened to do anything
but make a favorable impression. This was the irksome
issue of ballot reform. Hill was in an unenviable position
on ballot reform. He had taken a strong, almost contemp-
tuous stand against it in his veto of the first Saxton bill.
The movement, rather than wilting, had then seemed to
thrive on opposition. As the pressure for a reform measure
had mounted, Hill had been forced to retreat from his
more untenable arguments. His original contention that
there was no need for revision in the electoral laws was
transformed into an assertion that a change was "imperative." From his 1888 objection to restricting the "right of
the people to converse with and electioneer one another

at the polls," he had moved a year later to the position that a voter should be *compelled* to cast a secret ballot. From a complete rejection of publicly printed ballots as a needless and fruitless expense, he conceded that official ballots would be acceptable, as long as ballots were not exclusively official.[42]

These concessions did not begin to pacify the advocates of ballot reform, who would settle for nothing less than complete victory. The movement continued to gain adherents all over the nation. In Hill's own state, clubs sprang up with ballot reform as their cry. Pressure mounted within his own party, and prominent Democrats and Democratic newspapers endorsed the reform. The rumblings of discontent grew louder, when influential Democratic organizations like the Young Men's Democratic Club of New York joined the movement.[43] Even one of Hill's staunchest newspaper supporters, the New York *World,* publicly differed with him on the exclusively official ballot.[44] The great success of the new ballot law in neighboring Massachusetts, operating for the first time in 1889, added the weight of proven practicability to the demand for reform.

Hill was fully aware of the dangers in the ballot reform issue. He knew that he must somehow either become identified positively with this movement, or at the very least neutralize its political effects.[45] Yet an approval of the Saxton bill in its present form would imply an admission of earlier contumaciousness; and the official blanket ballot still gravely threatened Democratic voting strength. Hill's objections had already been trimmed to a minimum. There was nothing for him to do now but to stick by his guns, attempt to justify his position, and hope for the best. And this was the position that he now took.

To the legislature he again expressed his earnest desire for reform.[46] His sole objections were again directed against two features of the Saxton bill, the exclusively official ballot and the blanket ballot. As he had done in his veto of the Crosby bill in 1888, Hill relegated to the background all objections based on grounds of practicability and feasibility, and retreated to the ultimate defensive position, that of personal constitutional objections, already stated in his previous vetoes.

The Republican legislature again, however, refused to permit Hill to maneuver out of his tight spot, and once more passed the Saxton bill in essentially the same form as the previous year.

There seemed to be no way out of the spot. Throughout the bill's course in the legislature and while it lay on Hill's desk awaiting action, there were constant reminders of the drift of opinion on the subject. Mass meetings demanded the reform in increasingly violent tones. Even if Hill were ready to dismiss these meetings as opposition-inspired, he must have been disturbed by the appearance at the executive mansion of representatives of thirty-four Knights of Labor assembly districts who urged him to approve the bill. The popular demand for ballot reform was dramatized when a gigantic petition, weighing one-half ton and bearing some 77,000 signatures from New York City and Brooklyn alone, was carried by fourteen men to the floor of the legislature, there to rest during the debates.[47]

Hill had had enough. He was even willing, if necessary, to approve the bill as it stood, if a way could be found to save face and keep his earlier opposition from appearing petty, partisan, and obstructionist. Hill found that way. Shortly after the bill reached his desk, Hill sent a special message to the legislators.[48] As they well knew, he pointed out, he agreed with the objectives of the bill, but he could not approve it because of a "deep-seated and controlling" conviction that some of its provisions were unconstitu-

tional. Then Hill opened the escape hatch for himself. "I
have, however, no mere pride of opinion in this matter,
and will cheerfully acquiesce where convinced that my
views are unsound." Since the matter was of such great
importance, Hill suggested that it be referred to the Court
of Appeals for an informal opinion. Such a move was not
without precedent, noted the Governor, and a joint resolution by the legislature requesting such an opinion could
settle, once and for all, the constitutionality of the controversial provisions. The message breathed a spirit of fairness
and conciliation.

It was a shrewd political stroke. If the Republican legislators refused to do as Hill requested, at least some of the
onus for a veto would be put upon them. If they did refer
the question to the jurists, Hill would escape all the pitfalls
of the issue and emerge practically unscathed. A court
opinion agreeing with him would give him complete vindication. An adverse opinion would allow him to bow gracefully to the verdict of a judicial body, which had set at
rest his "deep-seated and controlling" constitutional misgivings, and he could then proceed to approve the bill
cheerfully. If the court were to split, Hill could exercise
his judgment and choose whichever course he deemed
wisest.

The legislature, seeing through the clever escape which
Hill had fashioned, blocked it as best they could by sending
the proposal to committee. Six days later the Governor
vetoed the Saxton bill, reciting once again his objections,
and making much of the legislature's refusal to submit
the bill to a judicial opinion. In rejecting his sincere offer,
fulminated Hill, the Republicans showed their contempt
for the best interests of the people. Their hypocrisy in
framing a bill which they knew must be vetoed was now
fully exposed, he asserted. Since the Republican obstruc-

tionism had prevented him from setting at rest his own objections to the bill, he had no choice but to veto it.[49] This tactic eased the pressure somewhat, although it was observed that if he had really wished an opinion, he could himself have asked the jurists, without a resolution from the legislature.

For all his cunning, inventiveness, and agility, however, the Governor still held the wrong end of the stick. He realized that, although he had managed to throw sand in many eyes, he was still in a poor position on ballot reform. At this point, however, aid arrived from an unexpected quarter, and through the efforts of the Ballot Reform League (a group of private citizens) and an incredible Republican blunder, Hill was rescued.

Shortly after Hill's veto of the Saxton bill, a series of conferences were held between members of the league, Senator Saxton, and Governor Hill. Anxious to salvage some measure of reform, the proponents of the Saxton bill decided to accept half a loaf, and worked out a compromise which satisfied Hill's demands.

The proposal, accepted by both Hill and Senator Saxton, resolved the impasse previously presented by the exclusively official ballot and blanket ballot. The new measure incorporated certain features of the blanket ballot, but separated them into strips, each separate strip containing the names of only one party's nominees. A blank strip was provided for those who wished to write in other candidates. The person who wished to vote a straight ticket merely deposited the strip which listed his party's nominees. These were the only ballots allowed, for the measure provided for an exclusively official ballot. No party or individual could supply other ballots. In their stead, however, they could supply pasters, which, when pasted onto the official ballots, became themselves official. The paster was considered the choice of the voter, regardless of which party strip it was pasted on. In this way the illiterate voter was cared for. Armed with a paster in his pocket, the non-reader could enter the voting booth, pick any of the strips out of the pack and affix his paster to it.[50]

This bill was promptly introduced in the senate and received immediate consideration. Hill was pleased with the compromise, and, using the veto of a minor bill as his vehicle, he announced his intention of accepting it:

> . . . A general act [he wrote] relative to the form of ballots and the manner of voting is now pending in the Senate, with fair prospects, as I am advised, of its passage by the Legislature. The act seems to meet with general approbation, and if passed in its present shape will probably become a law, inasmuch as it has been freed from constitutional and other objections which heretofore have made similar measures obnoxious to a part of the Legislature and to the Executive.[51]

It is doubtful that Hill was attempting to trick the Republicans into a false move with this declaration of intention. In all probability he meant to do no more than ease the bill on its course, salvage what he could by calling attention to his readiness to approve a bill which heeded his constitutional objections, and once for all be done with this troublesome issue. Yet even Hill's most cunning ruses rarely resulted so favorably for him. The Republicans, up to now holding the whip hand on ballot reform, now threw away all their advantage with an incredible blunder.

Reluctant finally to let Hill off the hook, a Republican caucus decided to drop the acceptable compromise measure and replace it with a bill which was objectionable to the

David Bennett Hill

Grover Cleveland, 1883

Harper's Weekly, *October 31, 1885.*

Hill's plight in the 1885 gubernatorial campaign, after
revelations linking the Elmiran with Boss Tweed in the
ownership of the *Elmira Gazette,* was pointed up by Thomas
Nast in this cartoon captioned: "THE SKELETON IN
HIS CLOSET: Mr. Hill's attempt to secrete a scandalous
volume of 'ancient history.' "

Harper's Weekly, *July 9, 1887.*

This cartoon of "LITTLE DAVID'S FIREWORKS" was captioned: "Well, by Jove, this is the only one out of the whole collection that will even sizzle."

Harper's Weekly, *June 16, 1888.*

"Hill's rejection of the Saxton ballot reform bill and his veto of another measure concerned with purifying elections, the so-called Fassett antibribery bill, promised to alienate a good deal of voting support in the November, 1888 elections."

New York State Executive Mansion, Eagle Street, Albany, N.Y. Built in 1857; acquired by state for $45,000 in 1877; expanded during Hill's governorship, in 1887.

New York State Capitol, Albany, N.Y. Cornerstone laid in 1871; first occupied in 1879; building completed in 1898.

T. C. Platt

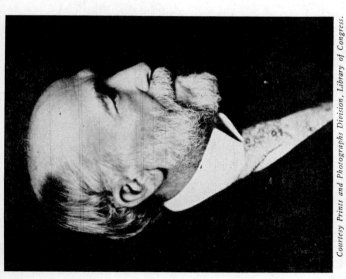

Richard Croker

Manton Marble

William C. Whitney

Governor and would be sure to be rejected by him. The substitute measure was pushed through the senate the following day. This exhibition of contumaciousness stirred a veritable hornet's nest in the independent press, both the *New York Times* and the *Evening Post* belaboring the Republicans for their cheap political antics.[52] Hill girded himself for battle, and sent out letters to Democratic editors announcing his readiness to fight in view of the Republican repudiation of the compromise.[53]

The Republicans were quick to see their error and, hastily receding from their antagonistic position, supported the compromise measure, which then passed the senate by a unanimous vote. The awakening, however, was too late, for their greed had already cost them dearly. In attempting to squeeze one last drop from the ballot reform issue, they had cast doubt upon the sincerity of their original support of it, and lent credence to Hill's earlier charges of hypocrisy. In three days they had forfeited much of the credit for ballot reform which would otherwise have been theirs.[54]

The bill was whisked through the assembly and Hill signed it immediately, using the occasion for an attack on Republican obstructionism and for a justification of his earlier vetoes.[55] It is not likely that Hill convinced anyone with his assertion that his fight for real ballot reform had finally been rewarded with victory, but by gaining this compromise, and with the aid of his opponents' tactical blunder, he did succeed in neutralizing the toxic political sting of the issue.

The Republicans, in throwing away this opportunity to embarrass Hill, lost the only such opportunity they were to have in 1890. On all other issues arising during this session, Hill showed to good advantage, and on two major issues, the World's Fair and rapid transit bills, it was the Republican senate which appeared in the role of factious partisans, while Hill was universally applauded for his statesmanlike efforts.

While Congress was considering a site for the great Columbian Exposition of 1892,[56] a bill designed to promote New York City's chances came before the legislature. When the Republicans tied up the bill in an effort to find some patronage in it, Hill promptly sent a message urging them to set aside petty partisanship for the greater benefit and glory of the state, and to pass the bill without further delay. The message was endorsed by an indignant public and press.[57] This plea and the clamor from the general public and numerous Republicans jolted the senate into passing the bill. Platt, however, was determined to keep the patronage connected with this mammoth undertaking out of Democratic hands in a presidential year. He proceeded to undercut the bill by spreading the word among Washington friends that he wanted the fair for New York only in 1893, one year later than planned. Platt's poorly disguised opposition and the initial indecisiveness of the legislature were factors in Congress' decision to award the fair to Chicago.[58]

New York's transit problem, which had become acute in recent years, was another concern of the state government in 1890. During the previous year a much-needed bill had been introduced authorizing a commission to work out a solution to the transportation problems of the metropolis. When the bill, despite its unquestioned merit, got through only the assembly, Hill had sent a special message to the senate urging its passage.[59] As was so often the case, the Governor's endorsement of the proposal was a kiss of death, and the senate buried the bill until the session expired. This measure, the Ives bill, was reintroduced in 1890. The bill left the choice of commissioners to Mayor Grant, in accordance with the principles of home rule. The Republican game became clear when Senator Fassett intro-

duced a rapid transit bill, identical in every respect with
the Ives bill, except that the commissioners were named
in the bill itself. The Fassett bill was an attempt to guarantee Republican representation on the commission, for
a number of those named were Republicans. Hill, of course,
threw his support to the Ives bill, and there was little question that it was the sounder measure. The press also generally favored it, especially after Mayor Grant publicly
designated a number of prominent qualified citizens whom
he intended to appoint when the bill passed. The Republicans held firmly to their demands, and when an eleventh
hour conference failed to break the deadlock, they were
roundly scored for the bill's failure.[60]

In addition to besting the Republican legislators on these
stalemated issues, Hill could also point to some constructive legislation which was at least partly the result of his
suggestions. The general registration act, without which the
new ballot act would have been ineffective, was actively
championed by Hill; and his suggestion that candidates
be required to file statements of expenses within ten days
following elections was also enacted. He was also instrumental in securing more adequate state care for the insane.
In addition, many of Hill's suggestions which did not
receive favorable action were unexceptionable. His desire
to extend the requirement of filing campaign expenses to the
executive committees of each party was based on a realistic
view of politics. The recommendation for improvement and
construction of county roads was a farsighted one, and his
renewed demands that the burden of taxation should be
more equitably adjusted between real estate and personalty
represented a workable solution to an increasingly knotty
problem.[61]

Perhaps the most interesting of all his suggestions was a
proposal for a constitutional amendment to transfer the

adjudication of contested seats in the legislature to the state courts, rather than leave it in the hands of a partisan legislature. While he undoubtedly intended to reflect upon the Republican majority's recent wholesale unseating of Democrats in the Congress, the suggestion was nevertheless a worthy one, supported by many reformers.[62]

Hill had taken giant strides since his inauguration into his second full term as governor. He had, as in the past, acquitted himself creditably in his annual battles with the Republican legislature, and his electoral victory in 1889 added further luster to his reputation as an all-conquering campaigner. With the party organization firmly in his grip, Hill was the undisputed leader of the state party. But bigger prizes lay ahead, and Hill now turned to extending that leadership to the national party as well.

CHAPTER VII

The "Governor-Senator"

THE ELECTION of 1890 figured large in the calculations of David Bennett Hill. During the two years following Cleveland's defeat, the ambitious Elmiran had labored tirelessly to make himself more widely known to the influential Democrats of the nation. Political leaders and editors had been cultivated and acquainted with the Governor's record through letters, personal visits, or consultations with personal emissaries. Admittedly, the record was an attractive one. Never once had Hill lost an electoral battle, whether as a candidate or as a strategist. He had molded from the divergent interests in the state party a smoothly working organization. He was a vigorous exponent of an unalloyed and unallied Democracy, and his devotion to party had been amply demonstrated. Twice he had carried the crucial state of New York. Yet despite this record and the wide publicity given it, David Bennett Hill, as the election of 1890 approached, was merely one of many contenders for his party's presidential nomination. In no sense could he be considered the leader of the national party.

As a realist, Hill was aware of this; as an opportunist, he was also alive to the possibility that the electoral contest of 1890 might be utilized as a spring-board by which he could vault himself into the vacant party leadership. Through a

vigorous, forthright, aggressive exposition of the Democratic
position on national issues and on a national scale, the New
York Democratic leader might well succeed in identifying
himself with the national Democracy, and thus give substance to dream and pretension.

The year seemed ripe for a Democratic victory. One and
one-half years of Republican control of the federal government had produced a record of recklessness, extravagance,
narrow partisanship, and pandering to special interest
groups. The treasury surplus, large enough under Cleveland
to convince him of the need for tariff cuts, withered under
the twin onslaught of congressmen hungry for pork and
veterans hungry for pensions—"God help the surplus"
proved to be more than a facetious remark by a Republican
official. To ease the passage of Republican legislation
Speaker Reed promulgated a series of arbitrary rulings
which soon earned him the nickname "czar," and his party
increased its shaky House majority of eight to a more
comfortable twenty-four by unconscionably unseating sixteen Democrats. To eliminate the need for repeating such
distasteful proceedings, the Republicans contrived to insure future control by means of a rigged federal census,
on which assignment of new House seats was based, and
through a federal elections bill—the so-called Force Bill—
which aimed at fettering elections in the Democratic South.
This bill failed to become law, but the two major measures
produced by the Republicans probably did their cause more
harm than the stalemated Force Bill. A high tariff, highest
in the nation's history, had angered thousands even before
its final enactment, and the Sherman Silver Purchase Act,
a temporizing attempt to allay the rising agitation for a
cheaper currency, alarmed the conservative East while
failing to appease the inflamed West.[1]

Hill, of course, was concerned with these facts, not only

as they affected national politics, but also as they might bear on the state elections; for victory, to be significant, had to begin at home. Although there was to be only one minor state-wide contest, a new assembly was to be elected, and its capture became one of Hill's major objectives. For six years he had had to struggle against a legislature controlled in both branches by the Republicans. This was normal in New York, where the under-representation of New York City in the legislature, along with a shameless gerrymander of the state's districts, tended to perpetuate Republican ascendancy. Winning the assembly would therefore represent no small triumph for Hill. It would amount to a resounding vindication and endorsement of his governorship and would attest to his mastery of New York politics. If, in addition, a large enough majority were secured, New York Democrats would select a United States Senator from their ranks, a feat not accomplished in many decades. Under these circumstances a Democratic senator from the Empire State, chosen by its governor, would be a constant reminder to the party's leaders of Hill's availability.

Democratic chances for a majority in the assembly were better than at any time since 1882, when the trick had last been turned. The Democratic tide deriving from reckless Republican rule of the nation was swelled by the petty obstructionism of the state legislature on rapid transit and the World's Fair bill, as well as its cynical tergiversations on ballot reform. Spring elections in the towns and villages showed Democratic gains in almost every area in the state.[2] Especially encouraging was the fact that eighteen of the seats now held by the Republicans had been won by margins of less than four hundred votes.[3] If these slim pluralities could be overcome, and if at the same time the Democrats could hold their own shaky seats, the day would be won.

The incentive was strong. Democratic success in state and nation, were he able justly to claim a share in the glory, could advance Hill far along the road to the White House. By 1890, therefore, Hill had nurtured a plan of action which, with few alterations, was to be pursued not only for this fall campaign but for the next two years as well.

In formulating this strategy, Hill was fortunate in having the experience of Manton Marble, former editor and publisher of the New York *World,* at his call. An acute observer and veteran of national politics, Marble had mastered its intricacies and vagaries. This wealthy ex-editor, who had been close to Tilden and shared the bitterness and frustration of his narrow defeat, had an unquenched ambition to be president-maker. In the summer of 1890 he opened an active correspondence with Hill. During the next two years Marble wrote most of Hill's major addresses and pronouncements, and was a continuous source of advice and admonition. While Hill reserved to himself all final judgments and not infrequently disagreed with his advisor, the course pursued by the Governor during the next two years was decisively influenced by Marble.[4]

The broad outlines of the strategy to be executed by Hill were laid out in a letter from Marble, written in late summer.[5] The crafty ex-editor warned Hill that a campaign waged exclusively on the tariff issues should at all costs be avoided, lest a Democratic sweep be interpreted as a personal triumph for Grover Cleveland and make him the logical standard-bearer two years hence. Marble pointed out another path to party victory, far safer for Hill: the Governor should attempt to turn his party's fire on the whole record of Republican disregard for promises, fairness, and justice. The McKinley tariff should be scored, but it should also be made to take its place as only one of a long list of Republican misdeeds. While placing the tariff in its proper perspective, Hill was to clothe himself in low-tariff robes, and vigorously expound the cause of tariff reform. This must be done, counseled Marble, in order "to prevent the tariff reform issue from wearing the exclusive aspect of a Cleveland issue," and to keep the future tariff debates in Washington from taking on "the character of a Cleveland boom." Moreover, added Marble slyly, it was in the best interests of the party to keep the tariff issue from an exclusive identification with Cleveland, "in case we were to be deprived of his [Cleveland's] leadership by death, disability, or the success of other ambitions. . . ." [6]

Marble also recognized the need for an identification with a new issue which could compete with the tariff for public attention. This issue he saw clearly emerging from the heated debates over the currency. Marble, who regarded bimetallism as "being clearly inevitable," urged the political wisdom of championing the movement before others had taken sides. Then, when it became a dominating issue—as dominate it must—Hill would personify it as completely as Cleveland did tariff revision, Jackson the bank fight, or Clay the American System. Pointing out the advantages of incorporating in a future speech a paragraph on bimetallism which he had prepared, Marble wrote revealingly, "It is 'safe.' It is true. It is enough for the West. It will do you no harm at the East." [7]

Hill demurred for the time being on this last suggestion, but in all other respects he concurred in Marble's advice. He had already given a strong indication of his intended course in an address delivered at the unveiling of a monument to Indiana's late Senator Hendricks. The event was an important one, as Hill's friend, Congressman William Holman, observed in his invitation, not only because "an unequalled attendance is assured, especially from the Central West," but also ". . . in view of the fact . . . that your predecessor in the N.Y. Executive Department—the Hon. Grover Cleveland—has sent his regrets." [8] Assured of top billing, Hill accepted. His address was an effective recital of Republican extravagance, high-handedness, and contempt for justice and popular feeling. The emphasis was entirely on Republican misdeeds, on which all Democrats could agree, rather than on any attempt at formulating a positive program.[9]

The fall campaign was officially opened on September 23, with the publication of a manifesto addressed "to the People of the State of New York." Issued through the Democratic State Committee at Hill's behest, the several thousand word "letter" was beamed at an audience wider than its salutation suggested. Its main emphasis was on national issues, and it spicily described Republican rule and policies as an "astounding misadventure," "undisguised revolution," and "taxation for the sake of protection." The Democratic road was exalted, of course, as the only path to political salvation.[10]

In a speech to the Brooklyn Democrats on the same afternoon, Hill echoed this indictment. During the course of this address, the Governor took a sounding on bimetallism. Couched in safe, conservative language, this feeler was nonetheless vigorous in its indictment of the Sherman Silver Purchase Act as the latest Republican act of fiscal folly in an unsound, vacillating monetary policy stretching over three decades. Declaring the act an expedient rather than a solution, Hill asserted that it "obstructs our progress toward that goal which we all desire to reach—the free coinage of silver under a proper international ratio." The launching of this trial balloon, however, on a subject ultimately to be the heart of Hill's bid for the nomination, passed almost unnoticed in the daily press (which failed even to note that an "international ratio" really begged the whole question), as reports of the speech featured the Governor's remarks about the McKinley tariff and the Force Bill.[11] Hill noted with some disappointment that "the remarks on the silver question did not seem to attract much attention, . . ."[12] and the subject was not again broached during that year.

The state campaign which followed proceeded smoothly, with Hill in command. Only in New York City was the Governor unable to hold the reins. There, a senate investigating committee, chaired by Hill's townsman, J. Sloat Fassett, had brought to light some unsavory facts about Tammany's corrupt rule, especially as regarded Mayor Grant. The public wrath which followed induced the County Democracy, declining in influence, prestige, and membership, to combine once more with the Republicans and run a fusion ticket against Tammany.[13]

During the last two weeks of the campaign, Hill left the state to stump for Democratic candidates in other areas. His most important speaking engagements were in the Ohio congressional district of William McKinley, running now for re-election on a high protection platform. McKinley's district had been gerrymandered by a Democratic legislature, which had wiped out the normally Republican majority. National interest was centered on McKinley's district, for each party looked upon the Ohio politician as the symbol of the tariff. Hill stumped the district for three days, making four major addresses and speaking to many thousands in the largest cities in the district. From Ohio, the New York Governor journeyed to West Virginia, where he made a major address in Wheeling, and whistle-stopped northward through the state. After a brief stop in New York to check on the progress of his own campaign, Hill crossed into Connecticut and addressed large rallies in Hartford and New Haven. In each of these out-of-state talks, the national administration was belabored for its bungling course in either domestic or foreign affairs.[14]

The outcome of the election exceeded even the most sanguine Democratic hopes. The Democrats swept into control of the House, gaining 155 seats, and almost won control of the Senate as well. In New York, a Democratic gain of twelve seats gave the party control of the assembly, sixty-eight to sixty. Since the Republicans had only a six-seat edge in the hold-over senate, the Democrats had a majority of two on a joint ballot and would elect the United States Senator. Even in New York City, the regular Democratic candidates were triumphant over the fusion Citizen ticket, headed by the County Democracy's Francis M. Scott.

Immediately after the election Hill issued a statement interpreting the great Democratic sweep. It meant, he declared, that the people disapproved the arbitrary course of the Republican Congress. It meant that the nation did not want a Force Bill, that it did not want the McKinley Bill, that it objected to the narrow partisanship of the Republican party. In the repudiation of Republican misdeeds, then, lay the significance of this election.[15]

Hill might well exult in the great victory of his party, for the triumph was in some measure his. He had worked in several states, and in every place he had campaigned, Democrats had been successful. The defeat of Major McKinley was especially noteworthy. It was true that the Major's district had been gerrymandered to poll a normal Democratic majority of some 1700 votes, and McKinley lost by only 200. Still, he had been beaten in spite of the time, money, and frantic efforts expended by his party to save him, and Hill could legitimately claim a hand in this important triumph.[16] Moreover, in his own state, he had led his party to a stunning victory in the capture of the assembly and the winning of a United States Senate seat.

Certainly his exertions on his party's behalf contrasted favorably to Grover Cleveland's inactivity during the campaign.

Yet ironically, the man whose presidential stock had made the greatest advance as a result of this election was not Hill, but Cleveland. For while the campaign had been waged on many issues, the one which had overshadowed all others was the tariff, and to millions, tariff revision was synonymous with Grover Cleveland. The attempt to transfer this identification to the party as a whole had not been successful, for while the party was traditionally low tariff, it was Cleveland who had deliberately pushed the issue forward in December, 1887, had forced his party to fight on it, and had been martyred on it. It mattered not whether Manton Marble was correct when he wrote that Cleveland had "dragged [the tariff] to an unprepared or untimely arbitrament," and that what was really suicide [had been] called martyrdom." [17] The tariff issue, in the public mind, was Cleveland's, and the victory, won on his issue, was his victory, though he lifted neither hand nor voice during the campaign to help achieve it.

The *New York Times* editorially wrote Hill's obituary: . . . the result of the Congressional elections makes the Presidential nomination in 1892 absolutely unattainable for him [Hill]. That tremendous demonstration was not of his making. The tidal wave did not sweep in his direction. The thoughts of the people are not fixed on him, but on another.[18]

While the *Times* was composing dirges, and the able Louisville editor, Henry Watterson, warned Hill that Cleveland's election was now inevitable,[19] most observers— including Cleveland himself—agreed that the battle was far

from over.[20] Although the election had been a disappointment in some respects, Hill had emerged from it with a
net gain. Certainly Hill's reputation for effective campaigning and strategy did not suffer from it. New York
Democratic leaders regarded him with something akin to
adulation, for there was no question in their minds that the
victory in the state was Hill's.[21]

Perhaps the most important result of the election for
Hill was the winning of a United States Senate seat. It was
generally conceded that, as the leader of the party and the
architect of the victory in the state, the choice of the
senator would be Hill's. This prize, however, so hard fought
for, turned out to be something less than an unmixed
blessing. The choice of a man to fill the seat confronted
Hill with a most difficult decision, and the final decision
became a turning point in his career.

The man who would go to the Senate would have to
meet certain specifications. Chief among these was the
stature and ability to command the respectful attention
of the other Senators. This man would have to be able to
make friends for Hill—it went without saying that he
himself must be friendly to Hill—and to speak for the
Governor in Washington circles. Manton Marble summed it
up neatly: ". . . don't send any man who cannot *capture
Washington's ablest men* for *you—that is all there is of it,*
and you should insist on *your* choice at all hazards." [22]

There was one active candidate for the senatorship,
Smith M. Weed of Plattsburg. A wealthy Tildenite prominent in party affairs for two decades, Weed felt that he
deserved the seat as a reward for his long party service.
Moreover, Hill had apparently encouraged him to believe
that the seat was his in the event of a Democratic victory.
Following the election, in which his yeoman efforts secured
the assembly and senate seats in Clinton County, Weed

put in his claims for settlement. He made no secret of his desire, talking freely to the press about his candidacy and broadly intimating that he had Hill's support.[23]

But Weed, though he had the required stature and ability, had two fatal shortcomings. His record on the tariff was spotty, and if Hill was to convince the party and nation that he could lead the fight for low tariff as well as Cleveland, it would not do to send a lukewarm tariff man to Washington as his representative.[24] The other obstacle to his candidacy was neither one of character, ability, nor philosophy, but one over which he had no control. He could not command the support of Tammany for the senatorship.

This latter barrier to Weed's hopes for the senatorship pointed up a peculiar problem facing Hill in making his choice. The Democratic candidate would be chosen in caucus by a majority of the eighty-one Democratic assemblymen and senators, and this man would then be officially elected over the Republicans' complimentary candidate by a vote of eighty-one to seventy-nine. What complicated the situation was the fact that, of the eighty-one Democrats, forty-two were from the New York and Brooklyn area. Since these two cities contributed so heavily to the Democratic representation, it was natural for them to desire a voice in the selection of a candidate.

Hill's grip on the party, while firm, was not absolute, and any attempt to force upon a majority of his party's representatives a candidate whom they were unwilling to take was not only unwise, but might also be unsuccessful.[25] The closeness of the final vote on a joint ballot also increased the bargaining positions of the downstaters. The slim margin of two could easily be dissipated by misfortune or knavery, neither of which was without precedent in the Democracy's history. Tammany was already showing its

teeth and snarling that it could not guarantee the delivery
of all its votes for an undesirable candidate.[26]

Hill foresaw this possibility, and shortly after the election he sent out letters to several Democratic county
leaders urging them to see that their assemblymen did not
"commit themselves on the subject of United States Senator
until I can see them." [27] Meanwhile, Hill parried Weed's
importunities for a clear-cut statement of support. By mid-
December, he was prepared to abandon Weed and in response to another request from the latter concerning a
definite commitment, he wrote coolly:

> I do not as yet desire to commit myself to your candidacy
> or to that of any one else, but for the present prefer as
> well as propose to remain perfectly free and untram-
> melled to take such action as may be deemed best for the
> interests of the Democratic party when the proper time
> arrives.[28]

Beyond Weed there was a dearth of senatorial timber.
Tammany indicated a preference for Edward Murphy, but
Hill ruled him out as too small a man. Hill's first choice
was Alton B. Parker, his old campaign manager who had
been making an admirable record as judge on the New York
Court of Appeals. But Parker was not well known in party
circles, and moreover, the judge himself was extremely
reluctant to make the financial sacrifice which six years in
Washington would demand of him.[29]

Days turned to weeks, and weeks to months, and still no
decision was reached. In the absence of an announcement,
rumor and speculation increased. More and more frequently
the press suggested the possibility that Hill intended to
take the seat himself.

Hill was, in fact, giving such a move serious considera-

tion. There was no question that the seat was his for the
asking. Indeed, he was the only Democrat who could with
certainty get the unanimous vote of the party representatives. Opposed to this certainty was the possibility that,
should he support another, the party might refuse to take
his choice. Such a refusal would be a severe blow to his
prestige. Even if he should succeed in forcing his candidate
—if he could but find one—on the party, the contest would
almost certainly result in ill feelings and dissension in the
ranks. This discontent could lead to Democratic defeat in
the state in 1891, which in turn would damage Hill's
reputation, and his chances for the Presidency. Moreover,
the specter of treachery on the final joint ballot was always
before him. To fail to elect a Democrat to the United States
Senate would be a calamity.[30]

There were other considerations which spoke for Hill's
taking the seat. The Senate might well be a convenient
steppingstone to the White House. It afforded the opportunity to mingle with Senators from all over the nation,
and presented its members with a nationwide platform
from which to expound their views. Moreover, Hill's term
as governor would expire at the end of 1891. While some of
his admirers boomed him for a third term,[31] he knew that
the two-term tradition would be a difficult one to break.
Hill thoroughly enjoyed public life and dreaded the
thought of leaving it. Were he to fail in his quest for the
Presidency, his retirement was likely to be, if not permanent,
at least lengthy. A Senate term, however, would not only
insure six more years in office but, in the event of failure
in 1892, would leave him in a position to challenge again
in 1896.

On the other hand there was good reason to be hesitant
about taking the seat. Senator Eaton of Connecticut, one of
Hill's strongest presidential boosters, warned the Governor

that the jealousies in the Senate, especially toward an ambitious freshman senator, could kill his chances for 1892.[32] Many friends and advisers, including Murphy, Sheehan, Dana, and Timothy Shaler Williams, Hill's private secretary, counseled him against the move, believing that it would darken the prospects for the presidential nomination.[33] They feared that in accepting the security of a six-year term Hill would be "indicating a lack of confidence on your part in your ability to win the fight for the Presidential nomination."[34] There was also the danger that choosing himself for the senatorship would make him appear inordinately ambitious for the honors of office. One friend suggested that Hill's stature would be increased if, rather than taking the seat, he could arrange to have the office tendered to him and then, like Caesar, refuse it. It would, explained this person, dispel any belief "that you are not 'so big a man' as to permit this dignified office to pass you by."[35]

The date of the Democratic caucus was nearing, and if Hill had made his decision, he kept his own counsel and said nothing to even his closest advisers and friends. It is likely that Hill was still debating the wisdom of a move to Washington as late as January 16, three days before the caucus. On that day, however, startling and unexpected news from down-state introduced a new factor which almost dictated the final decision. Frank P. Demarest, a Democratic assemblyman from Nyack, was suddenly arrested for swindling a steamboat company through forgery. Alarmed, Hill immediately wrote the local Democrats to see that bail was furnished and to arrange "that his [Demarest's] presence can be absolutely secured here [for the balloting]. . . . Everything depends upon Demarest's vote."[36]

Faced with the possibility of his already shaky margin of two being reduced to a lone vote, Hill made his decision. At a meeting in his office with Sheehan, Murphy, and Parker, he spoke his mind. One by one, Hill discussed the possible candidates—Weed, Murphy, Parker—and ruled them out. The gravest problem, he explained, was the fact that two desertions or abstentions from dissatisfied Tammany men— now perhaps only one—would cost the Democrats the fruit of their hard-fought campaign. The responsibility for electing a Democratic Senator rested squarely on Hill's shoulders. Failure to elect a Democrat would be catastrophic to his presidential chances. The risk, he continued, was too serious to take. Since he was the only one who could be elected with certainty, the situation compelled him to be the candidate.[37]

The decision had not been an easy one to make. Timothy Shaler Williams, who knew him as well as anyone, felt that the controlling factors in Hill's decision were his dread of retiring to private life, and the possibility that, should he not take the seat, the Democrats might fail to elect anyone. Murphy felt that Hill had "thrown away the Presidency." [38] Yet any other course would have involved a great gamble, and Hill was not by nature a gambler.

That night the decision was announced. Reaction was instantaneous. The opposition press howled and denounced Hill as a power-hungry self-seeker. Tom Platt affected jubilation and predicted the end of Hill's chances for the Presidency.[39] These judgments and prophecies were of course to be expected from opponents. What was far more disturbing was the reaction of erstwhile friends. Both Murphy and Williams believed that the Presidency was now out the window, and Charles Dana also concluded that the action marked the "abdication" of Hill's pretensions to the Presidency. T. C. Callicot's Albany *Evening Times,* while not taking exception to the announcement, had previously opined that a Senate seat would "shelve" the Governor

for 1892.[40] Only the New York *World* of all his most
influential supporters seemed to think the move was a wise
one. Shortly after the fall election it had suggested that Hill
take the seat, dismissing as "wholly fallacious" the contention that this would injure him as a presidential candidate.[41]

Hill's self-promotion to the Senate ruffled some, embittered others, disappointed many. Smith M. Weed, believing
himself the victim of unconscionable duplicity, nursed a
bitter hatred for the Elmiran from that time forward.[42]
The ascension to the Senate also became the target of
Dana's subtle and venomous pen.

In one telling column, the crotchety editor presented a
historical survey examining the validity of the notion that
the United States Senate had historically been a steppingstone to the White House. The survey showed that thirteen
presidents, a goodly number, had at some time served in the
Senate. Of course, observed Dana, there had been many
times thirteen Senators who had hoped that a Senate seat
would improve their prospects for the Presidency. And, as
another minor qualification, he noted that none of the thirteen succeeded to the Presidency while still serving as Senator. The article incorporated a table listing ten of the successful Senators, showing that anywhere from eight to thirty-
two years had elapsed between their first election to the
Senate and their eventual elevation to the chief executive's
chair. The article concluded with a dispassionate, statistical
observation: "The average period between election to the
United States Senate and inauguration as President in the
cases of those who have taken that road to the White
House is eighteen years." [43]

In restrospect it appears that Hill's acceptance of the
seat, by conveying an unfavorable impression of both
excessive ambition and lack of confidence in his own

chances for the Presidency, did hurt him. Yet Platt's estimate of the move as "the mistake of his political life"[44] seems a harsh, oversimplified verdict. For Hill, a man with no family and few outside interests, politics and public office was life itself. It was only human to seek to prolong this life by clutching at the security of a six-year guarantee. Even if Hill's understandable desire for security were discounted, to adjudge his decision a mistake one would have to accept several assumptions as valid: that, had he not taken it, a caucus contest over the seat, possibly disastrous to party unity, could have been averted; that an able man of proper stature could have been found and elected; and that on the final ballot for their candidate, all Democrats would stand firm to preserve their majority of one or two. Each of these assumptions by itself is shaky, and to assume the certainty of all three is unwarranted.

Hill's election to the Senate created a further problem, concerning the propriety and legality of continuing to serve as governor. Hill's friends and apologists insisted that it was both proper and consistent with law to remain as governor as long as he wished, for until he actually presented himself to the Senate, he was not a member of that body. Thus, Hill could retain the governorship without conflict at least until December, 1891, when the Senate reconvened, and even later, if he so desired. On the other hand, many argued that since a Senate term was exactly six years, and since each term ended on the fourth day of March, it followed that each must also begin on that date. To continue as governor beyond that date would be to hold two offices at once, certainly repugnant to the spirit, if not the letter, of the state constitution.[45]

These legal disputations may have interested Hill as a student of law, but as a practitioner of politics, he found them quite academic. While he made no formal announce-

ment, Hill's decision had already been made on the basis of
political exigencies. He would finish out his term as governor.[46] For one thing, he foresaw that a March resignation
would expose him to the charge of dodging troublesome
issues which might then be brewing in the legislature.
More important, as governor he could keep his hand on
the state machine which he had so painstakingly built, and
insure its smooth functioning for the manufacture of a
Hill delegation to the 1892 presidential convention. Hill
might have resigned, had his successor been a trusted aid,
but the lieutenant governor, Edward "He Pays the Freight"
Jones, had of late been manifesting an independence and
presumptuousness born of unrequited ambition for advancement. The wealthy Binghamton scales manufacturer had
already declared himself a candidate for the governorship.
There was little doubt that once installed as acting governor, he would use this office to press his candidacy, and
might well injure Hill in the process. Since Jones was
definitely not Hill's choice for a successor, this path of
advancement had to be closed to him.[47]

When it became apparent that Hill did not intend to resign, he became the target for renewed abuse. Hill was,
according to his detractors, greedy, drunk with power, corrupt, without conscience or sense of decency. More telling
than these abusive epithets was the simple "Governor-
Senator" which was from then on derisively applied to his
name.[48] The unpopularity of Hill's decision may well
have affected the outcome of the spring elections. Not only
were Democrats upset in several mayoralty races, but
Democratic control of many counties was either washed away
or seriously weakened by the loss of 131 county supervisors.
The Democratic defeat was widely interpreted as a rebuke
to Hill.[49]

During these trying months of decision, Hill continued

to pursue his duties as governor. These were made less burdensome than usual in 1891 by the presence, for the first time in his gubernatorial career, of a legislature not completely hostile to him. At the start of the session, Hill renewed his demands for a long-overdue enumeration and reapportionment, an equitable excise law, and a rapid transit bill, embodying the principle of home rule, for New York City.[50] He also repeated many other recommendations of earlier years: a law for compulsory voting, a bill providing for a constitutional convention, establishment of a state commission to supervise the gas, telephone, telegraph, and electric companies, provision for manual training in public schools, abolition of the senate's confirming power, except where expressly authorized by the constitution, and establishment of a system of county roads.[51]

On the subject of taxation, electoral reform, and labor, the Governor had some interesting comments and constructive suggestions. He repeated his objections to the present system of taxation, pointing out that, although the value of personal property and real estate in New York were about the same, real estate bore the burden of taxation, and personal property contributed almost nothing to the state treasury. This inequity was the result of laws which permitted holders of personal property to deduct their outstanding debts from the taxable personalty, only the difference being taxed, while no such benefit was given to the owner of real estate—notably the farmer—who could not deduct his mortgage. Moreover, taxes were evaded by unscrupulous holders of personalty who intentionally contracted debts just before their property was assessed, and discharged them immediately afterwards. Either holders of both real estate and personalty should be allowed to deduct outstanding debts from their taxable property, insisted the Governor, or neither should be allowed to do so. Hill suggested that one sure way of reaching personal property for purposes of taxation was through a graduated succession tax. After a reasonable exemption had been made on the estate of a deceased resident, the estate should be appraised and a graduated percentage tax should be levied.[52]

On the subject of elections and electoral reforms, Hill repeated three of his earlier suggestions, all sound and all constructive. He suggested the propriety of a constitutional amendment which would require the courts to settle contested elections rather than the legislature, thus eliminating partisanship as a factor in the decision. "A political majority," he noted, "usually exhibits judicial qualities only when it is large enough to be generous." In addition, Hill again recommended that the law requiring candidates to file verified accounts of their campaign expenses be extended to the committees of each political party. He urged also that a defeated candidate be allowed to institute quo warranto proceedings to unseat a successful candidate who was proven to have obtained votes through corrupt means on the part of either himself, his agents, or his political committees.[53]

The Governor suggested two additions to New York's labor laws, based on the experience of a strike on the New York City Railroad line during the previous summer. During the two-week tie-up, which had begun over a relatively minor issue, Pinkerton detectives had been called in by the employers. Though provoked, the workers had refrained from violence, and Hill had resisted pressure to call out the militia. Left uncoerced, the workers had reached a peaceful settlement with their employers.[54] The employment of Pinkertons, however, had rankled many, and Hill now asked for an anti-Pinkerton bill, which would prohibit or at least regulate the use of private detectives during labor disputes. He also suggested that the arbitration law of 1886,

which had proved so ineffective because of its voluntary
nature, be amended to provide for compulsory arbitration in
industrial disputes.[55]

During the following months the assembly, whose committees had been assigned in late December by Hill, Sheehan, Murphy, and Croker,[56] fulfilled its expected role as the
Governor's sounding board, echoing in legislation his every
spoken desire. The lower chamber quickly passed an
enumeration bill, a constitutional convention bill, a congressional reapportionment plan, a freedom of worship bill,
a tax reform bill, several labor bills including an anti-
Pinkerton measure, and an excise act. All of these were
killed in the senate.[57] While for the most part the senate's
opposition was on strictly political grounds, there were
measures to which they objected on principle. The excise
bill, for example, was sponsored chiefly by the Liquor
Dealers' Association, and was far too spineless a measure for
a high license party to support.

In the entire session only 389 measures survived the
scrutiny of the assembly, the senate, and the Governor to
become law. This unusually small number of bills[58] was
attributable not only to the legislature's unharmonious com-
position and an abbreviated meeting, but also to a two-week
deadlock between the parties in the senate. This paralysis,
coming at the very end of the session, prevented the enactment of the usual flood of bills during the closing days.

The deadlock occurred in early April when Republicans
moved that the committee on canals investigate the state
canals under the Hill administration. This resolution in an
election year was almost certainly politically motivated,
though newspapers had been circulating stories recently
about perversion of the canal patronage. The Democratic
minority determined to block this move, and with the aid
of the presiding officer, Lieutenant Governor Jones, they

used parliamentary tactics and the filibuster to prevent a vote. The Republicans stood pat, refusing to withdraw the resolution. The resulting deadlock continued until the day before the session was to end, when the Republicans gave in in order to pass their private bills before the legislature adjourned. The assembly, meanwhile, passed a bill creating an assembly commission—dominated by Democrats—to investigate the canals, and during the summer this group applied the whitewash liberally.[59]

Despite the jockeying and obstructions, some needed legislation was enacted. New York City got its long-awaited rapid transit bill, incorporating the principle of home rule. Some clarifying amendments were added to the ballot act of the previous year, and the inequities of the tax laws were diminished by the enactment of a 1 per cent inheritance tax.[60] But by and large, the session was a disappointing one from the standpoint of an ambitious political leader.

While the assembly was carrying out its assignments as a showcase for Hill, the latter did not neglect his interests outside of New York. With his friends and acquaintances he maintained an active correspondence. His growing recognition as a presidential aspirant was attested by the increasing volume of invitations to speak at Democratic club rallies, banquets, and receptions the nation over. Although he himself was too busy with state business to travel much outside of New York, a steady stream of friends and emissaries flowed from Albany to other states to stimulate interest in his candidacy.

Most of these good will ambassadors concentrated on spreading the Hill gospel to the southern states. North Carolina, South Carolina, and West Virginia were visited and revisited by Hill's friends, in a constant endeavor to stir activity and line up local leaders behind Hill. During the fall of the year Hill again journeyed South to deliver

the oration at the unveiling of the monument to the late
Henry Grady, who as editor of the *Atlanta Constitution*
had been one of the ablest spokesmen for the New South.
On the return trip from Georgia, the visiting Governor also
spoke at Richmond, Virginia and Charlotte, North Carolina.[61]

This continuous invasion below the Mason-Dixon line,
and Hill's own return to Georgia and the South two years
after an earlier triumphal visit, clearly indicated the importance which Hill attached to southern support. Traditionally, a Democratic candidate who could poll the full
electoral vote of the solid South, and in addition gather in
the four doubtful states of New York, New Jersey, Connecticut, and Indiana, was assured of election. A nominating
convention would therefore be likely to respect the pref-
erences expressed by the Democratic organizations of those
states. This seems to have been the underlying motive for
Hill's concentration on the South. With Georgia, where he
had strong organization support, as the keystone, Hill hoped
to swing the entire South behind him.

Along with the southern states, Hill hoped to enlist the
delegations from key states in the North. New York, the
most important, was his to give and his to receive. In the
neighboring states of New Jersey and Connecticut, he leaned
heavily upon influential friends. New Jersey's Governor
Leon Abbot, a kindred soul to Hill on such matters as ballot
reform and excise in his own state, had been aided by Hill
in his recent campaign for election. Hill counted upon
friendliness and gratitude to give him New Jersey's votes.
In Connecticut, too, a strong member of the Democratic
organization, United States Senator "Bill" Eaton, was a
powerful Hill supporter.[62] Hill's relations with the Indiana
Democracy were cordial, and he attempted to enhance them
by showing a friendliness toward the presidential aspirations

of the Hoosier Governor, Isaac Gray. The Governor arranged for several friendly editors in New York State to run
an editorial to the effect that "if a western man is to be
chosen," no better one could be found than Governor Gray.
The editorial observed that he would be satisfactory to the
South and West, could certainly carry doubtful Indiana, and
had a better chance to carry New York, New Jersey, and
Connecticut than any other westerner. "He never gives the
public the impression that he is sometimes ashamed of his
party," the ghostwritten editorial stated. "He is a Democrat
through and through, and that is the first essential required
for Democratic success in New York." [63] With this editorial,
Hill showed his kind feelings toward Gray as the most
available western candidate, without prejudicing his own
candidacy. It was more than coincidence that the same
qualities attributed to Gray were those generally associated
with a certain eastern candidate as well.

While friendship, wire-pulling, and backstage-maneuver-
ing—the hand tools of a skilled politician—quite obviously
were heavily counted upon to smooth the road to the White
House, these tools could not be used in the construction of a
personal platform which would meet with popular approval. Such a platform could be built only by public expressions and actions. As an emerging national figure, Hill
had already begun to establish his record on national issues.
His strong attacks upon the Republican Force Bill were
certain to make friends for him in the South, and his
advocacy of a lower tariff would meet with approval from
southern and western farmers as well as from consumers the
nation over. But, as Marble pointed out,[64] Hill could not
rely upon these two issues to lift him into the White House.
While his stand was sound on each, neither was regarded
as his own, for they had already become identified with
other prominent Democrats. The successful fight against the

Force Bill had been led by Senator Arthur Pue Gorman of Maryland, who had labored tirelessly debating, marshalling forces, and skillfully maneuvering to bring about its defeat. While many Democrats had fought the bill, it was Gorman who was the acknowledged leader in the struggle.[65] A man of no small ambitions, the Marylander was known to be an eager suitor for the hand of the convention. The elections of 1890, meanwhile, seemed to have demonstrated that tariff revision still was stamped indelibly with the name of Grover Cleveland.

But the success or failure of a candidate in 1892, Marble asserted, would not be determined by his identification with either the Force Bill or tariff revision, but by his position on a question that would shortly outweigh both in importance. A cautious yet vigorous stand by Hill on this question, continued the former editor, would not only induce support, but might well compel it. This potent issue grew out of the angry demands from the West and South for an inflated currency.

The currency issue in America was older than the nation itself. From the colonial era down to modern times debtor and depressed classes had periodically demanded an inflated currency as a solution to economic hardship. This demand had found expression over the years in a number of movements of varying significance, and encompassing a wide range of financial vagaries. None, however, were so widespread and intense as those undertaken in the last quarter of the nineteenth century.

The chief centers of discontent were in rural America. The farmer, burdened with a heavy mortgage acquired at high interest rates, squeezed between mounting costs and falling prices, sought relief from his distress in a cheapened currency. During the decades of the 1860's and 1870's, the advocates of inflation concentrated on demands for in-

creasing the number of greenbacks, the paper currency of
the Civil War. A Greenback party was formed, and polled
81,000 votes in 1876, reaching a peak presidential vote of
over 300,000 in 1880. With the return of higher farm prices
interest in the movement waned, and within a few years
the demand for greenbacks had substantially subsided.
Even before the movement had expired, however, it had
been superseded by a new darling of the inflationists—silver;
and when hard times returned, the cry for free and unlimited coinage of silver was insistent and threatening.

In 1873 the Congress, recognizing in law what had existed
as fact, had stopped the free coinage of silver, which many
years since had ceased to circulate as a result of undervalua-
tion at the mint. Shortly afterward the nation wallowed
in a severe depression, and many victims of falling farm
prices joined the marketless owners of burgeoning silver
mines in an agitation for the return of silver, now fast falling
in value, to the currency. The demonetization act of 1873,
so little noted at the time, was within a few years widely denounced as a "crime."

Attempts to restore the free coinage of silver were twice
within twelve years headed off by compromise. The first,
the Bland-Allison Act of 1878, required the Secretary of
the Treasury to purchase from two to four million dollars
worth of silver each month. The second, the Sherman Act
of 1890, raised the price of compromise to a monthly purchase of four and one-half million ounces of silver. These
silver purchases did little to inflate the currency, and with
the continuation of hard times the demands for free bimetallic coinage were swelled into an angry chorus. Silver,
already regarded as a panacea, became increasingly invested
with religious aura, and the cult of "sixteen to one" spread
throughout the land.

Meanwhile, frustrated farmers had already begun to

organize into Farmers' Alliances, seeking to deal with the various grievances of the agrarians. As the passing months brought neither satisfaction nor relief, the Alliances grew in size and number. By the early 1890's, farmers in and out of the Alliances were turning their attention more and more to the issues of credit and currency. Agrarians of the South and West accused the conservative financial East of restricting credit and thwarting free coinage, thereby continuing human misery for the sake of its own pockets. Wall Street became synonymous with the devil, and smoldering embers of sectional antagonism were fanned into flaming hatred.[66]

The increasing momentum behind the demand for a renewal of silver coinage convinced Marble that by the time of the 1892 Democratic convention, this issue would overshadow all others. Within the Democratic party, the drift of sentiment was evident. In twenty-one states west of New York, Democratic conventions had voted in favor of a return to free and unlimited coinage. When a free coinage bill came before the Senate in January, 1891, every Democratic Senator but one either voted in its favor or was paired for it.[67] Moreover, the sentiment was as strong in the South as the West, for there the members of the Farmers' Alliance, working within the Democratic party, represented a strong impulse for silver. "Hostility to free coinage or indifference," Marble therefore concluded, "is fatal to any Democratic candidate for the Presidential nomination, and even if nomination were obtained would be fatal to his election." [68]

Given this as a basic premise, the course for Hill was clear. The opportunity was immense. As an eastern candidate supporting free bimetallic coinage Hill would be the most available man before the convention, favored by the South and West because of his advocacy of free silver, and preferred by the East as a safer, more conservative alternative to a western candidate. (Eastern fears of free coinage could be set at rest by stressing the essentially conservative nature of bimetallism as "the money of the constitution.") Grover Cleveland's opposition to silver would suffice to sidetrack his candidacy.[69]

While Hill accepted Marble's conclusions on the political wisdom of ultimately championing free bimetallic coinage, he disagreed with his adviser on the important question of timing. Hill balked at Marble's persistent pleas for a prompt public statement in favor of free coinage. His few brief remarks on the currency issue during the 1890 campaign had passed almost unnoticed, and this indifferent reception seemed to have cooled him toward an early public commitment on the subject. Hill's long experience in public affairs and his cautious nature had made him wary of the treacherous undertows which so often race beneath inviting political waters. He preferred to move slowly and surefootedly, willing to sacrifice the greater rewards of daring leadership for the security of a more cautious commitment.

Marble, on the other hand, felt that all advantage lay in immediate action. In frequent letters to Hill, often accompanied by draft speeches, he urged the Governor to make his move. His arguments were forceful. He warned Hill that, with the South and West watching, he must follow up his earlier remarks concerning bimetallism "lest you appear to have taken your stake off the table." Moreover, postponement to a later season not only would appear more like opportunism than statesmanship but would acquiesce in the drift of eastern opinion away from silver. If this drift continued unchecked, it would cost Hill the East. It was still not too late, pleaded Marble. Many Democrats were already half committed, "but give them a case, a statement, an argument, & party hostility will soon reverse that."

An able, effective exposition by Hill would provide ammunition for his party, and the debates which were certain to follow in Congress would revolve about the arguments which the Senator-elect had presented. He would thus become the center of national attention.[70]

Still, Hill hesitated. One reason for his reluctance to champion free coinage immediately was the possibility that such a bill, almost certain to be passed by the new Democratic House and possibly by the Republican Senate also, might be signed into law by President Harrison. If this happened he feared that he would be left with a straw issue. Marble tried to reassure him of the value of an early pronouncement. If a bill were passed and approved, Hill would be vindicated. If vetoed, "no other issue would be possible in the canvass of 1892; & vetoed then or not, no other candidate than yourself would be possible, in the event that you had spoken now & staked all on it." [71]

Marble prodded Hill to choose an occasion and speak out. Immediately following the 1890 elections he urged the Governor to issue a statement interpreting the Democratic sweep as a rebuke to the Republicans, not only for their "Revolutionary tariff acts" but also for their "denial of free coinage." He also prepared an address on federal topics, including free coinage, to be delivered to the legislature. Each time Hill hesitated and finally decided against it, giving as his reason in the latter instance his reluctance to jeopardize the election of a United States Senator by "commit[ting] the party to a position it had not heretofore taken." [72]

There were other occasions as well that Marble regarded as both convenient and appropriate for speaking out without appearing to be meddling unduly in national affairs. One of these was the meeting of the Reform Club of New York City on February 10, 1891, to protest against free coinage. It was to this assemblage that Cleveland sent his famous "silver letter," denouncing the "dangerous and reckless experiment of free, unlimited, and independent silver coinage." [73] Marble urged Hill to seize this opportunity for a reply in behalf of free coinage, but the Governor remained silent.[74]

By the spring of 1891 Hill had decided to put off any declaration on silver until after the fall election.[75] Marble attempted to dissuade him from this postponement, warning that it would be awkward if New York was silent on silver while most other Democratic state conventions would be drumming for it. Moreover, he insisted that the wisest course was to commit New York to free coinage before the election. When the Democrats, under his leadership, were victorious, Hill would become the logical choice for the nomination, for he would have demonstrated his ability to carry crucial New York on a free coinage platform.[76]

In spite of Marble's woeful warnings and pollyanna predictions, Hill stood firm on his decision for two controlling reasons. Ever cautious, he did not want to commit himself irrevocably until he was convinced that the silver tide would remain strong. One test of that would be the 1891 elections, and until the results were in, Hill wanted to say nothing. Although he had planned to use an article in a national magazine to publicize his views on free coinage, he gave up the idea when he learned that the article would have to be printed before election for inclusion in the desired November or December issue. Hill insisted upon reserving "my final determination . . . as late as possible. . . . The November elections might change political conditions radically." [77]

A second reason for Hill's decision to wait was his reluctance to jeopardize the fall elections by throwing an untested issue into the campaign.[78] There was much at stake this fall. The governorship, a whole slate of state offices, and both the senate and assembly seats were up for election, and there was a good chance for a complete Democratic sweep. It would be difficult to overestimate the prestige that such a triumph would give to Hill on his send-off to Washington. A Democratic victory in New York would be interpreted as a Hill victory. His arrival in the nation's capital would be that of a conquering St. George, fresh from slaying the Republican dragon in New York and saving that fair state for the Democracy.

Therefore, Hill put aside until November a declaration for free bimetallic coinage, and concentrated on bringing victory to his party in the forthcoming elections. Although he himself was not running for office, he worked as assiduously as ever in rounding up friendly delegates from the many districts, and in seeing that the new state committee again reflected his views. And although there were some minor rebellions against his authority in a few country districts, these were little more than specks in the overall picture of allegiance to Hill.[79]

The ticket was arranged by Hill in consultation with Croker, Murphy, and Sheehan. The candidate for governor was known to almost everyone weeks in advance of the convention: Roswell P. Flower, whose perennial efforts to secure high office had finally blossomed into a nomination. The wealthy New York merchant was Croker's rather than Hill's first choice for the office, but in the absence of any likely candidate of his own, Hill accepted Flower quite willingly. Billy Sheehan, the youthful speaker of the assembly, was selected for second place on the ticket.[80]

The platform for the Saratoga convention, in accordance with Hill's wishes, was to say nothing about the currency besides a simple reaffirmation of the 1884 and 1888 national platform pronouncements. These planks were hollow ex-

pressions favoring the use of both gold and silver as the
circulating medium, and were about equivalent to declaring
in favor of good and against evil. For emergency use, Hill
sent along to the convention with T. S. Williams another
plank, prepared by Manton Marble. This plank, in pon-
derous phrases, denounced Republican fiscal policy, and
held up free bimetallic coinage to New Yorkers as sound
and conservative:

> N.Y. democrats steadfastly adhere to sound finance. We
> therefore denounce the new Sherman silver law under
> which 1/10 of our gold stock has been exported and all
> our silver out-put is dammed up at home as a false
> pretence but artful hindrance of return to free bimetallic
> coinage, a quickened step in the Rep. forward march
> from gold to silver monometallism. We . . . approve
> Gov. Hill's prompt & masterly expose at Brooklyn last
> Sept. already justified by time. . . .[81]

At Saratoga, Flower and Sheehan were nominated to
head the ticket. To safeguard the prearranged platform, a
handy Hill majority was put in charge of the resolutions
committee. As was expected, the County Democracy paid the
penalty for twice fusing with the Republicans by being
excluded from the convention. Its representation was given
to Tammany, which now was supreme in New York City.
Everything, in fact, followed the program except for the
final approval of the platform. Then, a colossal blunder by
Boss Croker completely upset Hill's careful plans on the
silver issue.

The platform committee, in Hill's camp by a three-to-one
majority, responded to convention sentiment for a declaration on the silver question by appointing a seven-man subcommittee to frame a currency plank. Hill men were in

control, five to two, and quickly beat down proposals from
the two Clevelandites for a declaration against free and
unlimited coinage. They then countered with Marble's
plank, and after dropping the reference to Hill's Brooklyn
speech of September, 1890 to pacify the Cleveland men, they
pushed through the plank with ease. Everything went off
smoothly until the subcommittee reported in favor of the
Marble plank. Then, wholly unexpectedly, Boss Croker
offered an amendment to the subcommittee's plank: "We
are against the coinage of any silver dollar which is of less
intrinsic value than any other dollar." This resolution, a
clear slap at the free silver movement, had been handed to
Croker by Jenks of Brooklyn, a Cleveland man; and Croker,
as T. S. Williams reported disgustedly to Marble, "was too
stupid to see its import."

Having expected no difficulty with the Marble plank,
most of Hill's floor leaders were out of the hall when Croker
offered Jenks's resolution. Since Hill delegates had previously been instructed to follow Croker's lead during the
convention, they made no objection to the resolution. When
Hill's lieutenants—Murphy, Williams, and Bourke Cockran
—realized what was happening, they made frantic efforts to
get to Croker and reason with him. But it was too late.
Croker's resolution was adopted.[82]

This unexpected turn of events left Hill in an awkward
position. He had hoped to by-pass the currency question
until after the campaign. At worst, he had planned no
greater committal than Marble's plank and a reaffirmation
of the 1884 and 1888 platforms. Yet this additional declaration for dollars of equal intrinsic value seemed to put New
York Democrats on record as being hostile to free coinage.
If this impression were left unchallenged, it would ruin
his appeal to western and southern silverites.

Hill was thus forced to declare himself earlier than he had

planned. In a speech on October 8 to a Democratic rally, at which Grover Cleveland presided, Hill undertook to interpret the plank as actually an endorsement—and an intended one—of free bimetallic coinage. Croker's troublesome contribution to the currency plank was blithely ignored, as Hill presented an elaborate analysis of the remainder. The plank, he noted, declared in favor of "honest money, the gold *and* silver coinage of the constitution," and opposed the Sherman Silver Law as an "artful hindrance" to the "return to free bimetallic coinage." Thus, New York Democrats had clearly declared for bimetallism, Hill asserted. "Those who would have switched us off the bimetallic track have had their hands tied," he declared. "Those who would have run us into collision with our fellow Democrats of other States . . . have had their plans frustrated. Our platform unites all Democrats upon the common ground of honest, bimetallic coinage. . . ." [83] Having thus straightened out the record, to his own satisfaction at least, Hill put the subject to rest for the remainder of the campaign.

The currency embarrassment was the only sour note of the campaign. The refusal of Andrew D. White, former president of Cornell University, to head the Republican ticket weakened Platt's chances of dethroning the Democrats. The job of standard-bearer went to J. Sloat Fassett, the state senator from Elmira. Fassett had run the Boss's errands too often to shake the charge that he was Platt's tool. Aid for both Flower and Fassett came from unexpected quarters. Hill's bitter enemy, the *New York Times,* supported Flower in the belief that he had been forced on Hill, and that Hill's power had been broken. Platt, on the other hand, managed to find new support for his candidate from, of all people, the liquor dealers, who dreaded the election of the teetotaling, water-serving millionaire.[84]

This surprising switch of the liquor men was not enough, however, and Flower was elected by over 50,000 votes. Sheehan's plurality, sliced by the defection of Clevelandites, was about 15,000 less than Flower's. The rest of the state officers were swept in by comfortable margins, and the assembly was once again Democratic, though by a narrow margin. Only in the senate did it appear that the Republicans had staved off defeat. There returns indicated an alignment of seventeen Republicans, fourteen Democrats, and one Independent. Even there, however, the Democrats threatened to take control, for in three of the seventeen Republican districts, Democrats reported irregularities, and claimed the victory for themselves. If Democrats were finally seated in all three districts, the positions of the parties would be reversed, and the Democratic majority would give the party a clean sweep of the state.

Hill, of course, was anxious for Democratic control of the senate. He had been plagued for seven years with a hostile senate, blocking legislation, hanging up nominations, and initiating embarrassing investigations. Democratic control would free Hill's successor from this millstone and make party sway complete. Moreover, if the sweep were achieved, it would be the first in almost a decade, and would boost his own prestige tremendously.

With such promising rewards for victory, Hill swung into action. All of the contests were managed from the executive chamber in Albany as Hill, drawing upon all his legal resources, mapped the strategy and issued his instructions. The ensuing struggle to wrest the three seats from Republican hands was marked by back-stage maneuvering, legal technicalities, charges and denials, court orders and counter-orders. For two full months, the action filled the political stage in New York.

Hill's strategy in each of the three contests was based upon

Democratic control of the several canvassing boards. According to prescribed procedure, the local officials in each voting district sent the returns from their polling places to the county board of canvassers. This board was simply the county board of supervisors, sitting in another capacity. Thus the canvassing board was not nonpartisan, for the supervisors had themselves been elected as political candidates.

The duties of the county board of canvassers were purely ministerial. It totaled the returns and certified to their accuracy, but it had no authority to go behind the returns or to make corrections, other than to send returns with clerical mistakes back to the district officials for correction. The certified returns were then sent from the county to the state board of canvassers. This board, too, was composed of elected officials—the secretary of state, state treasurer, comptroller, attorney general, and state engineer. Again, the duties of the board were simply ministerial, issuing certificates of election to the candidates with the highest total of votes. This board also had no power to go behind the returns, but merely awarded the certificate on the basis of the returns presented to it. Any contest over the validity of the returns or the eligibility of an elected member to take his seat was decided upon by the legislative chamber.

The three senate seats claimed by the Democrats were in the twenty-seventh, twenty-fifth, and fifteenth senate districts.[85] In all three districts, Democrats were in a majority in the county boards of canvassers. The contest in the twenty-seventh district, comprising Steuben and Chemung counties, was based on the ineligibility of the Republican victor, Frank Sherwood, to hold a senate seat. The Republicans had been aware of this fact when they nominated Sherwood, but they disregarded it, confident that an expected Republican majority in the senate would overrule any protest and seat him.[86] The Democrats had widely advertised Sherwood's ineligibility during the campaign, so that in the event of his victory, their challenge would be on firm ground.

Immediately after the election, Hill outlined the strategy to be followed by the Democratic canvassing board that was to deal with the Sherwood case.[87] The board was to canvass the vote as returned, instructed the Governor, but was also to pass a set of resolutions pointing out Sherwood's ineligibility and holding that his votes should be voided. The returns, along with these resolutions and necessary affidavits, were then to be forwarded to the state board of canvassers. That board would do the rest by withholding a certificate of election from Sherwood. A Republican protest over the state board's action would come before the court of appeals, where Hill was confident that the action would be upheld. If the Democrats succeeded in their other contests, they would have a sixteen-to-fourteen margin, and would then vote to seat Charles Walker, the Democrat whom Sherwood had defeated. Under no circumstances, Hill ordered, should the question of Sherwood's eligibility be argued before the county canvassing board, nor should his vote be thrown out, for ". . . then they would mandamus the Board in that district before the Republican judges and we would lose. . . . We don't want any decisions from Republican judges in that district. See that our programme is not changed." [88]

The "programme" was carried out. Sherwood took court action to prevent the resolutions from being sent to the state board, but without success. The chief headache to Hill came, not from Republican attempts to thwart his plans, but from Walker's loss of stomach for the contest, and his desire to drop it. If Walker balked, the chance for a Democratic senate would be gravely weakened.

Hill immediately wrote to a friend of Walker's asking him to bolster Walker's resolution:

I received, to-day, a rather queer letter from Charley Walker, expressing a disinclination to further contest the Sherwood matter. Has Charley been drinking some since the election? I judged as much from his letter or else he is weakening. I wish you would see him at once, and, without letting him know that you have heard from me, tell him to say nothing and take no action, but leave his case in the hands of his friends and the party leaders at Albany. He must abide by whatever is regarded as best by us here. We will not get him in any scrape, but will act for the best interest all around. . . . Get him to say nothing and do nothing; but simply abide events, and let us manage the affair further in our own way. This is very important as you can see! He ought to keep absolutely quiet! . . .[89]

Meanwhile Hill pursued his plans in the other two contests. In the twenty-fifth senate district, comprising Cortland and Onondaga counties, the Republican Rufus T. Peck had apparently defeated his Democratic opponent, Nichols, by 358 votes. The Democratic case in this district rested on a provision of the recent ballot act. Each election district had been provided with a quantity of official ballots, and as required by law, the designation of each district was marked on the ballots. Through some inexplicable error, the ballot strips containing the names of Republican candidates and marked for use in two heavily Republican districts had been mixed up, those marked for use in the first district being used in the second, and vice versa. The Democratic majority on the county board of canvassers contended that ballots bearing the wrong endorsement were invalid under the ballot act of 1890, as amended in 1891. If these ballots were not counted, Nichols would be the winner. The board therefore refused to certify Peck's election.[90]

The Republicans immediately went to court, insisting that the board had no right to go behind the returns, asserting that the intent of the voters had been clear, and hinting darkly that the ballots had not been mixed by accident. Judge Kennedy, the Republican judge who heard the complaint, issued a mandamus ordering the canvassers to certify Peck's election.[91]

While the board stalled, Hill sent Judge Morgan O'Brien of the New York State Supreme Court to hold an extraordinary term in Syracuse, where the case was being heard. A series of legal maneuvers ensued, designed to get the case before the court of appeals, which Hill felt sure would rule the disputed ballots as invalid. Meanwhile, the Governor warned Democratic lawyers to avoid presenting their motions before Judge Kennedy, who would not only deny them, but would probably sit on his decision until the legislature met, when it would be too late to appeal the decision. The maneuvering proved successful, and the case was assured of a hearing before the court of appeals in December.[92]

The most controversial and bitter of the three contests was that in the fifteenth senate district. Here, too, the struggle followed the familiar trail through the canvassing boards and courts. The outcome of this contest, however, was also affected by an act of questionable legality committed by a high state official, and was climaxed by a final award made in flagrant disregard of a court decision. Stigmatized by these actions, the entire episode became known as the Steal of the Senate.

The apparent victor in this fifteenth district was the Re-

publican Deane, with a plurality of 137 over the Democratic
candidate Edward B. Osborne. These returns were challenged by the Democrats, who claimed victory for Osborne.
There was no real disagreement in two of the three counties
in the district. Both parties gave Deane a plurality of thirty-
eight in Putnam, and the Democrats disputed only two of
his 136 vote plurality in Columbia. It was over the returns
in Dutchess County that the battle was waged. There the
Democratic majority of the canvassing board disallowed a
large number of Republican ballots which they contended
were illegally marked, and increased Osborne's plurality in
Dutchess from 37 to 186. This made Osborne the senator-
elect of the three counties by an over-all margin of 14 votes.
When the Republican county clerk refused to certify to
the accuracy of these revised returns, the Democratic majority ousted him, temporarily replacing him with one of
their number, John Mylod. The returns, later called the
Mylod returns, were then signed and forwarded to the
state board of canvassers in Albany.[93]

Thereupon, Governor Hill ordered the state board to
convene in the first week in December, two weeks earlier
than they usually met. His intention was obvious. It was
planned that the state board of canvassers, on the basis of
the returns before it, would issue a certificate of election to
William Osborne, before the Republicans could get a court
order restraining such action.[94]

Before the state board could carry out its part, however,
they were checkmated. Employing a battery of able attorneys
headed by the brilliant Joseph Choate, the Republicans
secured from State Supreme Court Justice Edwards a mandamus directing the state board not to canvass the vote of
Dutchess County on the basis of the Mylod returns. Democrats attempted to have this stay vacated, but Supreme
Court Justice Barnard denied their motion. The Democrats

received some consolation a few days later when Judge Edwards, in restraining the board from canvassing the returns of any of the contested districts, so stated his order as to assure that all these cases would come before the court of appeals.[95]

Meanwhile, matters had been further complicated by the death of the Republican candidate on November 21. Republicans continued the fight, but Deane's death darkened their hopes, for even if he were declared the victor, the seat would remain vacant until the Governor issued a call for a special election. If he so wished, Hill—and after him, Governor Flower—could keep the seat vacant simply by refraining from issuing a call. Few doubted that he would so wish, if the deceased Deane were declared the winner.[96]

With the canvassing board prohibited to canvass the Mylod returns for the time being, Hill's revised strategy aimed at preventing any other return from Dutchess from being sent to Albany. If the Mylod return were the only one before both the state board and the court of appeals, the day might still be won.[97] Within a week, however, these plans received a severe setback. On December 12 Judge Barnard granted a Republican request for an order on the Dutchess County board of canvassers and the newly appointed clerk, Storm Emans, to certify corrected returns showing Deane to be the victor, and to forward these returns to the state board of canvassers.[98]

This series of December decisions infuriated Hill. Both Edwards and Barnard, who had been handing down these adverse decisions, were Democrats. Hill, who sincerely believed that "we are clearly in the right," [99] was thoroughly disgusted with what he considered the "lack of backbone, pluck, and courage on the part of our Democratic Judges." [100] They seemed to be guided solely by Republican criticism: "They jump over one another in their haste to

grant stays when a returning board favors our side, but
when the other side gets a certificate none of our judges
want to interfere." [101]

In compliance with Judge Barnard's order, the new returns were reluctantly prepared by the county board of
canvassers and signed by Storm Emans. Instead of forward-
ing these returns as ordered, however, Emans held on to
them while Democrats attempted to have Barnard's order
stayed. The Republicans countered with a new order from
Judge Cullen, another Democrat, commanding Emans to
forward the new returns to the state board forthwith. This
order, issued on December 21, was served on Emans that
evening, and before 8:00 P.M. he mailed the three copies of
the returns, one each to the Governor, the Comptroller,
and the Secretary of State, as required by law.[102]

Within a few hours, a stay on Cullen's order, which had
been secured by the Democrats before Judge Ingraham in
New York City, arrived in Poughkeepsie and was served on
Emans. Emans immediately boarded a night train for
Albany, and went to Deputy Attorney General Isaac H.
Maynard, who was acting as attorney and counsel for the
board of state canvassers. Early the following morning,
Emans and Maynard repossessed the unopened envelopes
from the three offices to which they had been sent. By this
action the returns were kept out of Albany for the present,
and the Democrats secured a further order to keep the new
returns in Emans' possession.[103]

The court of appeals handed down its decision in all
three cases on December 29, 1891, and on the same day, the
board of canvassers issued their certificates of election. In
two of the cases the decisions were clear-cut. Frank Sherwood was ruled to have been ineligible in the twenty-seventh
district, and in the twenty-fifth, the court ruled that the
wrongly endorsed ballots should not be counted, giving the

election to the Democrat Nichols.[104] The ruling in the Dutchess case was somewhat less clear, but apparently forbade the canvassing of the Mylod returns.

The state board of canvassers met immediately after the decisions were handed down. Nichols was declared the winner in his district, and no certificate was issued in the twenty-seventh where Sherwood had been declared ineligible. In deliberate disregard of the court's decision in the Dutchess case, the board awarded the certificate of election to Democrat William Osborne, on the flimsy pretext that the only returns before it on which it could canvass the vote were the Mylod returns.[105]

Considered in the most charitable light, this action was high-handed. What was more inexcusable from the practical politician's viewpoint was that it was probably unnecessary. The Democrats could have controlled the senate without Osborne. With Nichols seated, there would be fifteen Democratic senators, fourteen Republican, and one Independent. Even if the independent voted with the Republicans—which was unlikely, since he had received Democratic backing in his race against a Republican opponent—the Democrats would have no worse than a tie, and the Democratic lieutenant governor as president of the senate would cast the deciding vote. With Sherwood ineligible, Walker could then be seated, and the Democrats would number sixteen. With special elections dependent upon the call of a Democratic governor, there would be no new Republican elected from the fifteenth district, or from any other where a vacancy occurred. Hill, however, seems to have been bent upon leaving the senate in certain control of his party, and it was apparently at his insistence that the board of canvassers awarded the certificate to Osborne.

The securing of a Democratic senate was Hill's final act as governor of New York. This concluding effort was almost symbolic of his seven stormy years in the executive mansion. Although these years were clearly not barren of achievement, they were distinguished primarily for their intense partisan struggles. From these struggles Hill had emerged, not unscathed, but victorious. He had led his party from victory to victory, and with its continued success, his own star had risen. Now with his party assured of complete control of New York's government, Hill turned his full energies to his quest for the Democratic presidential nomination.

CHAPTER VIII

The Elusive Brass Ring

THE MERRY-GO-ROUND of American politics has a fascination
all its own. Sometimes cycling predictably, more often
spinning with no apparent design, it has an irresistible
appeal to both the strengths and weaknesses of men. Its
big brass ring, the American Presidency, has been its greatest lure. It is part of the national legend that any native-
born can grab the brass ring, but in actuality few—through
training, perseverance, occasionally ability, and, more often
than not, chance—are ever in a position to reach for it.
As the presidential year of 1892 opened, David Bennett
Hill was one of those few who by fortune and circumstance
was in such a position. Whether he would succeed in clutching the brass ring, however, or whether it would elude his
grasp as it had eluded so many ambitious men before him
was a matter to be decided by the events of the months
which followed.

At once the keynote of Hill's grand drive for the presidential nomination and its chief single instrument was the
Elmira Address. Written for a December delivery by Hill's
chief adviser, Manton Marble, the address was aimed at a
far vaster audience than the roomful of local Democrats to
whom it was delivered. The speech dealt in the main with
two large themes: a course for Democrats for the forth-

coming session of Congress, and the growing currency question. It was hoped that through a full exposition of his views on both, Hill would nail together the chief planks of a platform that would fix him as the most available Democrat in the land.[1]

Marble had long held the conviction, based upon his study of economics and of recent Democratic state platforms, that no Democrat could receive his party's nomination without espousing the cause of bimetallism; that, indeed, free bimetallic coinage was inevitable.[2] What better course, then, than to meet the inevitable half-way, and not merely advocate but vigorously champion bimetallism? One portion of the speech, therefore, was designed to tie Hill firmly and finally to the bimetallist movement.

The second phase of the address was equally important in Marble's calculations. Outlining a blueprint for party action in the next Congress would enable Hill to display his talent for political strategy to the nation's Democracy. Politics abhors a vacuum; and with Cleveland virtually abdicating as the party's titular head through his almost total abstention from the political struggles since 1888, the party might very well rally to the man who boldly assumed the fallen reins and pointed the way to victory. Thus by championing free coinage and presenting a neatly packaged, sure-fire strategy for Democrats, the nomination must come to Hill. So, at least, reasoned Marble; and if his expectations seem extravagant in retrospect, they were not altogether unreasonable at the time.

Hill's first task was to establish himself solidly in the forefront of a silver movement already well underway. The difficulties involved in this chore were compounded by the necessity of bringing his state along with him, for unless the nation's Democrats were satisfied that New

York would stand behind a bimetallist standard-bearer, Hill's own candidacy was weakened.

Hill proceeded immediately to the task.[3] As his starting point, Hill paraphrased with approval the currency plank of the 1891 New York Democratic convention which, thanks to Croker's blunder, had declared against the coinage of any silver dollar of less intrinsic value than any other dollar. From there, he launched a vigorous and elaborately reasoned argument in favor of free bimetallic coinage. Castigating the Republican party as the "seventy-five cent silver-dollar party," Hill insisted that the only way to restore a sound currency, with parity of gold and silver dollars, was to resume the free and unlimited coinage of silver.

The reason for torturing the words of the New York Democracy's currency plank and tying them to his presentation in favor of silver was obvious. Lest anyone fail to grasp its significance, however, Hill spelled it out in bold terms: the New York Democratic party had intended their declaration in favor of dollars of equal intrinsic value as an endorsement of free bimetallic coinage. This strained and highly glossed interpretation was followed by an even bolder assertion: so conscious were New York Democrats of the importance of the silver issue, that they sent "me to the Federal Senate immediately after my public denunciation, in Brooklyn a year ago, of the Sherman Silver Law, and my declaration then in favor of free bimetallic coinage." This revival of a little noticed passage in a year-old speech was designed to make New York's alleged concern for free bimetallic coinage seem a long-standing one, and was aimed at countering any impression that either Hill or his state was a Johnny-come-lately to the bimetallist camp.

The Republicans, Hill noted, had desperately but unsuccessfully tried to dislodge New York from bimetallism by

decrying free coinage at staged public meetings in several
Eastern cities. ". . . Of Course," Hill caustically remarked
in an obvious stab at Cleveland and his followers, "they
enticed a few unwary Democrats to appear as convulsionists
at their scarecrow festivals." But, he continued, with those
few exceptions, New York remained firm for bimetallism.
Thus, "the Democratic party is now a unit for free bimetallic
coinage, and New York has refused to be disjoined from the
hard money doctrine professed by the Democratic Senatorial
body, and supported by the Democratic party in all the
great States of the West and South."

Having established—to his own satisfaction at least—
himself and his state firmly in the vanguard of the silver
movement, Hill turned to the second theme of his address,
that of projecting a policy for the Democrats during the
forthcoming Congress. Democratic strategy, he said, must
be determined by the overriding consideration of "*put*[ting]
*next November's contest upon the clear issues made by the
acts of the Billion Congress and not upon any other issue
whatever.*" The way in which this could be done was simple:
Democrats in both Houses should unite to demand repeal
of the McKinley Tariff and the Sherman Silver Purchase
Act, and nothing more.

Hill frankly admitted that attempts to repeal would be
unsuccessful; yet the reasons for pursuing this course Hill
regarded as unanswerable. Since both the Senate and the
Presidency were controlled by Republicans, he explained,
"excepting humdrum business, Democrats can not . . .
write a new line in the Federal Statute book." What better
course, then, than to keep the public's attention riveted to
those Republican misdeeds which had created the Democratic landslide of 1890, and which promised to result in an
even more sweeping verdict in 1892?

Moreover, Hill continued, such a policy would keep

Democratic forces united, while an attempt to settle upon details of new legislation could cause diversion in their ranks.

> Shall we break our party formation [he asked] and go to pieces in debating some small amendments toward taxation for revenue only, or some confusing details of scandalous tariff schedules; or shall we rather voice a great people's rebuke of the two McKinley Acts and demand their repeal?
>
> Shall we nibble at rates and percentages as if *that* were the size of our quarrel with Republican revolutionists, or shall we simply vote to repeal the two McKinley Acts? . . .

The cry for repeal was admittedly, then, a device for inaction, a convenient way both to keep the issues clearly before the electorate and to preserve Democratic unity. But as Hill pointed out, until the Democrats could gain control of both Houses of Congress and the Presidency, they would be powerless to enact remedial legislation anyway.

The argument had a convincing ring to it. While there would be a reform fringe among Independents who might become impatient or disgusted with such an expedient course, their loss would be more than offset by the gains to be realized by keeping alive and undiluted the issues which had already proved a scourge to the Republicans.

But if the strategy of foregoing the introduction of positive legislation for the sake of maintaining proven issues was a feasible one for the party, it was an essential one for Hill. For the introduction of any free coinage bill by zealous silverite Democrats in Congress might have nightmarish consequences to Hill's campaign. It was not inconceivable that a coinage bill might be pushed through both houses, for even in the Republican-controlled Senate there were enough silver Republicans who would vote with the Democratic majority. And it was always possible that Harrison might sign such a bill, if it had received appreciable support from his party. Were this to happen, free coinage as a party issue would be lost to Hill and the Democrats.

Even if such a bill were not enacted, once it was brought to the Senate floor Hill would be forced to vote on it. He would probably have little influence in framing the bill, and it might very well turn out to be a measure more extreme than he was prepared to support. A vote on such a bill— despite all the verbal reservations he might make—would cost support from either the conservative East or the fired-up West.[4] Thus, while presenting his case for maintaining the currency issue in the campaign, Hill had to convince his colleagues of the inadvisability of doing more than advocating repeal of the Sherman Silver Purchase Act.

His arguments were ingenious. He had already pointed out the danger of splitting Democratic ranks over the details of a silver bill. To this he added the caution that if a bill were introduced, the specific details of this bill, rather than the Republican failure to deal with the currency problem, would become the issue in the presidential campaign. "I would not," he said, "shift the silver issue from an evil to a remedy."

Moreover, he cautioned, the party would be throwing away an issue by enacting a coinage bill while the Republicans controlled both the Senate and the Presidency, for Harrison's signature would enable him and his party to pose as friends of bimetallism. For those Democrats who might be prepared to sacrifice the political issue for the sake of achieving their currency demands one year earlier, Hill had a warning. Their sacrifice, he prophesied, would

be in vain, for while claiming credit for its passage, the
Republican leaders would nullify the bill and discredit
free coinage through an unfriendly administration and
execution of its provisions. Thus, the Democratic party
would have neither issue nor substance.

Thus, by pointing to the dangers inherent in attempting
remedial legislation in 1892, Hill hoped to avoid both a
diminution of the issue for the party and an embarrassing
vote for himself. Western and southern enthusiasm for a
free coinage bill, however, was only one of the threats against
which Hill had to defend the wisdom of his policy. There
were many in the eastern wing of the party who protested
that the currency issue should be kept out of the campaign,
and that Democratic fire should be leveled at such things
as the high tariff and the force bill. Yet Hill had become
convinced that his chances for capturing the nomination
rested in large measure on the prominence of the currency
issue. He therefore lashed out angrily at those who wished
to see it dropped. "It is politics for babes and sucklings,"
he said, "to preach that the gold and silver question should
be kept out of the presidential election." For until a free
bimetallic coinage bill became law, the currency would have
to be an issue, and it would be an issue on which the
Democratic party could score heavily: "Democratic speakers
on every stump from Maine to Texas will be abundantly
equipped for irrefutable argument, with one silver dollar
and a melting pot."

While Hill insisted on the inclusion of the currency
issue in the campaign, he recognized that the desire of
conservative easterners to eliminate it reflected their fear
of a radical change in the currency. He also knew that
eastern Democrats would be unlikely to support, either for
the party nomination or national election, any candidate
who appeared radical on the monetary problem. Thus,

throughout the speech, conservative labels like "the currency of the constitution" and "hard-money doctrine" were applied to free bimetallic coinage, and a special effort was made to make it appear simply in the light of a restoration of sound currency from the twenty-year aberration of "gold monometallism."

Toward the end of his speech, Hill took pains to allay the fears of easterners in general, and New Yorkers in particular, by incorporating an assurance that he would follow a gradual course toward the goal of bimetallism.

It is offered to any Western or Southern friends who feel less keenly than it is felt in the great port of our foreign commerce that the Gold and Silver question is a world question, not only a federal or national question: Do not be impatient with our conviction in New York that every step toward Free Bimetallic Coinage must be safe and sure, no step backward, but also no step forward that puts in one hour's jeopardy the peace and prosperity of your commercial capital and so of your country at large, for these are inseparable.

On the whole, the Elmira Address was a cleverly phrased, calculated document. There were appeals to the interests and prejudices of voting blocs—a technique which Hill had exploited with great success in previous campaigns—judiciously sprinkled between the two major themes of the address. Throughout, appearance and reality were skillfully blended: breathing boldness while maintaining caution, exalting logic while appealing to emotion, clothing opportunism and partisanship with the cloak of statesmanship. There was something—either hope or reassurance—for everyone except those who were already lost to Hill's following. The address avoided a strictly sectional or

economic appeal, the market on which had already been
cornered by southern and western fire-eaters, and aimed at
presenting Hill as a truly national candidate, bigger than
any one section, and able to command the support of all.
In the Hill camp the speech was regarded as an overwhelming success. Marble somewhat immodestly waxed
enthusiastic over his own handiwork, and assured Hill that
his nomination was now almost a certainty:

> . . . You are safe on silver. You are already invulnerable
> as a tariff reformer, without another word; and *all* the
> Billion-Dollar Congress issues are rammed into the can-
> vass for *you*. . . .
>
> I consider that your reputation as the best candidate
> for any western or southern free c. man to vote for is
> *fixed*. The axis of the globe is not steadier.[5]

Much of the New York press, however, did not concur in
Marble's enthusiasm. The *Times* and *Tribune*, of course,
showered upon the speech ridicule and invective. Criticism
also came from the Democratic *Herald*. Far more ominous
was the defection of the New York *World*, heretofore an
unwavering supporter of Hill. The *World* took issue with
Hill's advocacy of free coinage, and also regarded Hill's
plan for congressional inaction as a brash attempt by a
still-unseated Senator to pressure his colleagues into a
course of expediency.[6]

This sudden change in temperament of an erstwhile
friendly paper alarmed Hill. At his urgent behest, Marble
visited Pulitzer in an attempt to persuade him to remain
at least neutral for the time being, but he was unable to do
more than leave a note for the editor-publisher, who was
confined with an illness.[7] Meanwhile, he attempted to quiet
Hill's fears about this sudden defection of his most influ-

ential press ally. He assured the Senator that the opposition
was only a passing one, and asserted that, in the long run,
it would prove to be an asset; for,

> without belittling Mr. Pulitzer's good feeling toward
> you, which is certainly as high as can exist in the breast
> of any tin-god-on-wheels, it is clear that the World must
> support you almost every other wise and that its support
> will be less liable to be discounted as prejudiced.[8]

This was small solace for Hill, as Pulitzer's assistants,
who were running the paper in their chief's absence, continued to hammer at the Elmira Address, and to reprint
columns from other papers which shared their views.[9]

On the other hand, there was some favorable response.
The *National Economist,* official organ of the Farmers'
Alliance, praised what it considered Hill's endorsement of
free and unlimited coinage of silver.[10] This was especially
encouraging, since the support of Alliance men in the
Democratic conventions in the South was being heavily
counted upon by Hill and Marble. Senator Pugh of
Alabama also indicated a favorable disposition toward Hill
after the address, and the other Alabama Senator, Morgan,
wrote a letter to Hill expressing interest in his stand and
requesting elaboration of some points in the address.[11]

Time, of course, would be required for the Elmira
Address to do its work fully; meanwhile, Hill busied himself in the more practical, tangible politics in which he was
so well schooled. At Hill's request, his old lieutenant
William Sheehan was selected to be Democratic national
committeeman from New York State.[12] This assured Hill
of a loyal spokesman in the deliberations of the national
committee. At the same time Hill maintained a correspondence with Senator Gorman which gave promise of a

working alliance, and kept in touch with tried and friendly elements in other states.[13]

A significant victory for the pro-Hill forces was scored in the election of Representative Charles F. Crisp as Speaker of the House. The contest for the speakership had been between the Georgian Crisp and Roger Q. Mills, long-time Congressman from Texas. Mills had fathered the tariff bill of 1888, around which the presidential campaign of that year swirled. As such, he represented the low tariff element of the party, and symbolized the desire for vindication on the tariff issue. Crisp, on the other hand, had had only a spotty, in-and-out record on the tariff, and was chiefly known as a silver supporter. His election on the thirtieth ballot thus seemed to augur a major shift in emphasis for the coming campaign from tariff to currency. Crisp lent support to this belief when he appointed William Springer, an old-line Illinois protectionist, to head the tariff-writing ways and means committee, and named one of silver's chief spokesmen, Dick Bland, to head the committee on currency and banking.[14]

Crisp's victory was thus a promising sign for Hill's candidacy. The New York Senator had conferred with Crisp in November, and it was public knowledge that he was supporting the Georgian. He had also advised his friends in Congress to vote for him in the party caucus.[15] Hill, of course, felt that the primacy of the currency issue would be ensured with Crisp as Speaker; but his support of Crisp was also part of a larger design to make Georgia his southern bellwether. This goal would be enhanced by reciprocal support from the speaker and his friends at the proper time.

These bold sallies into the national political arena were only a few of the events and decisions which made Hill's last month in Albany a busy one. Much of his effort and

attention during these weeks was devoted to masterminding
the battle for a Democratic majority in the state senate,
a struggle which was not concluded until the last days
of December. And while the outcome see-sawed from one
court ruling to another, Hill conferred with Sheehan,
Croker, Murphy, and Governor-elect Flower about committee selections for the legislature and outlined his
views on the program to be followed there. There was also
the inevitable winding up of affairs, both official and
personal, which demanded his spare moments. And, during
this last hectic month, Hill completed his preparation for
a final major address before leaving the New York scene.

Hill and Marble had agreed, even before the Elmira
address, that a follow-up speech would be desirable, and
the occasion of Hill's departure for Washington was
seized upon as a convenient one for the address. The
setting was to be a farewell dinner tendered to Hill on New
Year's eve by the state officers. It is very likely that Hill had
a big hand in arranging the party in order to provide a
platform for his speech, and the *New York Times*, sensing
this fact, made great sport of announcing the gathering
as "Hill's Dinner to Hill." [16]

The Farewell Address was essentially a reiteration of his
Elmira speech one month earlier, and a reply to the
criticism of it.[17] Hill again hammered at the necessity to
keep intact the issues of the Billion Dollar Congress for the
coming election, and repeated his plan for accomplishing
this: demand repeal of the Republican currency and tariff
laws, and do nothing else.

Hill then turned his fire upon those who criticized his
program as a policy of inaction.[18] "It is objected: 'You
cannot pass your repeal of the silver and tariff laws of the
Billion [Dollar] Congress. Perhaps we can pass a Binding-
Twine Act.' " For these critics, Hill had nothing but scorn.

Assume, he invited, that a Binding-Twine Act and other individual tariff reductions like it could be passed: ". . . were the decision mine to make," proclaimed the Senator, "I would not, for the sake of so small a difference in the interval before relief, whittle down the bulk of our indictment." For the same reason, and also that Democrats might not split on debating remedies, he urged Chairman Bland to postpone a free coinage bill, and to bring before the House only a bill for repeal of the Sherman law.

The Farewell Address was Hill's last utterance as governor of New York. Within a few days, he boarded the train for Washington and the Senate of the United States.

If Hill's thoughts drifted over the seven years just passed as the wheels of the train clacked off the miles to the nation's capitol, he must have found great satisfaction in his reflections. In those years of his governorship, he had seen through a large volume of legislation, much of it good, some bad. He had molded from diverse elements of the party a powerful political machine, prepared to do his bidding. In the ceaseless warfare with his Republican foes, he had almost always emerged victorious. He had combined with great success the skills of the craftsman in politics— canny appeals to voting blocs, pressure, influence, kindness and threats, skillful backstage maneuvering, and a sprinkling of occasional statesman-like acts. He had gauged the political temperament of his state with accuracy, despite his occasional insensitivity to the new awakening of a dormant political morality; and during those seven years, he had seen his star rise on the national horizon and glow with increasing brightness, until now he had just cause to hope that it might soon outshine all others in the political firmament. There was, indeed, much in which to find satisfaction.

Hill took his Senate seat on the seventh of January, 1892.

He was the center of attention as he entered the chamber for the first time. A number of Democratic senators filed by and cordially greeted their new colleague, and Hill shook hands warmly with them, as well as with the many Democratic representatives who had entered the chamber of the upper house to welcome the New York Senator. His committee assignments were relatively minor, as might be expected for a freshman senator sitting on the minority side. He was appointed to serve on the Interstate Commerce Committee, a committee dealing with Canadian relations, and two other standing committees on the territories and immigration.[19]

Hill found the task of adjusting to his new life in Washington a fairly easy one. He wrote delightedly to his former secretary that he had encountered none of the jealousy of which he had been warned, and told Marble that "there seems to be a very kindly feeling manifest towards me on the part of Southern senators and members. . . ." [20] Observing the rule that new senators do not talk much, Hill made no public addresses and granted very few interviews. This of course fitted well with his plans, for he had already spoken his piece on the political situation, and could add little more to it. He wrote Marble:

> Some good friends here suggest that I should say nothing further upon the issues raised in my recent speeches. They argue that I have said enough and that I should let well enough alone. They fear my efforts may be regarded as an attempt to improperly influence the action of the Democrats in Congress, especially in view of the fact that I am a new Senator.[21]

Not only was Hill not heard in Washington, but he was seldom seen. During the first two months of the session he spent only two and one-half weeks in his Senate seat. Most of those two months was spent in visits to New York City and Albany, where he conferred with state party leaders. His frequent visits to New York also helped him to keep his hand firmly on the party machinery. He continued to have a large, and on some matters a controlling, influence in the new Flower administration. In addition to having already selected the assembly speaker and many committee heads, and having aided in the formulation of the legislative program, he wielded a large influence in patronage matters. Like all politicians, Hill found it impossible to satisfy all the requests for appointments, and the dispensing of jobs was often a headache. When Boss McLaughlin continued to press Hill for several appointments, Hill wrote in disgust to Williams, "Like Oliver Twist these politicians are always crying for more." [22]

One appointment of Flower's, made rather obviously at Hill's behest, stirred up great indignation. Isaac Maynard, so recently involved in the distasteful court proceedings over state legislative seats, was appointed to the court of appeals. To many it appeared that this was Maynard's reward for his part in the Steal of the Senate, as indeed it probably was; and once more the invectives and accusations of political immorality were showered upon Hill. But that was old hat to Hill, and the appointment stood.[23]

During the early part of 1892, then, the direction of the political tides was quite favorable to Hill. Perhaps the most encouraging sign for his prospects was the absence of many contenders of large stature who might challenge him. It was felt in some quarters that Maryland's Gorman might make a race for the nomination, and there was always the strong possibility that the West might unite behind a candidate from the other side of the Mississippi, perhaps Iowa's popular Governor Boies. Governor Gray of Indiana could also be considered a potential threat. But none of

these were men of great stature and fame, and each would
be faced with a decidedly cool reception in many areas.
The most formidable obstacle in Hill's path, former president Cleveland, was generally being counted out of the
race. It was felt that his famous "silver letter" of February,
1891, as well as Hill's control of the party machinery in
New York State, made him unavailable.

This was not merely the cheerful, optimistic view of
Hill's supporters. Many of Cleveland's friends told him at
the time of the silver letter that it would end any hope of
his candidacy, and even Cleveland's old tariff ally, Roger
Q. Mills, now stated that he expected the fight to be
between Hill and some western candidate.[24] Tammany's
great orator, Bourke Cockran, summed up Hill's prospects
in a letter to Stephen M. White of California:

> I firmly believe that he [Hill] will be nominated for the
> Presidency. I base this belief not upon his personal
> popularity but upon the conditions of the political situa-
> tion. If Hendricks were living now, or if Thurman were
> 8 or 10 years younger I would expect to see either
> one or the other chosen by the National Convention.
> Cleveland is out of the race by universal consent. Nobody
> dreams of forcing his nomination against the opposition
> of his own State. Hill has demonstrated his ability to
> carry the State of New York and the Convention will be
> forced either to take him or incur the risk of naming a
> candidate weaker than he is. I cannot see anywhere
> above the horizon a rallying point for the opposition
> and I rather expect him to be nominated on the first
> ballot.[25]

The events of the National Committee meeting in mid-
January seemed to support the conclusion that the tide

was flowing in Hill's direction. The committee chose
Chicago as the site of the nominating convention, and set
the opening date for June 24. Hill was quite pleased with
the selection of Chicago as the convention site. "Everything
passed off in the meeting of the National Committee just
as I desired," he wrote with satisfaction to Marble.[26] The
vote of the committee was significant, too, in that Brice and
Gorman had supported Hill's preference for Chicago.

To all appearances, then, the outlook was bright. But
what could not then be seen was that, in an attempt to
influence the delegates to the national convention, Hill and
his advisers had already decided upon a course which, as
much as any other single event or circumstance, would
deny to him his party's greatest gift. That fateful decision
was to call an early convention in New York.

Because of the vital importance of New York as the largest
of the so-called "key" states, the Empire State delegation
had always enjoyed a considerable influence at Democratic
conventions. Since the ability to carry New York was a
prime prerequisite for any Democratic aspirant, the candidate who received New York's endorsement enjoyed a great,
and not infrequently an insurmountable advantage over
the rest of the field.

Hill and his lieutenants, of course, had little doubt that
they would control the New York delegation. The party
machinery seemed in his grip, and barring an unforeseen
rebellion, the New York convention would select delegates
who would do their master's bidding. But the New York
convention was not normally held until May, or late
April at the very earliest. Meanwhile, there would be other
state conventions deliberating, and pledging their delegates
to avowed candidates or to favorite sons. If the New York
delegation could be securely pledged to Hill before other
state conventions met, this would be a weighty, perhaps even

a controlling, consideration in the determinations of these conventions. A leading Kansas Democrat friendly to Hill succinctly put forth the case for an early convention in a letter to the New York Senator:

I also think that it is the general sentiment of the democracy [sic] of the country that the choice of New York must eventually govern, and this impression is becoming stronger daily. In view of this fact, pardon me for the suggestion, whether it would be prudent to have the New York Convention for the selection of delegates, meet at an early day and express in unmistakable terms, her wishes. I think that such action would substantially settle the question as to the nominee of the national convention.[27]

If this letter was intended to convince Hill of the advisability of calling an early convention, it was superfluous; for Hill and his advisers had already made their decision. Whether Hill or his counselors first proposed the idea is not clear. Allan Nevins, Cleveland's biographer, states that Murphy and the leaders of the Democratic State Committee convinced Hill of the efficacy of calling a winter convention.[28] It is certain that Marble favored the plan, and it is even quite possible that he fathered it.[29] While the proposal does not appear to have originated with Hill, he apparently concurred in the suggestion without much prodding.

The convention was to be held on Washington's birthday. The state committee was scheduled to issue the call on January 26, but news of the plan leaked out two weeks earlier. E. Ellery Anderson, a prominent reform Democrat and Clevelandite, told a meeting of the Reform Club on January 16 that there was reason to believe that an early convention would be called. Several days before, in a letter to the state committee, he had pleaded that the right of the people to be heard in selecting a candidate not be denied by suddenly calling a mid-winter convention. William Whitney also drafted a protest to the state committee, and several prominent reform Democrats gathered at Anderson's home to consider further action.[30]

Such a protest was to be expected from Cleveland men. Far more alarming was the second rupture within two months with the *World* on a matter of policy. Upon hearing that the state committee intended to call an early convention, George Harvey, then managing editor of the *World*, hastened to Washington to dissuade Hill from the project. Failing in this, Harvey brought the rift into the open with an editorial entitled "Don't," which appeared several days before the committee issued the call. The editorial urged Hill to call off the plans, warning that this unfair procedure would split the party in New York, offend the Democratic delegations of other states, and might have unforeseen consequences which could wreck his candidacy.[31]

The opposition of the *World*, whose support he greatly valued, alarmed Hill enough to consider calling off the program, but when he suggested this to Marble, the latter counseled "not the least change in your plans." Not only were the reasons which led to the decision for an early convention still valid, insisted Marble, but it was also too late to back down. "With the public you and the committee will become a laughing stock, as bull dozed from the world, if you change from Feb. 22." [32]

So, on January 26, at the appointed time, the call went forth. Within a short time opposition to this attempted coup assumed alarming proportions. The New York press was almost unanimous in its denunciation. Several Demo-

cratic groups passed condemning resolutions, and a group
of reform Democrats, among them former Mayor Grace,
Isador Strauss, Charles Fairchild, and Francis M. Scott,
met again at Anderson's home to discuss means of organizing
these cries of outrage into an effective political force. This
group, which was as much pro-Cleveland as anti-Hill, issued
a strong statement denouncing the "snap convention" and
invited the public to voice its protest at a mass meeting in
early February. A committee of twenty-five was organized
to lead the fight against the snap convention, and this
committee gave unmistakable notice that its opposition
would be more than a passing fancy by establishing itself
in permanent quarters on Wall Street.[33]

These repercussions were far greater than Hill had
anticipated, and immediately attempts were made to discredit the committee of twenty-five. Murphy labeled them
Mugwumps and bolters, and Hill, shrugging off the uproar,
assured a Philadelphia friend that

> My friends in Philadelphia need not be disturbed over
> the efforts of Messrs Grace and Company of New York
> City. They are the same malcontents who called a mass
> meeting to oppose my nomination and election in 1888.[34]

But despite this affected unconcern, the uprising must
have caused Hill many a sleepless night. To the *World*,
the selection of several pro-Hill delegations within two days
of the call for the convention clearly demonstrated that
"methods which are undemocratic, unfair, and dangerous
to the party" had been used.[35] Throughout the following
weeks, the newspaper urged Hill to accept its friendly
advice, and withdraw the call for an early convention.
The *St. Louis Republic* was less kind in its appraisal of the
situation:

Mr. David B. Hill is now engaged in being unusually silent. His entire attention is devoted to a strenuous effort to chew the very large mouthful he has bitten off.[36]

But criticism or no, plans went ahead on schedule. On February 22, delegates trudged through the light blanket of snow that covered Albany's streets and filed into the convention hall. The convention, as was expected, was all Hill. The local elements of the Hill machine, alerted to the plan for the early convention, had done their job effectively. Some local conventions had been held less than a week after the call had been issued, and opposition had had little time to organize effectively. In the few areas where anti-Hill men succeeded in being elected, a pro-Hill slate was sent along to contest their seats. The convention hall on February 22 was packed with Hill supporters, prepared to participate in a play for which they needed no script.

The proceedings were cut and dried. Hill was nominated as New York's candidate for the Democratic presidential nomination; delegates stamped and cheered on cue; and New York's seventy-two votes were pledged to Hill. Hill's acceptance speech was filled with appropriate phrases of modesty and humble gratitude to the delegates. He also used the occasion to restate the position on national issues already laid down in his Elmira and Farewell addresses.[37]

There was only one off-key note amid all this harmony. A short distance from the convention hall another meeting was being held. In order to dramatize their protest, the anti-snappers had arranged to convene in Albany on the same day as Hill's cohorts with the avowed intention of contesting the authority and decisions of the snap convention. It was announced that local conventions would be held again to select delegates for a second state convention to be held at the end of May.[38]

Yet criticism and bolters notwithstanding, Hill had achieved his goal. New York's influential delegation of seventy-two was bound tightly to him, and other state conventions and would-be candidates would have to reckon with this fact. Opposition there had been and continued to be, and cries of outrage, and threats of challenging delegations, and solemn predictions that the snowshoe convention would be his undoing. But Hill had heard outraged cries and threats and forecasts of doom many times before in his political career, and he had always managed to set them at naught. And what had happened so often before could be made to happen again.

Indeed, within a few days after the convention there were signs that, the deed having been done, events and opinions would become reconciled to it. Charles Dana, embittered by Hill's decision to take the Senate seat a year before, had already brought his New York *Sun* four-square behind Hill, and the *World*, despite earlier protests, now urged that the anti-snappers preserve party unity by accepting the convention's verdict and disbanding.[39]

On Hill's return to the Senate chamber, he was congratulated by a bevy of Senators and Representatives who seemed not at all shocked or disturbed by the recent proceedings in New York. Georgia's Senator Colquitt undoubtedly voiced the mind of all "practical" politicians when, in announcing for Hill, he remarked that this was no time for prattle about "virtue, purity, and such abstract talk." [40]

During the next few weeks there was a surge of support for Hill. Senators from many southern and mid-western states gave a favorable nod to Hill's candidacy, and all indications pointed to substantial support from their state delegations.[41] There were reports that New Jersey would also swing in to the Hill column by the second ballot at the latest.[42]

There were some minor set-backs. Town elections held in New York State went against the Democrats, and much of the press heralded the results as a rebuke to Hill's snap convention. This view was supported by the fact that Hill's handpicked candidate for mayor of Elmira, his home town, was soundly whipped by an Independent Democrat-Republican coalition.[43]

But these were mere specks in an over-all bright horizon. And with the New York delegation tied to Hill, Cleveland appeared—if previous campaigns were a reliable criterion—more unavailable than ever. The *New York Times*, for whom there had heretofore been only one candidate, obliquely conceded this when they began to talk of "Cleveland or some other available Democrat" stopping Hill.[44] The distinguished editor of the Louisville *Courier-Journal*, Henry Watterson, agreed that "Mr. Cleveland is no longer a possibility," although he still believed that the convention would not take Hill: "The transition is too abrupt, the wrench is too violent." [45]

During the weeks which followed the snap convention, it appeared that Marble's predictions would be justified by events, and that Hill might ride the crest of a growing wave of support into the Chicago convention. But in reality, Hill was riding not the crest of a wave of support, but of a false prosperity. What neither he nor Marble realized was that by mid-March, the bottom to his campaign had already fallen out.

One of the chief causes for the sudden crumbling of Hill's candidacy was the adverse reaction to the snap convention in the state and nation. Far from exerting a gravitational pull on other conventions, the snap con-

vention turned many Democrats away from him. Hill had
badly miscalculated. The indignation over the snap convention, rather than dying down, mounted and spread, abetted
by the influential anti-Hill press which now had a *cause
célèbre* upon which to fasten.[46] The anti-snappers, now
well-organized, conducted a full-fledged registration of
New York Democrats in order to hold new local conventions. From these, delegates would be sent to a second
state convention to be held at the end of May. Great care
was taken to present a clear contrast with machine methods
by making the registration as complete, thorough, and just
as possible. The anti-snappers obviously intended to contest
Hill's pledged delegation at the national convention.

This revolt in New York confirmed the uneasy feelings
of many Democrats outside the Empire State that the snap
convention had been machine politics in its most naked
form. The revulsion against the unsavory methods of the
New York Senator was widespread.[47] Hill's insensitivity to
political morality had finally betrayed him, and the *World*'s
warning that he might win New York but lose the other
forty-three states in the process began to appear hauntingly
prophetic.[48]

Another great factor in the change in Hill's fortunes was
the decision of Grover Cleveland to re-enter the political
arena. Following his defeat in 1888, Cleveland had retired
to private life, quite delighted to be relieved of the cares
and burdens of public office. Though he continued to take
an interest in state and national affairs, he showed no desire
to take an active role in politics, and in the few public
addresses he delivered during 1889 and early 1890, he
resolutely steered clear of political issues.

By mid-1890, however, Cleveland's concern over Republican rule, and also over the unchecked advances of David
Hill toward the party leadership, modified his resolution

somewhat, and he began to speak out publicly on political matters. During the 1891 state campaigns, he delivered addresses at Democratic rallies in New York and Massachusetts.[49] Although still disinclined to resume an active role in politics, this disinclination was being strained by his irritation over the successes of Hill, whom Cleveland regarded as the antithesis of everything he stood for.

Cleveland's rising ire can be traced in his letters of this period. In 1889, he sounded like little more than an interested observer in his comments on Hill's obvious designs on the Presidency.[50] The following year he expressed his disquiet over a friend's complacent estimation of Hill's chances, and added:

I am a simple looker-on with no ambition except the attainment of peace and quiet, and yet with an intense desire that all that we by the hardest work accomplished may not be lost to the country.[51]

By mid-1891 he wrote to Bissell with indignation:

. . . It is getting to be very hard to endure and submit to a continuance of the prevailing bossism, and look honest men in the face.[52]

And again, four days later to Lamont:

My only thought about politics is that we are great fools if we allow ourselves to be hauled about by Hill and his gang.[53]

Cleveland added in his letter that he would gladly remain in retirement and remain faithful to the party "except in one contingency"—obviously, the nomination of Hill.

By December, the prospect of Hill's capturing the state delegation to the national convention brought Cleveland's wrath to the boiling point.

It seems to me [he wrote Bissell] that the only way for a decent Democrat to live in New York and maintain his self-respect, and at the same time stand by his party, is to break this thing up.[54]

During 1891 Cleveland was faced with increasing pressure from friends to declare himself a candidate, and while he still withheld permission to use his name, it is clear that he was already conditioned to the idea of entering the race. If a final spur was needed, the snap convention provided it. This latest act of high-handedness by the political masters of New York appears to have moved Cleveland to a final decision. On the day that the snap convention opened, Cleveland addressed the law students at the Universty of Michigan. "Interest yourselves in public affairs as a duty of citizenship," he counseled; and in an obvious reference to the Albany proceedings, he added, "but do not surrender your faith to those who discredit and debase politics by scoffing at sentiment and principle, and whose political activity consists in attempts to gain popular support by cunning devices and shrewd manipulation." [55]

Two weeks later Cleveland, in a letter to an old supporter, General Edward S. Bragg, revealed that he would consent to run if the party and the nation wanted him. With the publication of this letter in the press, the green light was on for Cleveland sympathizers.[56]

A third factor in Hill's decline—in part a product of the first two—was his disappointing showing in the South. The southern states were important in the arithmetic of the electoral college, and so of a Democratic national convention. Hill already had many strong indications of good will from influential southern senators, and in mid-March he embarked on a tour to convert this cordial feeling into pledged delegations.[57] On this three-day tour Hill made major addresses to large crowds in Roanoke, Knoxville, Atlanta, Birmingham, and Savannah, and in Jackson he addressed not only a public gathering but also the state legislature of Mississippi. In addition, Hill whistle-stopped through Virginia and Tennessee.

The speeches were all filled with expressions of friendship and praise for the New South, denunciation of the Force Bill and other Republican legislation, and repetition of his oft-outlined program of Congressional inaction. Free coinage was promised as the panacea for the farmer's ills. During these three days, there were also backstage conferences with political leaders which L. Q. C. Lamar reported were concerned with the *quid pro quos* of national politics—cabinet positions and foreign ministerships.[58]

It is hard to evaluate accurately the effects of Hill's southern tour, for most of the accounts were written by men friendly to Cleveland, and they all insisted that the trip was a failure.[59] Hill wrote Marble that he felt the trip went off well;[60] but if an empirical judgment is valid, based on the decisions of the southern conventions during the next two months, the tour failed to achieve its objective: to bring the South into the Hill fold.

In still another respect, Hill's plans and calculations went awry. Chairman Bland of the House Committee on Banking, ignoring Hill's frequent pleadings to postpone a coinage bill until 1893, reported a silver measure out of committee in late February. Hill and Marble had tried to forestall such a measure in this session, believing that no good could come of it for the party or for Hill, no matter what the outcome. Marble immediately tried to counter

the introduction of the bill, and urged Hill to issue jointly
with Speaker Crisp the same proclamation he had wanted
the New York snap convention to declare—that Democrats
would postpone all action on the currency issue until they
had won all branches of the government in November, and
would then call a special session to deal with free coinage.
Hill discussed the plan with Crisp, who showed some
interest, but after due consideration the Speaker decided
against it. Marble then urged Hill to go it alone and
incorporate the manifesto in the form of a Senate resolution,
but Hill feared that he would get no support for it, and the
matter was dropped.[61] Meanwhile, in late March, a test
vote on the Bland bill resulted in a tie. Following a brief
filibuster against it, Bland conceded that the bill was
dead, and he made no further attempt to push it.[62]

Since the bill never reached the Senate floor, Hill was
spared the trial of casting a vote upon it. But the House
vote had already done the damage. The fact that House
Democrats, in the majority, could not push through a free
coinage bill must have disillusioned many of those who had
believed that the Democratic party would be the instrument
through which free coinage would be enacted. Moreover,
only one of the New York Democrats in the House voted
in favor of the measure. This was H. H. Rockwell, an old
friend of Hill, who owed his House seat to Hill's machine
and influence. The votes of the New York members dis-
credited Hill's claim that New York could be carried on a
free coinage platform.[63]

At about the same time, the New York City Bar Association dealt a serious blow to Hill's prestige. A committee
had been selected to investigate the conduct of the newly
appointed appeals judge, Isaac Maynard, in the recent
struggle for state legislative seats. On March 22, the com-

mittee's report was issued. It condemned Maynard's conduct as unethical and immoral, if not illegal, and petitioned the legislature to remove him. Since Maynard had been Hill's appointee and his chief instrument in the fight for the disputed seats, the report was an indirect condemnation of Hill.[64]

The bursting of Hill's campaign bubble was evidenced, and completed, by the decisions of the state Democratic conventions. The earliest of these occurred in Rhode Island, where on March 2, all ten delegates were instructed to vote for Grover Cleveland. Two more conventions in March brought twenty-four more delegates into the Cleveland camp. North Dakota sent a solid Cleveland delegation, and Minnesota, binding its delegates by the unit rule, declared that they should work for the renomination of the former President.[65]

In April Cleveland's total began to swell. Massachusetts, while not instructing, selected a slate composed largely of pro-Cleveland delegates, and Pennsylvania sent a full complement of Clevelandites, bound by the unit rule. Although Nebraska sent an uninstructed delegation, a resolution endorsing Cleveland was passed by the convention; and when the convention beat down William Jennings Bryan's resolution for free silver, it was clear that Clevelandites were in the saddle.[66] Although some of the delegates were favorably disposed toward Hill, the Nebraska results were nevertheless a disappointment to the Senator and Marble, who had been receiving encouraging reports from a prominent Nebraska Democrat.[67] On April 21, Kansas also instructed for Cleveland. Paradoxically, the same convention which supported for president the author of the "silver letter," declared for "free and unrestricted coinage of gold and silver."[68] The ability of Kansas, and several other states as well, to declare for free silver and then instruct for a man committed to fight against it was one of the most remarkable aspects of the entire campaign.

While these results underlined the startling rise in Cleveland sentiment, they were not in themselves extremely damaging to Hill. Except for Nebraska, little had been expected from these states, and Hill had hoped only for uninstructed delegations which might be swayed in Chicago.

The first blow of real consequence came from Indiana. Hill had not expected to have the Indiana delegation in his hip pocket, but he was confident that Governor Gray would be supported as a favorite son, and that Indiana could be counted upon after the first ballot. Instead, the convention named Cleveland as its first choice, and the best that Gray could get was a pledge that, if Cleveland's nomination were deemed inexpedient, Indiana's votes would go to her governor. The blow was tempered, however, by the fact that the delegation had not been formally instructed, and might still be open to persuasion at the convention.[69]

Far worse news came from Georgia. In Hill's concerted effort to win the South, Georgia had been designated the key state. Hill had numerous friends there, and he had made three trips since 1889 to curry favor in Georgia. The Hill boom was launched in earnest during his last trip, two months before the state convention. The tip-off that things were amiss came a week before the convention when the *Atlanta Constitution*, which had for weeks been claiming the state for Hill, now called for an uninstructed delegation. Cleveland sentiment was growing, and through careful planning and organization, the Clevelandites gained control of the convention. At least 20 of the 26 delegates selected were Cleveland men. Hill's friends salvaged what they could by blocking an attempt to bind the delegation by the unit rule.[70]

Early in May, Wisconsin and Michigan added their delegates to the Cleveland column, and Connecticut, another of the key states, chose a predominantly Cleveland slate. In New Jersey, Cleveland supporters substituted his name for that of Hill in the resolution to instruct the delegates, and the motion was passed.[71] Thus of the four key states, Hill had managed to secure the votes of only one, his own New York. And even here, there was a challenge, for the anti-snapper convention, meeting in Syracuse at the end of May, elected a slate of delegates to contest the seats of Hill's snappers at the national convention.[72]

The results from Georgia set the pattern for the rest of the South. In North Carolina, the Alliance men turned out in force, and passed a free silver resolution, but the 18 delegates were bound by no instructions, and may of them were known to be Cleveland supporters. Virginia, with young Carter Glass working for Hill, had been a center of Hill strength, but the best that Hill men could get there was half of the delegation. Tennessee not only instructed her 22 delegates for Cleveland, but also demanded that the national convention refuse to seat the snappers from New York. In Alabama, where Hill hoped to sweep the delegation, the results were in doubt, for the convention split into two separate factions and elected separate delegations. Missouri's representatives were instructed for Cleveland, despite a strong silver sentiment in Dick Bland's home state. And so it went. Only in South Carolina, where Pitchfork Ben Tillman ruled supreme, was Cleveland wholly repudiated by the state convention.[73]

By the beginning of June the complexion of the preconvention campaign had changed radically. Three months earlier, Hill's prospects had been bright and promising; now his situation had become almost hopeless, as delegation after delegation boarded the Cleveland bandwagon. There was still one outside chance: if enough of the uncommitted delegates could be kept from gravitating to Cleveland, he would fall short of the necessary two-thirds on the early ballots, and the convention might still turn to Hill.

The efforts of Hill and his advisers during the three weeks before the convention were directed to this end. Despite the strong showing of the anti-snappers at Syracuse, there was serious doubt in many quarters that Cleveland could carry New York against the will of the regular party organization. This doubt Marble wanted to exploit to the fullest. Chairman Murphy called a meeting of the New York delegation for June 7. Marble planned to have the delegates adopt a resolution stating that Cleveland could not carry New York, and hinting that he would receive less than full support from the party organization, if nominated. T. S. Williams, Hill's former secretary, opposed such a resolution, lest Hill's delegation appear to have a "dog-in-the-manger" attitude which would hurt Hill as well as Cleveland. In the end, the delegation adopted a milder resolution affirming their continuing loyalty to Hill. The substance of Marble's resolution found its way into some unofficial pamphlets of a Hill campaign club.[74] At the same meeting, the delegation voted to leave for Chicago almost a week before the convention was to open, in order to work for their candidate.

Before the delegation embarked, Hill journeyed to New York City for a final huddle with Murphy, Croker, Sheehan, and McLaughlin. From that point on, the struggle for delegates was in their hands. Hill's spirits were still high when he wrote to Marble on the sixteenth:

I am doing everything in my power to bring about a
favorable result. . . . I am always overcautious in reference to results. All our friends are quite enthusiastic.[75]

In the same letter, however, the Senator revealed that
he recognized he might have to step aside for another
candidate if Cleveland were to be stopped:

I do not think Cleveland can be nominated unless our
delegates are purchased away from us by Whitney & Co.
If they stand firm, either myself or some friend will be
nominated.[76]

One final-hour effort was made to swing uncommitted
silver supporters to Hill. A letter from Hill to a Kansas
Democrat dated December, 1891, in which Hill promised to
sign a free coinage bill if elected president, was published
in the press three days before the convention opened.[77]
This was done in deference to Marble, but Hill was
adamant when Marble urged him to make one final speech
on silver, stating that he wished to "leave well enough
alone." Hill confessed that he had little faith in last-minute
efforts to swing delegates on issues, for by this time, he had
realized what Marble still refused to accept: they had
miscalculated on the role of the currency issue in 1892.
"The question," Hill realistically wrote to Marble, "does
not turn upon free coinage, but is, who can be elected?" [78]
Senator Hill's hopes for stopping Cleveland now rested
almost entirely on the deterrent power of the New York
delegation pledged to him.

In Chicago, both sides worked feverishly to swing over
uncommitted delegates. In this endeavor, Murphy, Sheehan,
and Croker were no match for the able forces of Cleveland.
Led by the polished, brilliant William C. Whitney, Cleve-

land's workers won over one group after another. Indiana's tiny boom for Governor Gray fizzled out, and Senator Voorhees, once a Hill supporter, went along with the rest of the delegation into Cleveland's camp. Senator Gorman, also previously inclined to Hill, capitulated to Whitney when his own boom collapsed. Skillfully, Whitney led his forces, now enchanting one delegation, now charging into and breaking up a combination of silver states against Cleveland. With things well in hand, the anti-snappers were persuaded not to contest the seats of the New York delegation, lest there ensue a convention fight which might harm Cleveland.[79]

Marble, who at Hill's request had postponed a European trip in order to be at Chicago, made a last desperate effort to stop Cleveland. When he saw that Gorman, Voorhees, and Watterson, all previously opposed to Cleveland, had "gone up," he felt that the only way to stop a stampede was, as he later wrote, "to plant the whole delegation from N.Y. in the path of the Gadarene swine." [80] Marble drew up a petition, signed by all but one of the New York delegation, which warned the convention that Cleveland could not carry the Empire State. This petition, which was circulated through the convention hall, stated that

> with a deep sense of responsibility to the democracy of the United States [we] are constrained to . . . [say] that in our best judgment Mr. Cleveland's nomination would imperil the success of the party and would expose it to the loss of the electoral vote of the State.[81]

The story of the convention itself has been fully told elsewhere:[82] how the Cleveland forces, in command, beat down delaying motions; how at two o'clock on the morning of June 23, with a pouring rain sifting through the huge canvas top covering them, the Cleveland leaders prevented any re-grouping of enemy forces by refusing to adjourn; how the brilliant Tammany orator, Bourke Cockran, fatigued and disheartened, held his audience spell-bound for three-quarters of an hour with a superb appeal for Hill; how in the early hours of the morning the balloting began; and how, before dawn had broken, the Democratic party had nominated Grover Cleveland as its candidate.

In the perspective of a half-century, several factors stand out as basic in Hill's failure to capture the presidential nomination. One of these was the snap convention. Had the prize been a gubernatorial nomination, and the securing of the state delegation an end in itself, the snap convention might have been highly effective. But in this national contest, the pledge of seventy-two votes was more than offset by the revulsion to machine methods felt by many of the nation's Democrats and expressed in their state conventions. Moreover, the obvious irregularity of the mid-winter convention gave Hill's opponents within the state Democracy an excuse for effecting an extra-party organization. The anti-snapper revolt, by demonstrating the widespread antipathy to Hill and the large following of Cleveland in the Empire State, dealt a severe blow to Hill's campaign.

Cleveland's decision to re-enter politics was another basic factor in the Senator's defeat. Prior to Cleveland's announcement, Hill's bandwagon had rolled along smoothly, with no man of national stature in the field to stop it. All signs pointed to the selection of enough pro-Hill delegates to give him a commanding lead at Chicago. With the reappearance of the popular former President, however, Hill's national campaign fizzled, as many states from which he had expected support turned instead to Cleveland.

Still another factor which accounted for Hill's failure was Marble's miscalculation of the role of the currency issue in 1892. This miscalculation had been dramatically illustrated when many state conventions passed resolutions endorsing both free coinage and Grover Cleveland, without being bothered by the apparent inconsistency. Marble had been correct in his belief that free coinage would eventually become the dominant issue in a national campaign, but he had erred in assuming that the year would be 1892.

To these basic causes for Hill's failure should be added an additional factor, the brilliant Chicago performance of William C. Whitney in behalf of Cleveland. Although the former President had far more pledged votes than any other candidate, he still lacked the necessary two-thirds majority when the convention opened. It was the peerless Whitney who charmed, influenced, and cajoled enough uncommitted delegates to give Cleveland his first ballot triumph. Had the former President failed to win on an early ballot, the convention might still have turned to Hill.

The defeat at Chicago left Hill a bitter and disappointed man. He was especially angered by the desertion of men like Gorman and Voorhees, who were counted upon to block a first ballot stampede for Cleveland. A week after the convention, Hill wrote to T. S. Williams:

The treatment of the N.Y. delegation was most outrageous and makes our people bent on revenge as they now feel. Gorman and everybody else have been explaining ever since they returned—but I think I know how it was.[83]

And to Marble: "I am keeping quiet and saying nothing." [84]

For the next two months Hill kept to his own counsel. He declined an invitation to the ceremony formally notifying Cleveland of the nomination, and he refused also to serve on the national advisory committee. His long silence

inclined Whitney and Cleveland to the belief that the
defeated candidate was either planning to sit on his hands
during the campaign, or worse, was plotting some treachery.
Evidence supporting the latter possibility came in the
annual report of Charles F. Peck, the New York Commissioner of Labor and a Hill Democrat. This report, which
appeared in late August, concluded that the McKinley
Tariff had had a favorable effect on wages and production.
It was widely assumed that Hill was behind this report, and
that he had used it to warn Cleveland and Whitney that
he would have to be dealt with.[85]

Cleveland stubbornly insisted that he would prefer
to look outside New York for electoral votes rather than
deal with the regular organization, but Whitney was too
realistic to forfeit the vital vote of the Empire State. He
set upon a policy of wooing Sheehan, Murphy, Croker,
and other state leaders to support the national ticket.
If they could be won over, he reasoned, Hill would be
isolated, and would either fall into line or be nullified as a
force in the fall campaign.[86]

Whether such a course was necessary is doubtful. It is
true that Hill did not lift a finger on behalf of the national
ticket during the summer months. But it is not unreasonable
for a defeated candidate to hibernate for a period, during
which he could reconcile himself to his defeat, assuage his
disappointment, heal his injured pride. And Hill was a
man of intensely proud feelings.

In his letter to Williams shortly after the convention,
he wrote:

> I personally feel relieved from all responsibility for the
> canvass this fall. It will be the first fall in many years
> when I shall not have to stew and worry. If I should work
> ever so hard, and Mr. Cleveland should then fail, they

will again falsely accuse me of treachery. It is a difficult situation.[87]

These were the words of a man trying to find solace in his own defeat. At last, a respite from the political wars and relief from responsibility—no stewing, no worrying, just complete relaxation; let someone else do the hard work of campaigning and organization for a change.

But it was not in Hill to follow such a course. On September 19, he broke his long silence. In a speech to a mass meeting of Brooklyn Democrats, Hill reminded his audience that seven years before, on the same spot, he had first proclaimed his famous "I am a Democrat" slogan. "Under the existing political situation," he continued,

I know of no more appropriate place or presence than here to declare that I was a Democrat before the Chicago Convention and I am a Democrat still. The National Democratic Convention of 1892 has passed into history with its record, its triumphs, and its disappointments. The wisdom of its action is not now to be questioned. It was the court of last resort established by party usage as the final arbiter to determine the conflicting interests and claims of candidates, states, and sections, and its decision will be accepted with loyal acquiescence by every true patriotic Democrat who recognizes the necessity of party organization and discipline and respects the obligations which he assumes in its membership.[88]

His position stated, Hill launched into a slamming attack on the Republican record, and a vigorous appeal for support of the Democratic ticket. From this moment on, Hill was in the campaign with both feet, speaking up and down the state on behalf of Cleveland.

In the November elections, New York gave Cleveland a heavy majority, and the Democrats swamped the opposition. Following the victory, there were wild celebrations in New York; but for Hill, there was little to celebrate. The Democracy had triumphed, and that was gratifying. But his own ambitions had been crushed. Carter Glass assured him that the party would turn to him in 1896,[89] but this was small consolation to the disappointed Senator. The big brass ring, once almost within reach, had eluded him after all. Perhaps Hill knew, even then, that he would never again have an opportunity to grasp it.

CHAPTER IX

"I Am a Democrat"

THE STRUGGLE to secure the Democratic presidential nomination marked the high point in the political career of David Bennett Hill. In the years following this unsuccessful battle, Hill's political prestige and influence were gradually but steadily eclipsed. It was almost as though all the energy and potential of his career had been mustered and spent on the one great effort. There were a few occasions during the years which followed when the embers glowed brightly once more, but the moments were fleeting, and the flickering embers soon settled into ashes. Never again did Hill's hopes, prestige, and fame—or notoriety—reach the peak that they enjoyed in 1892.

Hill served out his term in the Senate until it ended in 1897. His senatorial career was active, and not without distinction. While in the Senate he turned his attention to the need for expediting the business of that body. An able parliamentarian, he proposed to accomplish this by a revision of the hoary and complex rules which deterred the smooth flow of business and permitted obstructionism by a small minority. He introduced resolutions to institute a rule of relevancy, make cloture easier to obtain, prevent dilatory quorum calls, and count as present those who sat in the chamber but refused to answer quorum calls. But tradition was too strong, and he met with no success in his attempts to change the Senate rules.[1]

On most legislative matters he supported his party, and frequently defended the Cleveland administration against Republican and Populist attacks, even when criticism of Cleveland had become fashionable and some of the President's own party were deserting him. But in spite of his frequent defense of administration policy, there was no love lost between Hill and the President. Over Cleveland's strenuous objection, Hill and Croker combined to elect Murphy to the United States Senate in 1893.[2] In matters of patronage affecting New York State, Hill was almost completely ignored by the President. The ill feelings flared up when Cleveland attempted to fill a vacancy in the Supreme Court with William B. Hornblower, a New York attorney. Hornblower had been one of the authors of the New York Bar Association's damning report on Maynard in 1892, and Hill regarded this nomination as a direct insult to himself. By exercising the prerogative of senatorial courtesy, Hill defeated the nomination. Cleveland then submitted the name of Wheeler H. Peckham, an old foe of Hill who was even more anathema to the Senator than Hornblower. Hill bristled, and again caused the nomination to be defeated in the Senate.[3]

On foreign affairs, Hill had little to say. His only notable entry into that sphere was the introduction of a resolution in December, 1896, declaring that a state of war existed in Cuba, and that the parties involved should be accorded belligerent rights. This resolution never reached a vote.[4]

On only one issue—the income tax amendment to the tariff bill of 1894—did Hill bolt his party. Hill believed an income tax to be unconstitutional and wrong, and while he favored a tariff revision, he refused to support a bill with an unconstitutional feature in it. Hill fought vigorously

against the measure. At first he directed the attack against
the income tax provision, citing legal arguments to support
his view. At the same time he pointed out to Democrats
that although their party platform pledged a tariff revision,
it said nothing about an income tax. Insistence upon the
latter, he warned, would jeopardize the fulfillment of the
former.[5] When this approach failed and the income tax
provision was incorporated into the tariff bill, Hill
attempted to sabotage the entire bill. He voted for every
delaying motion, and supported and proposed amendments burdening some goods with extreme tariffs and
giving others a duty-free status. Hill hoped that in the end,
the final bill would be so obnoxious as to be unacceptable,
either to the Congress or the President. Despite all his
efforts, however, the bill became law.[6]

Hill's desertion of the Democrats on this bill left him
open to the jibes of his critics, who submitted this as
evidence of insincerity in his professions of party loyalty.
But in that same year, the New York Senator gave indis-
putable evidence of his willingness to sacrifice his own
interests when called upon by his party to do so.

Things had gone badly for the Democracy of New York
between 1892 and 1894. The Flower administration, with
the aid of a Democratic legislature, had compiled a shameful record. The revelations of the Lexow investigating committee and the Reverend Charles Parkhurst's shocking and
amusing tales of the unchecked vice he encountered while
touring New York City in disguise pointed up the corruption in the Tammany-ruled metropolis. When Judge Isaac
Maynard, against the private advice of Hill, insisted on
running for re-election to the New York Court of Appeals in
1893, the wrath of the voters exploded, and he was swamped
by over 100,000 votes. All these developments bode ill for

the gubernatorial campaign of 1894. The outlook for the New York Democracy was dark indeed.[7]

The state convention met in Saratoga to choose a slate of lambs to be led to certain slaughter at the polls. Hill was chairman of the convention. When the nominations began, a cry for Hill went up as if by prearrangement, and stomping, cheering delegates acclaimed Hill their nominee for governor. Hill tried desperately to check the movement. He thanked the delegates for their courtesy, but insisted that he could not be a candidate. But as the roll call proceeded, each county fell in line for Hill. The professionals declared it Hill's duty to accept. "The party has honored him," Bourke Cockran told the convention, ". . . let him now serve his party." Again Hill declined, but he had no control over the convention, which refused his declination and adjourned shortly afterward. Hill pleaded with the state committee to substitute another candidate, but he was rebuffed. Murphy told him, "You run in the fat years and now you must take your chance in the lean year." Hill knew he was being sacrificed, but he agreed to run.[8]

So, with absolutely nothing to gain, and facing almost certain defeat and the consequent loss of prestige, Hill made the hopeless fight. All of his old techniques were again called into play—appeals to labor, liquor interests, religious groups. But the obstacles were insurmountable. Cleveland not only refused an endorsement, but threatened to blurt out "in straight United States language" what he thought of Hill.[9] A third ticket, the State Democracy, was entered by Hill's foes in the party to siphon off votes from the regular Democratic slate. The desperateness of the Senator's situation was unconsciously caricatured by a campaign document urging bicyclists to vote for Hill because he had signed a bill in 1887 permitting them to ride in state parks. On election day, the Republican nominee, Levi P. Morton, buried Hill by 150,000 votes.[10]

One thing more should be noted of the senatorial period of Hill's career. From 1892 on, his views on the currency— the burning issue of the era—changed from a staunch advocacy of free bimetallic coinage to a more orthodox position. This change stemmed from his concern for the preservation of a sound currency, then jeopardized by the rapidly dwindling supply of gold in the Treasury, and from his alarm over the rising radical spirit which was pushing the demand for free silver. Time and again he made bitter speeches against the Populists and those in his own party who were prepared—even eager—to drive the nation onto a silver standard.[11] By 1895, although still proclaiming his belief in international bimetallism, he was leaving the door ajar. In a resolution he stated that

> . . . if our efforts to establish or maintain such bimetallism shall not be wholly successful, and if for any reason our silver coin shall not hereafter be at parity with gold coin and the equal thereof in value and power in the market and in the payment of debts, then it is hereby declared that the bonds of the United States . . . which by their terms are payable in coin, shall nevertheless be paid in standard gold dollars. . . .[12]

In practice, he had joined the ranks of the financial conservatives. When the Cleveland administration deemed necessary, to maintain the Treasury's stock of gold, a private sale of bonds to financiers, Hill defended it vigorously against all comers in the Senate.[13]

By 1896, the middle ground between gold and silver in the Democratic party had become untenable, and Hill aligned himself with the gold interests. At the national convention he was one of the floor leaders in the fight to stem the silverite tide, but the effort was in vain, as the fervor of western delegates and the oratory of young William Jennings Bryan carried the day.[14]

Following the convention, Hill was undecided as to his course in the campaign. Bryan and the new order were anathema to him; yet he, Hill, was the high priest of party loyalty. Lamont invited the Senator to join him and many other financially orthodox Democrats in the new Gold Democratic party. Hill, however, elected to remain with his party in the hope that he could at least salvage the wreckage of the New York Democracy after its aberration. Moreover, to bolt and be beaten, as beaten he would be, did not appeal to him: "I do not like the martyr business as a steady job," he wrote.[15] Still, he could not bring himself to campaign for Bryan. When asked whether he would support the national ticket, Hill made his famous remark, "I am a Democrat still—very still." [16]

In the elections, the Republicans swept into control of the nation and the state, as the voters indicated their preference to crucifixion on a cross of gold to inundation in a sea of silver. The return of a Republican legislature in New York meant the end of Hill's senatorial career. It was ironic that the Republican legislature chose as his successor his old enemy, Thomas C. Platt.

Although Hill was never again a candidate for public office, he remained active in politics. For the next few years he was still a power in state party circles; but his resounding defeat in 1894, the almost total denial of patronage by the Cleveland administration, his retirement from office, and his long absence from the New York scene had taken their toll on his influence. The Tammany tiger had been mustering strength, and was waiting on the sidelines for an opportunity to replace Hill as the state leader. In the state convention of 1898, Hill had a falling out with Boss Croker and Tammany, and his loss of control was all but completed.[17]

For seven more years he continued to labor for the party and campaign for its candidates. The high point of these years was his management of Alton B. Parker's campaign for the Presidency in 1904. Hill managed his friend's campaign ably, but Theodore Roosevelt's popularity was too much for the Democrats. One writer remarked that the Dutch boy with his finger in the dyke was the greatest example of human fortitude until "Parker ran for the presidency against Theodore Roosevelt and was defeated by acclamation." [18]

In 1905, Hill retired from politics. With the sale of his shares in the *Elmira Gazette* to a young journalist named Frank Gannett,[19] Hill devoted himself almost entirely to his Albany law practice and a quiet life at Wolfert's Roost, a modest estate which he had bought from the actor Franz Emmett in 1892. There he spent the remaining years until his death in 1910.

Hill's political career was in many ways a remarkable one. Through native ability, a consuming interest in politics, and a skill in dealing with men, he rose to high political office. His political skill enabled him to become politcal overlord of the greatest state in the Union, and for a time, a prominent candidate for his party's presidential nomination. With his carefully built organization in upstate New York, he was able to do what few other Democrats of the century had succeeded in doing: to force Tammany into an alliance in which it acknowledged fealty rather than proclaimed supremacy.

Hill was essentially a conservative. Like most men, he was a product of his age, and his concept of the relationship of the government to its people was a nineteenth-century philosophy. The role of government was, in the main, a passive one:

> People should not be educated to the belief that the government is powerful enough to override the laws of trade and supply and demand, prevent overproduction of crops or guarantee favorable results to every business venture. The people must support themselves, and their measure of prosperity must depend on their own industry. It should be understood that success in life does not depend on governmental measures.[20]

The natural laws would take care of events, and the government could best serve its people by letting these laws operate with a minimum of interference. Even in a depression, recourse to governmental action would be futile. "I confess," he stated, "that I know of no adequate remedy for hard times within the power of the government to bestow." [21]

Hill was dismayed by what he considered the tendency of the federal government to enlarge its functions and assume doubtful powers, which he believed was "leading plainly in the direction of paternalism." "Paternalism," he insisted, ". . . can only flourish under a liberal, broad, and generous construction of constitutional restrictions." A strict construction was the bulwark that prevented the ship of state from helplessly drifting "towards every modern dogma and dangerous scheme for relief which a fickle and unintelligent public sentiment may desire to have foisted upon the government." [22]

In fine, Hill believed in a strictly limited federal government, whose activities were carefully circumscribed by a rigid constitution. ". . . The true theory of our institutions," he once remarked, "is that the state should do nothing that can better or as well be done by the free and un-

trammelled action of the individual citizen." [23] Jefferson
had said it more pungently almost a century earlier, but the
philosophy was still the same.

Like most true conservatives, Hill did not believe in a
rigid maintenance of the status quo, but he did believe that
change should be approached cautiously and deliberately.
Hill had the element of realism—his detractors called it
cynicism—which is so often lacking in pollyanna reformers.
He recognized that governmental schemes and devices
framed by humans are imperfect at best. To those who
would discard present systems and institutions in haste Hill
frequently issued the reminder that "all change is not reform." [24]

For men of more radical temperament Hill had less
patience. Doctrines like that of Henry George were anathema to him, and some of his bitterest words were directed
at them. In the Senate, Hill spent as much time battling the
rising Populists as he did the traditional Republican foe.

Even on the currency issue, Hill followed a conservative
course. In a politically expedient move, he had adopted the
cry for free bimetallic coinage in 1891 and 1892; and in the
Senate he had been a leader in the fight to repeal the
Sherman Silver Purchase Act, regarded by free coinage
advocates and gold standard men alike as an obstacle in
their path. To the extent that he believed in free coinage,
he understood it to be a safe, conservative solution to the
currency problem. But during the following years, when he
saw the radical spirit behind the demand for free silver,
he shrank from the movement. Although he still clung
to a vague ideal of international free bimetallic coinage, he
realized its impracticability and in practice he abandoned its
support. By the mid-1890's, Hill was in almost all regards
lined up with the conservative interests on the currency.[25]

As in his philosophy, so in his personal life, Hill was a

conservative. A non-drinker and non-smoker, his habits were abstemious. He kept regular hours, rarely indulged in social functions not required of him, ate simply, and lived frugally and unostentatiously. Only once was there even the remote likelihood of marriage, but Hill was apparently too absorbed in his career to follow through. Lawbooks were Hill's only indulgence. He frequently ordered large quantities of them and kept an up-to-date legal library. Even Hill's costume did not change over the years. Long after his retirement from politics, he could be seen bicycling through the streets of Albany, wearing his black Prince Albert statesman's frock and soft black hat. Nor did he rush after new inventions. Not until 1908 did he buy an automobile, and while governor at Albany, he refused to have a newfangled long-distance telephone installed in his office.[26]

But while his philosophy of government and the tenor of his outlook on life help to explain Hill, they are tangents to the main line of his thought and interest: politics. Hill's political beliefs are best summed up in his own oft-proclaimed phrase: "I am a Democrat." Hill was a partisan through and through, and he gloried in the fact. Few, indeed, were his actions which were not dictated by a partisan approach to politics. His criterion for most events and proposals was essentially simple: that which advanced the party's fortunes was good, that which opposed its interests bad. It brings no discredit upon Hill to add that in his judgments he frequently considered the effect on his own advancement within the party as well. Thus Hill believed in a partisan press and in the usefulness of party organs. He believed also in the fostering of Democratic clubs which would stand by the party in stormy periods as well as in fair weather.[27]

There is a case to be made for the partisan approach to politics. To Hill, as to most people, a party represented, in the ultimate sense, certain ideals, political, social, economic, and philosophical. The end of politics is, after all, the attainment of one's principles; and Hill believed that these could best be advanced by supporting the party which espoused them. "Parties," he noted, "represent great political principles; partisans are men with political convictions; partisanship is courageous devotion to those principles and convictions. If there is anything wrong in that . . . I have yet to learn it." [28]

Hill believed further that a party's triumph was achieved through a careful, thorough organization. A party may advocate great principles, "but no matter how high the standards of any political party may be, how brilliant its past achievements, or how excellent its principles, it cannot hope for valuable, practical, and successful results without a thorough organization of its adherents." [29] For those who considered the work of organization beneath them, Hill had an answer: "Organized effort and vigorous partisanship are not political qualities to be ashamed of. They are necessary to the triumph of every political principle." [30]

Hill's attitude toward patronage was that of a spoilsman, but not a cynical spoilsman. There was never an element of nepotism in Hill's appointments, nor did he, like Croker and others of this period, ever use his official position or his power of appointment to line his own pockets. His views on civil service were largely molded by his belief in the efficacy of organization. It was all well and good to talk of higher standards and performance in the civil service, and in theory and limited practice, Hill concurred. But man being what he is, patronage is necessary for the efficient functioning of a party organization. A decrease in patronage meant a decrease in organizational efficiency, and the consequent damage to a party's chances for success. Therefore, Hill set himself stolidly against civil service reformers. It was said that while governor of New York, he told his civil service commissioners that they could draw their pay and draw their breath, but they were not to draw resolutions.[31]

It is no surprise that a partisan like Hill could not understand the Independent and Mugwump in politics, who he felt considered themselves above dirtying their hands in the necessary work of party organization. "There is no place in honorable American politics," he told an audience of partisan Democrats, "for the political guerillas who do not attach themselves to either of the great political armies, but who, while swearing allegiance to neither, criticize them both and fight first upon one side and then upon the other." [32] Such people were "neuter politicians," a caste for which Hill had no use.[33]

Hill regarded partisanship also as necessary for the maintenance of responsible government. Responsibility for its actions should be placed squarely on the party that rules, and a less than partisan course would blur this responsibility. Hill had as little use for the bipartisan as for the nonpartisan. Bipartisanship, a theory then coming into vogue among political reformers, was a "travesty upon government," a creation invented "to enable political parties ostensibly to divide the responsibility for bad municipal government." [34]

Hill realized that there was bound to be a difference in values among the millions of party adherents, but he insisted that these individual values must bow to the general will of the party, if a practical result were to be achieved. Differences there were and would always be, but "those differences should be harmonized and adjusted in a spirit of unselfish patriotism, to the end that some practical measure of relief, embodying the things upon which we all can agree, may be speedily enacted, and thereby the honor and credit of our party may be advanced. . . ." [35]

It was easy, of course, for one who for so long had held the whip hand to counsel others to submerge their disagreements with party policy. But there were many occasions—especially later in his career—when Hill found himself required to follow his own advice. Only once in his long career—on the income tax issue in 1894—did he break from the party discipline which he preached, when in the struggle to reconcile his beliefs on discipline and constitutionality, he resolved the conflict in favor of the latter. On other occasions—even in the presidential conventions and campaigns of 1892, 1896, and 1900—he swallowed the pill which he himself had prescribed without complaint, albeit with varying degrees of grace. While campaigning in 1900 for Bryan, whom he had twice opposed for the nomination, he explained his position:

I repudiate the idea so persistently inculcated by impracticable [*sic?*] doctrinaires that every time a citizen is outvoted in a convention . . . even upon a material matter—he is honor bound to bolt and form another party. . . . It is not expected, nor is it practicable, that . . . parties will, at all times, fully and accurately, represent the sentiments of every individual member. It is sufficient that some leading principles in which a citizen believes, are advocated by the party with which he is associated, to justify his support of that party, regardless of its attitude on subordinate questions which he may or may not approve. He need not endorse every line or plank of a platform in order to maintain his orthodoxy. . . .[36]

To explain Hill solely in terms of his essentially conservative beliefs and his philosophy of party government, however, would be to present an incomplete portrait of the man. There were, indeed, principles and beliefs; but expediency and opportunism were also large factors in determining his course. At times these factors operated in the absence of a worthier cause; and not infrequently, his actions represented a skillful blend of the higher and baser motives. But there were also numerous occasions throughout his career when principle was callously set aside in favor of opportunism.

To conclude that the key to Hill's rise to political power and prominence lay in his mastery of the skills of the politician, and to describe and analyze these skills, presents little difficulty. Yet a politician must be judged not only on his success or failure in attaining power, and the means used to attain it, but also on the uses to which he puts his power. It is here that Hill becomes an enigma. One puzzled critic, after asserting that all politicians could be divided into the three classes of reformers of, conformers to, and deformers of, the body politic, neatly expressed the difficulty of trying to classify Hill: "No sooner does he exhibit a symptom of being a reformer," remarked this contemporary, "than he does something that as plainly indicates he is a conformer, on the heels of which will come some dastardly act that stamps him a deformer. I hesitate to call him either, I want to call him all three, I can't think of a name that means so much," he concluded, "and yet so little, unless it be the name he already bears, David Bennett Hill." [37]

The language is a bit unkind, perhaps; but even David Hill would have found it difficult to quarrel with the judgment.

Notes

CHAPTER I

1. The name of the village was changed in the 1890's to Montour Falls.

2. Elmira *Telegram*, Nov. 21, 1886.

3. Hill Papers (New York State Library, Albany, N.Y.), D. D. Turner to G. S. Bixby, Feb. 13, 1922; Charles R. Watkins to Bixby, n.d.; Havana *Journal*, Nov. 29, 1862. Some forty years ago, George S. Bixby undertook to write a commissioned biography of Hill but, because of a number of untoward circumstances, never completed the work. He did, however, gather and preserve many of Hill's papers, which are now in the possession of the New York State Library at Albany. This George S. Bixby collection is referred to in this volume as Hill Papers.

4. Elmira *Telegram*, Mar. 9, 1913; Charles A. Collin, "David Bennett Hill: A Character Sketch," *Review of Reviews*, V (Feb.–July, 1892), 19.

5. Elmira *Star-Gazette*, Nov. 2 (3?), 1940. In David B. Hill Scrapbook, Montour Falls Memorial Library.

6. Collin, *op. cit.*, p. 19; Elmira *Advertiser*, June 10, 1868. This incident occurred in December, 1865.

7. Elmira *Star-Gazette*, Nov. 2 (3?), 1940; Collin, *op. cit.*, pp. 20–21; Hill Papers, D. D. Turner to Bixby, Nov. 23, 1921; Charles R. Watkins to Bixby, n.d. At just about this same time, in the back room of a drugstore in near-by Tioga County, a young

Republican named Thomas Collier Platt was manifesting an identical fascination in the grand and petty strategy of politics, the mastery of which was destined to earn him not only the title of the Easy Boss of the New York machine but also the implacable political enmity of Hill.

8. Hill Papers, D. D. Turner to Bixby, Nov. 23, 1921; Collin, *op. cit.*, p. 20; Elmira *Star-Gazette,* Nov. 2 (3?), 1940; Tilden Papers (New York Public Library, New York, N.Y.), Hill to William Cassidy, Oct. 19, 1869.

9. *Infra,* pp. 45–46.

10. *New York Times,* Mar. 29, 31, 1871; Oct. 10, 1885; New York State Legislature, *Assembly Journal, 1872,* Vol. II, pp. 1629–50.

11. De Alva Stanwood Alexander, *A Political History of the State of New York* (4 vols.; New York: Henry Holt & Co., Inc., 1906–23), III, 381.

12. For example, Tilden Papers, Hill to Theodore Miller, September 21, 1874.

13. Aside from wanting to end Judge Jeremiah McGuire's decisions which favored the Canal Ring, Tilden was also irritated by Steve Arnot's unreasonable demands for patronage in the Elmira Reformatory. Alexander C. Flick, *Samuel Jones Tilden: A Study in Political Sagacity* (New York: Dodd, Mead & Co., 1938), p. 275.

14. Hill Papers, E. K. Apgar to Hill, Mar. 20, 1875.

15. Elmira *Telegram,* Mar. 16, 1913; Elmira *Advertiser,* Sept. 4, 1875; Hill Papers, E. K. Apgar to Hill, Sept. 2, 1875.

16. Tilden Papers, Hill to E. K. Apgar, Sept. 5, 1875.

17. Collin, *op. cit.,* p. 20.

18. Elmira *Star-Gazette,* Nov. 2 (3?), 1940.

19. Flick, *Samuel J. Tilden,* p. 493; Timothy Shaler Williams Memorandum in Hill Papers, n.d.

20. Hill Papers, E. K. Apgar to Hill, July 30, 1875; Apgar to Hill, Feb. 27, 1875; Apgar to Hill, Apr. 21, 1876. Tilden Papers, Hill to W. T. Pelton, May 2, 1876.

21. De Alva Stanwood Alexander, *Four Famous New Yorkers*

256

(A Political History of the State of New York, Vol. IV [New York: Henry Holt & Co., Inc., 1906–23]), p. 63.

22. De Alva Stanwood Alexander, *Political History,* III, 380–83.

23. Collin, *op. cit.,* p. 20.

24. Hill Papers, campaign document of 1888; Beman Brockway, *Fifty Years in Journalism* (Watertown, N.Y.: Daily Times Printing and Publishing Co., 1891), p. 404.

25. Elmira *Telegram,* May 27, 1923.

26. Elmira *Advertiser,* Mar. 2, 7, 8, 1882.

27. *Elmira Gazette,* Mar.–Dec., 1882, *passim.* The files for this period are incomplete.

28. Hill Papers, William Purcell to Hill, Sept. 10, 1881; R. A. Maxwell to Hill, May 31, 1881.

29. For example, Hill Papers, F. G. Babcock to Hill, Aug. 24, 1882; E. K. Apgar to Hill, Aug. 29, 1882; E. W. Chamberlain to Hill, Aug. 29, 1882; D. C. Fowell to Hill, Aug. 31, 1882; also John B. Stanchfield to Bixby, Dec. 17, 1919.

30. Cleveland Papers (Library of Congress, Washington, D.C.), Hill to D. S. Lamont, Sept. 2, 1882.

31. Tilden Papers, Hill to Tilden, Sept. 2, 1882. When Hill received the nomination, several of the congratulatory telegrams he received stressed the point that he deserved it on the basis of his service to the party. Hill Papers, Alton B. Parker to Hill, Sept. 23, 1882; T. Miller to Hill, Sept. 25, 1882.

32. Allan Nevins, *Grover Cleveland: A Study in Courage* (New York: Dodd, Mead & Co., 1933), pp. 100–101; *New York Tribune,* Sept. 23, 1882.

33. *Appleton's Annual Cyclopaedia, 1882,* p. 610; *New York Times,* Dec. 8, 1882.

34. New York *World,* Mar. 14, 1883; *New York Times,* Mar. 14, 1883. The New York State constitution required the presence of three-fifths of the membership of each house and the affirmative vote of one-half the full membership to pass bills involving appropriations of money. The eighteen Democratic members who voted to approve constituted one more than the required vote

but one less than the required quorum, and the fourteen Republicans sat in silence.

35. William A. Robinson, *Thomas B. Reed, Parliamentarian* (New York: Dodd, Mead & Co., 1930), p. 210.

36. Hill Papers, Thomas E. Benedict to Bixby, Dec. 12, 1920; De Alva Stanwood Alexander, *Four Famous New Yorkers*, p. 64.

37. Nevins, *Grover Cleveland*, pp. 147, 150, 152; *Albany Evening Journal*, June 5, 1884.

38. Alexander C. Flick (ed.), *History of the State of New York* (10 vols.; New York: Macmillan Co., 1933–37), X, 173. The 1910 figure is for Greater New York.

39. Nevins, *Grover Cleveland*, p. 125.

CHAPTER II

1. *Messages from the Governors,* Charles Z. Lincoln, ed. (Albany, 1909), VIII, 1–40.

2. "Three Executive Messages," *Harper's Weekly,* XXIX (Jan. 17, 1885), 34; New York *Evening Post,* Jan. 6, 1885.

3. The *Times* turned upon Hill immediately, apparently because of his advocacy of a "freedom of worship" bill, which the *Times* considered a pandering to the Irish Catholic population. *New York Times,* Jan. 7, 8, 1885. See also New York *Star,* New York *Sun,* and *New York Tribune,* Jan. 7, 1885.

4. Hill Papers, C.S.B. [Charles S. Beardsley] to Hill, Dec. 1, 1884. *New York Times,* Jan. 8, 1885.

5. *New York Herald,* Feb. 16, 1885; "Freedom of Worship," *Harper's Weekly,* XXIX (Feb. 7, 1885), 82. Governors Robinson and Cleveland had rejected similar bills.

6. *New York Times,* Mar. 12, 1885.

7. *New York Herald,* Apr. 2, 1885; *New York Times,* May 16, 1885.

8. To a certain extent the movement to capture the labor vote was tied to the attempt to win the Irish vote, since many Irish were included in the laboring class.

9. *Messages from the Governors,* VIII, 35.

10. The prison labor bill, assembly bill 652, passed the assembly but failed in the senate. Yonkers *Gazette,* July 4, 1885.

11. Hill Papers, C.S.B. [Beardsley] to Hill, Dec. 1, 1884.

12. *Messages from the Governors,* VIII, 35–36.

13. *New York Times,* Apr. 8, 1885. The problem of competition in the open market between prison-made goods and those produced by free labor was finally resolved in part in 1888. In that year a statute was enacted providing for the sale of goods made by prison labor to other state institutions.

14. *Messages from the Governors,* VIII, 40–43.

15. *New York Times,* Mar. 11, 22, Apr. 5, 1885; *Messages from the Governors,* VIII, 57–61, 66–70.

16. *New York Times,* May 22, 1885.

17. *New York Times,* May 23, 1885.

18. Hill Papers, R. Ransom to Hill, Jan. 8, 1885.

19. *New York Times,* Feb. 24, 1885.

20. *New York Times,* Mar. 4, 1885. The Davidson case was a holdover from Cleveland's administration. An investigation by Assemblyman Theodore Roosevelt had resulted in the charges.

21. *Nation,* XLI (July 23, 1885), 64; *New York Times,* Mar. 13, 1885; Hill Papers, Thompson to Hill, May 19, 1885; Thompson to Hill, June 16, 1885.

22. Hill Papers, C.S.B. [Beardsley] to Hill, Dec. 1, 1884.

23. *Messages from the Governors,* VIII, 124–25; *New York Times,* June 14, 1885.

24. For example, the census issue, the careful veto of items in the appropriations bill, and his memorandum filed with his approval of an inheritance tax act. In the latter, Hill suggested that the minimum exemption of $500 should be raised to $5,000 so that persons of "limited means" would not suffer. See *Messages from the Governors,* VIII, 71–76, 102, 106–19.

25. *New York Times,* July 1, Sept. 18, 1885.

26. Albany *Journal,* July 14, 1885; *New York Times,* July 14, 22, Aug. 10, 1885.

27. *New York Times,* July 15, 22, 1885.

28. Hill Papers, James W. Covert to Hill, Sept. 3, 1885.

29. Hill Papers, Alonzo B. Caldwell to Hill, Sept. 15, 1885.

30. *New York Times,* July 6, 1885.

31. *New York Times,* June 1, 1885.

32. Albany *Express,* July 15, 1885.

33. *New York Times,* Sept. 2, 1885.

34. *New York Herald,* Aug. 17, 1885; *New York Times,* Aug. 3, 1885.

35. Mark D. Hirsch, *William C. Whitney, Modern Warwick* (New York: Dodd, Mead, & Co., 1948), p. 354.

36. *New York Times,* June 6, Aug. 15, 1885.

37. Brooklyn *Daily Eagle,* July 17, 1885.

38. *New York Times,* Aug. 22, 1885; William C. Hudson, *Random Recollections of an Old Political Reporter* (New York: Cupples & Leon Co., 1911), p. 259; Hill Papers, Dominick Roche to Hill, Nov. 6, 1885.

39. Kelly and Tammany bolted the regular ticket in 1879 and ran a third ticket, resulting in a Republican victory.

40. Albany *Press and Knickerbocker,* Aug. 17, 1885; *New York Times,* July 6, 1885.

41. *New York Herald,* Aug. 11, 18, 1885; *New York Times,* Aug. 19, 1885; New York *Evening Post,* Aug. 19, 1885; New York *World,* Aug. 19, 1885.

42. Hudson, *op. cit.,* p. 254; Hirsch, *op. cit.,* p. 354. Only Lamont, Cleveland's secretary, seems to have favored Hill. Cleveland Papers, Hill to Lamont, Nov. 15, 1885.

43. George F. Parker, *Recollections of Grover Cleveland* (New York: Century Co., 1909), pp. 244–45.

44. New York *Sun,* Aug. 30, 31, 1885; *New York Times,* Sept. 3, 1885; *New York Herald,* Sept. 1–14, 1885; Hill Papers, D. T. Arbuckle to Hill, Aug. 31, 1885; E. F. Jones to Hill, Sept. 4, 1885; E. R. Tanner to Hill, Sept. 7, 1885; G. W. Smith to Hill, Sept. 7, 1885; E. K. Burnham to Hill, Sept. 4, 1885; H. O. Cheseboro to Hill, Sept. 4, 1885.

45. Hill Papers, James Lyddy to Hill, Sept. 11, 1885; Lyddy to Hill, Sept. 14, 1885.

46. *New York Times,* Sept. 18, 24, 1885.

47. *New York Times,* Sept. 25, 1885. Mr. Eaton, who released

the letter, claimed that he did not receive it until September
23, at which time he gave it to the press.

48. Hill Papers, E. R. Keyes to Hill, Jan. 11, 1886.

49. New York *Sun*, Sept. 25, 1885; *New York Times*, Sept.
25, 1885.

50. *New York Times*, Sept. 26, 1885.

51. New York *World*, Sept. 26, 1885; De Alva Stanwood
Alexander, *Four Famous New Yorkers*, p. 69.

52. New York *World*, New York *Sun*, *New York Tribune*,
New York Times, Sept. 25, 1885.

53. *New York Times*, Sept. 25, 1885. Hudson attributes
slightly different words to the General, but the intent is essentially the same. Hudson, *op. cit.*, p. 262.

54. *New York Times*, Oct. 1, 1885.

55. *Infra*, pp. 102–109, 115.

56. Hill Papers, Willis Paine to Hill, Oct. 3, 1885; Alton B.
Parker to Hill, Oct. 12, 1885; *New York Times*, Oct. 8, 9, 1885.

57. *Nation*, XLI (Oct. 8, 1885), 292; *New York Times*, Oct. 25,
1885.

58. "The New York Democratic Nomination," *Nation*, XLI
(Oct. 1, 1885), 272.

59. Hill Papers, Thomas Grady to Hill, Sept. 25, 1885. Copy
of Pomeroy handbill in Hill Papers.

60. Hill Papers, William L. Muller to Hill, Oct. 12, 1885;
New York Times, Oct. 7, 1885.

61. Hill Papers, Grover Cleveland to Alton B. Parker, Oct.
22, 1885. See also Cleveland to Daniel Manning, Sept. 18, 1885,
in Allan Nevins (ed.), *The Letters of Grover Cleveland, 1850–
1908* (Boston: Houghton Mifflin Company, 1933), p. 76. On
hearing of Hill's nomination, Cleveland had expressed to his
close friend William Bissell the hope that Hill "will pull
through." *Ibid.*, p. 78.

62. *New York Times*, July 22, 1885.

63. *Documents of the Senate of the State of New York, 1876*,
Vol. VI, No. 78, pp. 426, 447–51, 477–78, 516–28, 555–59.

64. *Ibid.*, pp. 555–59.

65. *New York Tribune,* Oct. 3, 5, 1885.

66. *New York Times,* Oct. 1, 2, 1885.

67. Flick, *Samuel Jones Tilden,* p. 208.

68. *Harper's Weekly,* XXIX (Oct. 31, 1885), 705.

69. *New York Times,* Oct. 3, 1885; Hill Papers, Muller to Hill, Oct. 3, 1885.

70. *New York Times,* Oct. 18, 1885.

71. Broadsides and handbills in Hill Papers.

72. Florence E. Gibson, *The Attitudes of the New York Irish toward State and National Affairs, 1848–1892* (New York: Columbia University Press, 1951), p. 395.

73. Campaign literature in Hill Papers.

74. New York *Journal of Commerce,* Oct. 12, 1885, clipping in Hill Papers; also Hill Papers, pamphlet *Address of the Merchants and Business Men of New York City* (N.p., 1885).

75. De Alva Stanwood Alexander, *Four Famous New Yorkers,* p. 73; *New York Times,* Oct. 22, 1885.

76. New York *Sun,* Oct. 29, 1885.

77. De Alva Stanwood Alexander, *Four Famous New Yorkers,* p. 72.

78. *Ibid.,* p. 73.

CHAPTER III

1. *Messages from the Governors,* VIII, 25–26, 298; Rice Papers (New York Public Library, New York, N.Y.), Rice to Walter Bunn, Feb. 7, 1889. The legislature finally yielded in 1889, and a commission to scrutinize legislation was set up during that year.

2. For example, see veto messages in *Messages from the Governors,* VIII, 197, 229.

3. *Ibid.,* pp. 47–48, 52, 54–55.

4. *Ibid.,* pp. 342–48.

5. For example, Hill secured a general law for the incorporation of trust companies, after vetoing individual acts for two years. *Statutes of the State of New York, 1887,* chap. 546. Also *Messages from the Governors,* VIII, 476.

6. *Ibid.*, pp. 158–161.

7. *Supra,* p. 20.

8. New York *World,* May 20, 1886; *New York Times,* May 25, 1886.

9. *Messages from the Governors,* VIII, 278–89. In 1889 Hill vetoed a similar bill designed to change the system of selecting Brooklyn aldermen. *Ibid.,* pp. 739–49.

10. See vetoes in *ibid.,* pp. 211–12, 377–78; Rice Papers (NYPL), Rice to Mayor D. D. Whitney, Mar. 22, 1886; Rice to William R. Grace, Jan. 26, 1886; Rice to Grace, Apr. 9, 1886; Rice to H. D. Graves, Feb. 5, 1886.

11. *Messages from the Governors,* VIII, 152–55, 158–61, 168–75, 179, 180–81, 304–308, 311–12, 319–20.

12. Vernon B. Santen, *The Administration of the New York State Civil Service Law, 1883–1917* (Syracuse, N.Y.: Maxwell Graduate School of Citizenship and Public Affairs, Syracuse University, 1952), Appendix.

13. New York *World,* Nov. 6, 1885.

14. Boston *Daily Globe,* June 19, 1886.

15. *New York Times,* Jan. 13, Feb. 13, 1886; *Harper's Weekly,* XXXI (May 14, 1887), 343.

16. New York *Sun,* Mar. 11, 1886; *Messages from the Governors,* VIII, 235–37. Hill repeated his rebuke the following year. *Ibid.,* pp. 426–27.

17. *Harper's Weekly,* XXXI (May 14, 1887), 343.

18. Hill Papers, Hill to T. C. Platt, May 27, 1887; New York *World,* May 27, 28, 1887; *Nation,* XLIV (June 2, 1887), 460.

19. *New York Times,* July 29, 1887.

20. *Nation,* XLV (Dec. 29, 1887), 516.

21. Thomas C. Platt, *The Autobiography of Thomas Collier Platt* (New York: B. W. Dodge & Co., 1910), p. 194; *New York Times,* Jan. 14, 1888; Hill Papers, Abram Hewitt to Hill, [?] 1888. The case was carried to the highest courts and was finally sustained by the state court of appeals. *New York Times,* Nov. 27, 1889.

22. *Messages from the Governors,* VIII, 155–58, 178, 298–99, 302.

23. *Ibid.,* pp. 393–99; *New York Times,* May 7, 1887. For the Democratic plan as proposed by Hill, see *Messages from the Governors,* VIII, 309–11. For Republican scheme, see *New York Times,* Apr. 14, 1887.

24. For a history of the Prohibition movement, see David L. Colvin, *Prohibition in the United States: A History of the Prohibition Party and of the Prohibition Movement* (New York: George H. Doran Co., 1926) or Ernest H. Cherrington, *The Evolution of Prohibition in the United States of America* (Westerville, Ohio: American Issue Press, 1920).

25. Colvin, *op. cit.,* pp. 134–35.

26. De Alva Stanwood Alexander, *Four Famous New Yorkers,* p. 99.

27. *New York Times,* Mar. 24, 1887. The existing rates in New York and Brooklyn were $250 and $30 for liquor and beer licences, respectively. The minima and maxima permitted by state law were as follows: for cities, from $30 to $250 for liquor and beer; in towns and villages, $30 to $150 for liquor, not less than $10 for beer. See *Messages from the Governors,* VIII, 685.

28. Colvin, *op. cit.,* p. 188.

29. *New York Times,* Apr. 6, 1887.

30. *New York Times,* Mar., 1887, *passim.*

31. *Messages from the Governors,* VIII, 340.

32. *Ibid.,* pp. 342–48.

33. See veto in *ibid.,* pp. 355–65. There were other objections as well, chiefly a constitutional objection to the clause permitting a holder of a beer and wine license to be prosecuted for having liquor in his possession on the licensed premises.

34. *Ibid.,* pp. 436–39; *New York Times,* Apr. 28, 1887.

35. *Nation,* XLIII (Dec. 2, 1886), 446.

36. *Messages from the Governors,* VIII, 162–65.

37. *Statutes of the State of New York, 1886,* Chap. 409. A labor historian, crediting Hill with "material assistance," writes that "the Factory Law of 1886 forms the real basis for legislation for the protection of working children in New York State." Mary S. Callcott, *Child Labor Legislation in New York* (New York: Macmillan Co., 1931), pp. 1, 12.

38. *Statutes of the State of New York, 1886,* Chap. 410. Because decisions of the board were not binding and submission to arbitration was voluntary, this board was ineffective.

39. *New York Times,* May 19, 1886; Hill Papers, Hill to Terence V. Powderly, June 10, 1890.

40. *Messages from the Governors,* VIII, 312–19, 320–23. Hill had uttered similar sentiments in a speech on September 19, 1886. *Nation,* XLIII (Sept. 23, 1886), 241–42.

41. *Statutes of the State of New York, 1887,* Chaps. 63, 84, 288, 289, 461.

42. For a fuller explanation of the role and methods of the State Trades Assembly, see Howard Hurwitz, *Theodore Roosevelt and Labor in New York State, 1880–1900* (New York: Columbia University Press, 1943), pp. 25–26.

43. *New York Herald,* Sept. 7, 1887; also, for example, *infra,* pp. 70–72.

44. *New York Times,* Mar. 18, Apr. 2, 21, 1887.

45. *New York Times,* Apr. 26, May 4, 6, 12, 1887; *Messages from the Governors,* VIII, 373–75.

46. *Albany Evening Journal,* Oct. 8, Nov. 19, 1887; *New York Tribune,* Nov. 19, 1887.

47. *Albany Argus,* Nov. 19, 1887.

48. "The Labor Party," *Harper's Weekly,* XXXI (Aug. 27, 1887), 606.

49. "The United Labor Party," *ibid.,* XXXI (May 21, 1887), 358.

50. Quoted in the *Nation,* XLV (Aug. 25, 1887), 143.

51. *New York Times,* June 16, 1887.

52. Rochester *Union and Advertiser,* Sept. 6, 1887; *New York Times,* Sept. 7, 1887. Five of the nine factory inspectors then in office were present as delegates to the State Trades Assembly convention. Moreover, the chief of the Political Branch of the assembly, George Blair, was a friend of Hill's. *New York Herald,* Sept. 7, 1887.

53. Utica *Morning Herald,* Sept. 8, 1887.

54. *Appleton's Annual Cyclopaedia, 1887,* p. 551.

55. De Alva Stanwood Alexander, *Four Famous New Yorkers*, p. 94.

56. *Appleton's Annual Cyclopaedia, 1887*, p. 551.

57. *Ibid.*, p. 552.

58. Speeches at Penn Yan, N.Y., Oct. 6, 1887; Bath, N.Y., Sept. 29, 1887; Academy of Music, Brooklyn, N.Y., Nov. 1, 1887. Copies in Hill Papers. "The Election," *Harper's Weekly*, XXXI (Nov. 12, 1887), 814.

59. Speech at Academy of Music, Brooklyn, N.Y., Nov. 1, 1887.

60. De Alva Stanwood Alexander, *Four Famous New Yorkers*, p. 99.

61. Hill Papers, Hill to William Steinway, Oct. 26, 1889.

62. *Appleton's Annual Cyclopaedia, 1887*, p. 552; *Nation*, XLV (Nov. 10, 1887), 361.

CHAPTER IV

1. Speech to the Young Men's Democratic Club of Brooklyn, Feb. 22, 1887. Copy in Hill Papers.

2. Address to the New York Democratic Men's Banquet, Jan. 8, 1886. Copy in Hill Papers.

3. *Messages from the Governors*, VIII, 150.

4. "Rallying the Young Men," *Nation*, XLIII (July 1, 1886), 6.

5. Rice Papers (NYPL), Rice to John Jay, June 28, 1887; Santen, *op. cit.*, pp. 42–43. An 1888 court decision upheld Hill and exempted these positions. *Ibid.*, p. 47.

6. Speech to the Young Men's Democratic Club of Brooklyn, Feb. 22, 1887.

7. Hill Papers, William P. Tomlinson to Rice, Nov. 17, 1886.

8. Hill Papers, W. S. Ray to Hill, Nov. 9, 1886; Shelbyville *Daily Democrat*, Nov. 18, 1886. Clipping in Hill Papers.

9. *New York Times*, Mar. 8, 1887; *Nation*, XLIII (Sept. 2, 1886), 186; Rice Papers (NYPL), Rich to C. H. Peck, Feb. 17, 1887.

10. Hill Papers, C. A. Coryell to Hill, Oct. 13, 1886. Coryell cited figures from a poll by the St. Louis *Globe-Democrat*.

11. Rice Papers (NYPL), Rice to W. S. Ray, Nov. 23, 1886.

12. *New York Times,* Jan. 9, 1886. The relationship was polite at best, rather than friendly. Cleveland had written to his friend Bissell describing Hill as a "whelp, morally and politically," when he learned that Hill had tried to entice Lamont, the President's secretary, to return to Albany and work for the Governor. Cleveland Papers, Cleveland to Bissell, Aug. 12, 1886.

13. Speech to the Young Men's Democratic Club of Brooklyn, Feb. 22, 1887.

14. Albany *Express,* New York *World,* Feb. 23, 1887.

15. *Albany Argus,* Feb. 23, 1887.

16. Nevins, *Grover Cleveland,* p. 395.

17. Hill Papers, William P. Tomlinson to Rice, Nov. 17, 1886.

18. *Infra,* pp. 104–105.

19. *New York Times,* July 6, 1886.

20. New York *Mail and Express,* 1886. Clipping in Hill Papers. Hill Papers, Dominick Roche to Hill, Oct. 20, 1886.

21. *New York Times,* Sept. 11, 1886.

22. The *Nation,* XLII (Feb. 11, 1886), 118; *New York Times,* July 1, 1887.

23. *New York Times,* May 3, 1886; Hudson, *op. cit.,* p. 271.

24. *Nation,* XLIII (Sept. 23, 1886), 244.

25. Flick, *Samuel Jones Tilden,* p. 486; Nevins, *Grover Cleveland,* p. 394.

26. White Plains *Standard,* July 17, 1886. Clipping in Hill Papers.

27. After Hill's victory in 1888, Pulitzer sent Hill a diamond pin in the shape of a rooster, the Democratic symbol. Hill Papers, Hill to Pulitzer, Dec. 29, 1888.

28. New York *Sun,* June 24, 1886.

29. *Nation,* XLIV (Feb. 10, 1887), 108.

30. De Alva Stanwood Alexander, *Four Famous New Yorkers,* p. 96.

31. *Ibid.*

32. *Ibid.,* p. 104; Nevins, *Grover Cleveland,* p. 248.

33. New York *Sun,* New York *World, New York Times,* Aug. 31, 1887.

34. *New York Times,* New York *Evening Post,* Aug. 31, 1887.

35. New York *Sun,* Aug. 31, 1887.

36. Troy *Telegram,* Sept. 1, 1887. Clipping in Hill Papers.

37. *New York Herald,* Aug. 31, 1887.

38. De Alva Stanwood Alexander, *Four Famous New Yorkers,* p. 96; *New York Times,* Oct. 6, 1887.

39. De Alva Stanwood Alexander, *Four Famous New Yorkers,* p. 96.

40. Nevins, *Grover Cleveland,* pp. 285–86.

41. *Ibid.,* p. 381.

42. *Ibid.,* p. 399.

43. New York *World,* Jan. 27, 1888.

44. Cleveland Papers, Cleveland to Bissell, Jan. 13, 1888.

45. Cleveland Papers, James Shanahan to Cleveland, Feb. 5, 1888.

46. For example, see *Nation,* XLVI (Feb. 16, 1888), 125.

47. De Alva Stanwood Alexander, *Four Famous New Yorkers,* p. 107; *Nation,* XLVI (Mar. 1, 1888), 165.

48. De Alva Stanwood Alexander, *Four Famous New Yorkers,* p. 108.

49. *New York Times,* Apr. 6, 1888.

50. *New York Times,* May 14, 16, 1888.

51. Robert McElroy, *Grover Cleveland, the Man and the Statesman* (2 vols.; New York: Harper & Brothers, 1923), I, 289–90.

52. Copy of speech, June 12, 1888, in Hill Papers.

CHAPTER V

1. *Messages from the Governors,* VIII, 478–80, 484–85, 487–91; *Statutes of the State of New York, 1888,* Chaps. 77, 489, 578.

2. *Messages from the Governors,* VIII, 509–16.

3. Veto message in *ibid.,* pp. 540–46.

4. *Ibid.,* pp. 640–43.

5. For a full treatment of electoral reform, see the pamphlet by the Society for Political Education, *Electoral Reform* (N.p., 1889); also, Eldon C. Evans, *A History of the Australian Ballot System in the United States* (Chicago: University of Chicago Press, 1917), pp. 1–26; and William M. Ivins, *Machine Politics and Money in the Elections in New York City* (New York: Harper & Brothers, 1887), pp. 37–38.

6. *Ibid.*, Chaps. III and IV, especially pp. 54–58.

7. "Paying the Piper," *Harper's Weekly*, XXXI (Aug. 6, 1887), 554.

8. The law prescribed that the ballots of all parties must be white, but this requirement was circumvented by using different shades of white.

9. The Society for Political Education, *op. cit.*, pp. 1–22.

10. *Messages from the Governors*, VIII, 566–80. De Alva Stanwood Alexander errs in stating that Hill's motive for vetoing the Saxton bill was to win further support in his quest for the Democratic presidential nomination of 1888. The veto came on June 9; the convention met on June 8. De Alva Stanwood Alexander, *Four Famous New Yorkers*, pp. 105–106.

11. The so-called Fassett antibribery bill, passed during this session, had many defects, and was vetoed by Hill. See *Messages from the Governors*, VIII, 598–603.

12. *New York Times*, Feb. 28, 1888.

13. *New York Times*, Oct. 15, 1887; Mar. 16, 1888.

14. Document No. 57, *Documents of the Senate of the State of New York, 1889*, 112th sess. (Vols. VI–IX), VI, 81. Hereafter cited as *Senate Documents, 1889*. Also, Committee Report, *ibid.*, p. 4.

15. *Ibid.*, pp. 4–5, 82–170.

16. *Ibid.*, p. 35.

17. *Ibid.*, pp. 117–18.

18. *Senate Documents, 1889*, VIII, 1612.

19. *New York Times*, Aug. 7, 1886.

20. *New York Times*, Aug. 26, 1886.

21. *Senate Documents, 1889*, VI, 5–10, 240; VII, 698–713.

22. *Ibid.*, VI, 18.

23. For example, see "The Squire Investigation," *Harper's*

Weekly, XXXII (May 5, 1888), 314; also, *New York Times,* Aug., 1888, *passim.*

24. *Senate Documents, 1889,* VI, 87.

25. There is a strong suggestion of this in the Hill Papers, John H. Douglass to Hill, Sept. 21, 1886.

26. *Messages from the Governors,* VIII, 644. The legislature did pass a prison labor bill, Chap. 586 of the laws of 1888. *Supra,* p. 258, n. 13.

27. *Messages from the Governors,* VIII, 652–55.

28. *Ibid.,* pp. 656–58.

29. *New York Times,* New York *Evening Post,* Aug., 1888, *passim.*

30. Quoted in De Alva Stanwood Alexander, *Four Famous New Yorkers,* p. 111.

31. *New York Herald,* Sept. 8, 1888.

32. Nevins, *Grover Cleveland,* p. 424; Cleveland Papers, Cleveland to Bissell, July 17, 1888; Cleveland to Grace, July 14, 1888; George F. Parker, *Recollections of Grover Cleveland,* p. 245.

33. Allan Nevins, *Abram S. Hewitt: With Some Account of Peter Cooper* (New York: Harper & Brothers, 1935), p. 521.

34. *Ibid.,* pp. 510–16; New York *World,* Mar. 7, 8, 9, 1888.

35. Hirsch, *op. cit.,* pp. 359–60.

36. Nevins, *Grover Cleveland,* p. 425.

37. See Hill Papers for Aug. 20–30, 1888.

38. Hill Papers, Hill to Peter Harelenbeek, Sept. 5, 1888.

39. *New York Herald,* Sept. 8, 1888.

40. *Appleton's Annual Cyclopaedia, 1888,* p. 609; De Alva Stanwood Alexander, *Four Famous New Yorkers,* p. 112. The rest of the ticket was Edward Jones for lieutenant governor and Clinton Gray for court of appeals.

41. *Albany Argus,* Sept. 14, 1888; Hill Papers, Rice to Albert Moore, Oct. 22, 1888.

42. Hill Papers, Hill to Peter J. Leonard, Oct. 23, 1888; Hill to F. G. Lupien, Nov. 3, 1888.

43. For example, see speeches during the 1888 campaign in Binghamton, Sept. 19; Elmira, Sept. 20; Rochester, Sept. 28; Auburn, Sept. 29. Also, Nevins, *Grover Cleveland,* p. 426.

44. Hill Papers, Hill to W. S. Ray, Sept. 22, 1888; Rice to J. B. Sargent, Oct. 11, 1888; Hill to John Foley, Oct. 22, 1888; Rice to C. J. Canda, Dec. 26, 1888.

45. Nevins, *Grover Cleveland*, p. 427, quoting Henry Watterson in the Louisville *Courier-Journal*, Apr. 11, 1904. Cleveland had also been advised by former Mayor Grace that to support Hill publicly would be "absolutely suicidal." Cleveland Papers, Grace to Cleveland, Sept. 20, 1888.

46. Nevins, *Grover Cleveland*, p. 427, quoting San Francisco *Examiner*, Sept. 21, 1888.

47. *Ibid.*, pp. 426–27.

48. Copy in Hill Folder, New York Public Library, New York, N.Y.

49. This plank, like the one in 1887, avoided the words "high" and "license," as well as "saloon" and "Crosby bill," though it did refer to the latter indirectly. It stated, "We approve the efforts of the Republicans in the last legislature upon the liquor question, especially the act nullified by Executive action, to restrict that traffic by charges which would lift some of the burdens of taxation caused by the liquor traffic from the home and farm; and we believe such charges should be advanced to standards similar to those successfully enforced in other States under Republican control." This last phrase was intentionally vague. The "standards" ranged from $200 in Ohio and Connecticut to $500 in Illinois, all under Republican control. See De Alva Stanwood Alexander, *Four Famous New Yorkers*, p. 123.

50. *Ibid.*, p. 126.

51. *Nation*, XLVII (Oct. 11, 1888), 285.

52. See, for example, a denunciation of Hill by Elmira Local Assembly 1965, Knights of Labor, contained in broadside: *David B. Hill. Knights of Labor Repudiate and Denounce Him*. Library of Congress Broadsides.

53. De Alva Stanwood Alexander, *Four Famous New Yorkers*, p. 127.

54. Hill Papers, Hill to Elisha Winter, Oct. 5, 1888; Rice to William Murtha, Oct. 1, 1888; campaign literature, copy of Oct. issue of *Hotel Register*, 1888; Alton B. Parker to Bixby (mem-

orandum), Oct.–Nov., 1919; also, Harold F. Gosnell, *Boss Platt and His New York Machine* (Chicago: University of Chicago Press, 1924), p. 41.

55. Hill Papers, Hill to William Sheehan, Sept. 2, 1888.

56. As, for example, they had organized against the outlawing of Sunday beer in New York City in 1887, and brought about relief in the Cantor-Giegerich bill. Nevins, *Abram S. Hewitt*, p. 479.

57. This measure forbade the wholesaling of liquor in areas where the population had chosen to prohibit its retailing.

58. Copy of campaign speech used in 1888, in Hill Papers.

59. *Nation*, XLVII (Oct. 11, 1888), 285.

60. Hill Papers, Rice to Nelson J. Waterbury, Sept. 29, 1888; copies of documents in Hill Papers.

61. *Nation*, XLVI (Feb. 23, 1888), 147. Ben Butler had been a minor-party candidate in 1884 and had drawn votes away from the Democratic ticket.

62. *Messages from the Governors*, VIII, 535–37.

63. Hill Papers, Rice to William Murtha, Oct. 6, 1888. The papers also contain a number of samples: Labor Record, Rickard Document, and Prison Labor Document.

64. Henry Cabot Lodge (ed.), *Selections from the Correspondence of Theodore Roosevelt and Henry Cabot Lodge, 1884–1918* (2 vols.; New York: Charles Scribner's Sons, 1925), I, 72–73.

65. Hill Papers, Rice to John Riley, Oct. 16, 1888; Rice to Theodore Basselin, Oct. 16, 1888.

66. *Appleton's Annual Cyclopaedia, 1888*, p. 609; Nevins, *Grover Cleveland*, p. 439.

67. These papers had stated this point of view even before Hill was renominated. See Nevins, *Grover Cleveland*, p. 424; *Nation*, XLVII (Nov. 15, 1888), 385.

68. Nevins, *Grover Cleveland*, pp. 423–27.

69. Hill Papers, Lamont to Hill, Nov. 7, 1888.

70. Hill Papers, Calvin Brice to Hill, Nov. 12, 1888.

71. To George F. Parker, in George F. Parker, *Recollections of Grover Cleveland*, pp. 342–43.

72. Albany *Times-Union*, June 25, 1919. Clipping in Hill Papers.

73. Nevins, *Grover Cleveland*, Chap. XXIV, *passim;* Harry Thurston Peck, *Twenty Years of the Republic, 1885–1905* (New York: Dodd, Mead & Co., 1906), pp. 162–63. There is a strong suggestion that Miller was chosen as the gubernatorial candidate and ran on this issue with the intention of keeping Republican voters in the ranks to vote for the national ticket, regardless of what might happen to the state ticket.

74. George F. Parker, *Recollections of Grover Cleveland,* p. 344.

CHAPTER VI

1. *New York Times,* New York *World,* Jan. 2, 1889.

2. *Messages from the Governors,* VIII, 662–96.

3. Rice Papers (NYPL), Rice to William S. Andrews, Sept. 5, 1888.

4. This suggestion had also been put forward by Governor Edwin D. Morgan in 1867.

5. Hill Papers, Hill to Nelson J. Waterbury, Jan. 24, 1889.

6. *New York Times,* Mar. 15, 1889; Hill Papers, Rice to Charles Dana, Mar. 14, 1889; Rice to William Purcell, Mar. 14, 1889; Rice to E. P. Bailey, Mar. 14, 1889.

7. *New York Times,* Apr. 10, 26, 1889.

8. *Messages from the Governors,* VIII, 762–89.

9. Hill Papers, Hill to Frank Jones, July 17, 1889.

10. *New York Times,* Jan. 8, 10, 11, 1889.

11. *New York Times,* Feb. 1, 1889.

12. *New York Times,* May 8, 1889.

13. *Messages from the Governors,* VIII, 801–14. On the same day, Hill vetoed another excise bill, sponsored by Senator Vedder and only slightly less objectionable than his measure of the previous year. *Ibid.,* pp. 797–801.

14. The law of 1888 permitting the sale of prison-made goods to other state institutions was extended to allow their sale to county institutions as well.

15. *New York Times,* Apr. 11, May 9, 1889.

16. For example, see *Messages from the Governors,* VIII, 697–98, 704, 713, 719–21, 738–39, 817–19, 837–38. Hill vetoed a bill to provide for women factory inspectors—a bill which he wanted very much—because it was defectively drawn. *Ibid.,* pp. 837–38; Hill Papers, Hill to Terence V. Powderly, June 18, 1889.

17. *New York Times,* Feb. 10, 15, 1888.

18. *New York Times,* Feb. 19, 27, May 23, Oct. 1, 1889.

19. *Messages from the Governors,* VIII, 839–70; *New York Times,* June 18, 1889. Grover Cleveland, after perusing Hill's vetoes, congratulated him on his "first-class Executive work." Nevins (ed.), *Letters of Grover Cleveland,* p. 208.

20. *New York Times,* Aug. 20, 1889.

21. *Ibid.*

22. New York *World,* Oct. 2, 1889. The rest of the ticket: secretary of state, Frank G. Rice; state treasurer, Elliot Danforth; state engineer, John Bogart; and judge of the court of appeals, Dennis O'Brien.

23. *New York Times,* Oct. 25, 30, 1889.

24. *New York Tribune,* Sept. 26, 1889. The ticket was: secretary of state, John I. Gilbert; comptroller, Martin W. Cooke; treasurer, Ira M. Hedges; attorney general, James M. Varnum; state engineer, William Van Renssalaer; and judge of the court of appeals, Albert Haight.

25. *New York Times,* Nov. 2, 1889.

26. Hill Papers, Hill to William Steinway, Oct. 26, 1889.

27. *New York Times,* Nov. 3, 1889.

28. *New York Times,* Nov. 6, Dec. 6, 1889.

29. See Hill Papers, Aug. 20–Sept. 20, 1889, *passim; New York Times,* Apr. 9, 1889.

30. New York *Sun,* Oct. 2, 1889.

31. *New York Times,* Feb. 4, 1889; *New York Times,* Apr. 9, Dec. 17, 1889.

32. Hill Papers, George Bradshaw to Hill, Jan. 9, 1890; Hill to Stanley N. Wood, Dec. 20, 1889; Hill to Joseph D. Ellis, Dec. 20, 1889; Hill to Joseph L. Williams, Dec. 20, 1889; George W. Davis to Hill, Nov. 15, 1890.

33. Hill Papers, Hill to General Daniel Sickles, Dec. 9, 1889.

34. Hill Papers, Hill to John A. Sleicher, Dec. 16, 1889.

35. *New York Times,* Dec. 23, 24, 1889.

36. *New York Times,* Feb. 7, 8, 1889.

37. *New York Times,* Feb. 8, 1889.

38. *New York Times,* Apr. 8, 20, 1889.

39. *New York Times,* Dec. 11, 1889; Jan. 21, 1890.

40. New York *World,* Oct. 16, 17, 18, 19, 1889.

41. Hill Papers, Jefferson Chandler to Hill, Feb. 11, 1890.

42. *Messages from the Governors,* VIII, 576–77, 578, 664, 666, 667.

43. *New York Times,* Feb. 26, 1889. Former Mayor Grace, Grover Cleveland, and other prominent Democrats endorsed ballot reform.

44. Williams Papers (New York Public Library, New York, N.Y.), T. S. Williams to George Eggleston, Jan. 6, 1890.

45. See interview of an "intimate friend" of Hill's in *New York Times,* Nov. 18, 1889. Hill was also inquiring about the court decisions on the ballot acts of other states. Hill Papers, Hill to Robert L. Taylor, Dec. 9, 1889.

46. *Messages from the Governors,* VIII, 895–920.

47. *New York Herald,* Jan. 17, Feb. 9, 1890; *New York Times,* Mar. 4, 29, 1890.

48. *Messages from the Governors,* VIII, 946–49.

49. *Ibid.,* pp. 949–67.

50. *New York Times,* Apr. 19, 22, 1890.

51. *Messages from the Governors,* VIII, 973.

52. *New York Times,* Apr. 23, 1890; New York *Evening Post,* Apr. 23, 1890.

53. Williams Papers, Williams to Andrew McLean, Apr. 22, 1890. Copies to E. P. Bailey, St. Clair McKelway, M. H. Northrup, and William Purcell.

54. New York *World,* Apr. 25, 1890; *New York Times,* Apr. 23, 25, 1890. The bill as finally passed incorporated Hill's recommendations for limiting election districts to one per three hundred inhabitants, setting aside two hours on election day to al-

low employees to vote, and making the use of pay envelopes for purposes of intimidation a crime.

55. *Messages from the Governors,* VIII, 1005–15.

56. Originally planned to commemorate the five hundredth anniversary of the discovery of America but, because of a number of delays, postponed one year.

57. *Messages from the Governors,* VIII, 938–41; *New York Times, New York Herald,* New York *World,* Feb. 8, 1890.

58. *New York Times,* Feb. 18, 22, 1890. A number of Platt Republicans, confident of the outcome, had even purchased land in Chicago for speculative purposes. *New York Times,* Oct. 9, 1891.

59. *Messages from the Governors,* VIII, 759–61.

60. *New York Times,* Mar. 16, Apr. 11, 25, May 9, 1890.

61. Hill Papers, Hill to Edward Fleming, Apr. 26, 1890; *Statutes of the State of New York, 1890,* Chap. 94; *New York Times,* Apr. 16, 1890; *Messages from the Governors,* VIII, 790–92, 923–26; *infra,* pp. 175–76.

62. *Messages from the Governors,* VIII, 982–89. The proposal was adopted by two successive legislatures but was rejected at the polls in 1892 by the electorate. *Ibid.,* p. 982.

CHAPTER VII

1. Ellis Paxson Oberholtzer, *A History of the United States since the Civil War* (5 vols.; New York: Macmillan Co., 1926–37), V, Chap. XXXIV, *passim;* Peck, *op. cit.,* Chap. V, *passim.*

2. *New York Herald,* Mar. 6, 1890.

3. *New York Times,* Oct. 8, 1890.

4. Hill's other close friend and adviser in New York politics, Judge William L. Muller, had died suddenly in January, 1891.

5. Marble Papers (Library of Congress, Washington, D.C.), Manton Marble to Hill, Aug. 27, 1890. Although this is the first letter between the two men in either the Marble or Hill papers, it is evident from its tone and contents that there had been previous correspondence. The strategy discussed in this

letter had obviously been formulated and agreed upon before.

6. *Ibid.*

7. *Ibid.*

8. Hill Papers, Holman to Hill, June 19, 1890.

9. Hill Papers, "The Great Political Issue," speech at Indianapolis, Ind., July 1, 1890.

10. *New York Times,* Sept. 24, 1890.

11. *New York Times,* New York *World, New York Herald,* Sept. 24, 1890.

12. Marble Papers, Hill to Marble, Nov. 26, 1890.

13. *New York Times,* Sept. 24, Oct. 10, 1890.

14. New York *World, New York Times,* Oct. 22–Nov. 3, 1890. Hill Papers, "An Attempt to Deceive the Farmer," speech used widely by Hill in his swing through the farm areas belaboring the McKinley Tariff.

15. New York *World,* Nov. 6, 1890.

16. Warwick, the congressman-elect, sent Hill a telegram thanking him for his aid. Hill Papers, Warwick to Hill, Nov. 5 [?], 1890. See also T. S. Williams to Bixby, Aug. 18, 1920; New York *Sun,* Oct. 24, 1890.

17. Marble Papers, Marble to Hill, Aug. 27, 1890.

18. *New York Times,* Dec. 26, 1890.

19. This letter was sent with Cleveland's approval. Nevins, *Grover Cleveland,* pp. 472–73. The letter was reproduced publicly in the *New York Times,* Feb. 12, 1891.

20. Nevins (ed.), *Letters of Grover Cleveland,* pp. 235–36.

21. *Ibid.*

22. Hill Papers, Marble to Hill, Jan. 9, 1891.

23. *New York Times,* Jan. 1, 1891; Nevins (ed.), *Letters of Grover Cleveland,* pp. 234–35, 238.

24. *Ibid.,* p. 238; Hill Papers, T. S. Williams memorandum, Jan. 28, 1891.

25. Cleveland thought this a very real possibility. Nevins (ed.), *Letters of Grover Cleveland,* p. 238. Also, see *New York Times,* Nov. 11, 1890; Hill Papers, T. S. Williams memorandum, Jan. 28, 1891. Williams was troubled by Hill's acceptance of the Senate seat, and a week after the event, he wrote a lengthy diary-like

memorandum, recounting the events leading to and the factors involved in Hill's decision.

26. *Ibid.*

27. Hill Papers, Hill to David Miller, Nov. 14, 1890; Hill to Charles Barnum, Nov. 14, 1890.

28. Hill Papers, Hill to Smith M. Weed, Dec. 10, 1890.

29. Hill Papers, T. S. Williams memorandum, Jan. 28, 1891.

30. *Ibid.*

31. Albany *Evening Times,* Dec. 22, 1890.

32. Hill Papers, D. C. Birdsall to Hill, Nov. 24, 1890.

33. Hill Papers, Williams memorandum, Jan. 28, 1891; Charles Dana to Hill, Dec. 1, 1890. There are several suggestions that Dana's protestations grew from his own desire for the seat, which had been given some encouragement by Hill. E. G. Riggs to Bixby, 1919; De Alva Stanwood Alexander, *Four Famous New Yorkers,* p. 144.

34. Hill Papers, A. C. Eustace to Hill, Nov. 14, 1890. Cleveland did not believe Hill would take the Senate seat for the same reasons. Nevins (ed.), *Letters of Grover Cleveland,* p. 235.

35. Hill Papers, A. C. Eustace to Hill, Nov. 14, 1890.

36. Hill Papers, Hill to George W. Wieant, Jan. 16, 1891; *New York Times,* Jan. 17, 1891.

37. Hill Papers, T. S. Williams memorandum, Jan. 28, 1891.

38. *Ibid.*

39. *New York Times, New York Tribune,* New York *Evening Post,* Jan. 18, 1891; *New York Times,* Jan. 20, 1891.

40. New York *Sun,* Jan. 20, 1891; Albany *Evening Times,* Dec. 22, 1890. Marble also opposed the move to the Senate.

41. New York *World,* Nov. 7, 1890.

42. Nevins (ed.), *Letters of Grover Cleveland,* p. 238 n.; Plattsburg *Republican,* Jan. 31, 1891; Marble Papers, Smith M. Weed to Marble, Feb. 28, 1892.

43. New York *Sun,* Jan. 26, 1891.

44. *New York Times,* Jan. 20, 1891.

45. De Alva Stanwood Alexander, *Four Famous New Yorkers,* pp. 146–47; *New York Times,* Mar. 9, 1891.

46. Hill Papers, Marble to Hill, Feb. 25, 1891.

47. De Alva Stanwood Alexander, *Four Famous New Yorkers,*
p. 146; *New York Times,* Nov. 27, 1890; Jan. 18, Mar. 1, 6, 1891.
Jones's nickname came from the fact that he was originally selected as a candidate for office in order to make his money available
for financing the campaign. His efforts to advance himself to
the governorship fizzled by late spring.

48. De Alva Stanwood Alexander, *Four Famous New Yorkers,*
p. 147. The *Times* and *Tribune* made frequent use of this
phrase.

49. *Ibid.; New York Times,* Mar. 5, 1891.

50. *Messages from the Governors,* VIII, 1055–57, 1058–60,
1070–71.

51. *Ibid.,* pp. 1054–88.

52. *Ibid.,* pp. 1062–66, 1067. Cleveland had pointed out the
same loopholes in the tax laws on personalty in 1884. Nevins,
Grover Cleveland, p. 138.

53. *Messages from the Governors,* VIII, 1075, 1079. For constitutional amendment, see *supra,* p. 275, n. 62.

54. *New York Herald,* Aug. 9–21, 1890.

55. *Messages from the Governors,* VIII, 1071–74.

56. *New York Times,* Jan. 4, 5, 1891.

57. *New York Times,* May 2, 1891. The only Hill-supported
measure which failed to pass the assembly was a state roads bill
to provide two state roads in each county of the state. It was
beaten by one vote. *New York Times,* Apr. 22, 1891.

58. As compared to 586 in 1888, 570 in 1889, and 569 in 1890.

59. *New York Times,* Apr. 22, 25, May 1, June 3, 1891.

60. *Statutes of the State of New York, 1891,* Chaps. 4, 215,
296.

61. *New York Times,* Jan. 2, 19, Mar. 16, Oct. 19–21, 1891;
Hill Papers, Hill to John H. Inman, Sept. 9, 1891.

62. New York *Star,* Oct. 11, 1889; *New York Times,* July 1,
17, 1891.

63. Hill Papers, Hill to R. R. Soper, May 28, 1891; Hill to
William Purcell, May 27, 1891; *Elmira Gazette,* May 29, 1891.

64. Hill Papers, Marble to Hill, Feb. 2, 1891.

65. *New York Times,* Feb. 4, 1891.

66. Nevins, *Grover Cleveland,* pp. 201–205, 465–66; Ober-holtzer, *op. cit.,* V, 112–15, 126–32, 138–39; Peck, *op. cit.,* pp. 267–68.

67. Nevins, *Grover Cleveland,* pp. 466–67; Hill Papers, Marble to Hill, Feb. 2, 1891. The lone Democrat opposing free coinage was Senator Gray of Delaware.

68. *Ibid.*

69. *Ibid.*

70. *Ibid.;* also, Marble to Hill, Feb. 20, 1891.

71. Hill Papers, Marble to Hill, Feb. 20, 1891; Marble to Hill, Feb. 2, 1891.

72. Marble Papers, Marble to Hill, Nov. 7, 1890; T. S. Williams to Marble, Dec. 31, 1890; Williams to Marble, Jan. 11, 1891.

73. Nevins, *Grover Cleveland,* pp. 467–68.

74. Hill Papers, Marble to Hill, Feb. 19, 1891. T. S. Williams, in an undated memorandum, noted that Marble had drafted a strong letter for Hill to send to the meeting, but Hill decided against using it.

75. Hill Papers, Marble to Hill, Feb. 25, 1891.

76. Hill Papers, Marble to Hill, July 18, 1891; Marble to Hill, Feb. 2, 1891.

77. Hill Papers, Marble to Hill, July 26, 1891; Hill to Marble, Aug. 5, 1891; Marble to Hill, Sept. 5, 1891.

78. Hill Papers, Marble to Hill, July 18, 1891.

79. For example, see Hill Papers, Hill to C. D. Moore, Aug. 24, 1891; Hill to George Hall, Sept. 2, 1891; Hill to Frank Campbell, Aug. 21, 1891; *New York Times,* Sept. 7, 11, 1891.

80. Hill Papers, T. S. Williams memorandum to Bixby, [?] 1919. Alfred Chapin, mayor of Brooklyn, would have been Hill's choice, but he had recently been involved in a scandal. During the week before the convention, newspapers gave wide currency to the story that Flower, Sheehan, and the rest of the slate were chosen against Hill's will and that Hill had been shoved into the background. Subsequent events proved these stories to be groundless. Instead, there is evidence that this impression was intentionally cultivated in order to ease the way for

Sheehan's nomination. Sheehan was bitterly hated by Clevelandites, of whom there were many in the convention. An expression
of disapproval of Sheehan by Hill would confuse these men,
who also disliked Hill. Meanwhile, Hill's friends could be quietly
instructed to vote for Sheehan. Williams wrote to Marble after
the conventions, "Of course you saw through the newspaper reports of friction between the Governor and Messrs. Murphy,
Croker, and Sheehan. That move was very adroitly made and
resulted in the best of harmony and good feeling. It made
Sheehan the most popular man in the convention." Williams
Papers, Williams to Marble, Sept. 17, 1891.

   81. Willams Papers, Marble to Hill, Sept. 12, 1891.

   82. The whole incident is related in Williams Papers, Williams to Marble, Sept. 17, 1891. Cleveland thought that Oscar
Straus was the one most responsible for the pro-gold clause in
the plank, and wrote him a warm note of thanks. Nevins (ed.),
Letters of Grover Cleveland, p. 267. Straus did work hard for
the plank, but it was incorporated only through Croker's
blunder.

   83. Hill Papers, "Cooper Institute Address," Oct. 8, 1891.

   84. New York Times, Sept. 17, 25, 30, 1891; Wine and Spirit
Gazette, Sept. 28, 1891. Clipping in Hill Papers.

   85. There was also a fourth contest, in the Sixteenth District, but the Democrats did not expect much to come of it
and did not press it hard. The Republican was finally seated.

   86. Sherwood had held the office of park commissioner of
Hornellsville within one hundred days of the election. This
made him ineligible to sit in the legislature under Article III,
Section 8 of the New York State constitution. New York Times,
Nov. 11, 1891; De Alva Stanwood Alexander, Four Famous New
Yorkers, p. 158.

   87. Hill Papers, Hill to C. F. Peck, Nov. 8, 1891. Although
Sherwood won by a large majority, Hill was so confident of
success that on the day after the election he sent a telegram
to the Democratic candidate congratulating him on his victory.
Hill Papers, Fred J. Millener to Bixby, Dec. 6, 1920.

88. Hill Papers, Hill to Frank Campbell, Nov. 6, 1891; Hill to C. F. Peck, Nov. 9, 1891.

89. Hill Papers, Hill to John B. Stanchfield, Nov. 24, 1891.

90. *New York Times,* Nov. 20, Dec. 16, 1891.

91. *New York Times,* Nov. 29, 1891.

92. *New York Times,* Dec. 2, 1891; Hill Papers, Hill to William B. Kirk, Nov. 28, 1891. There was another contest in this district which came before Judge Kennedy. This concerned the race for assembly seat, where David A. Munro won over the Democrat, Patrick Ryan. The returns from the several districts had listed Munro as D. A. Munro, David Allen Munro, etc. On this flimsy technicality, the Democratic canvassing board declared Ryan the winner, giving him 5,229 votes to 4,398 for David Allen Munroe, Jr., 752 for David A. Munro, and 138 for D. A. Munro. The outraged Republicans secured a mandamus ordering the returns sent back to the several districts for correction, but a Democratic member of the canvassing board, Welch, disappeared with the copies of the returns. Meanwhile, Hill removed the Republican county clerk, George Cotton, who had refused to sign the false returns. Judge Kennedy later fined the disappearing Welch and sentenced him to thirty days, but Hill, in a clear abuse of his pardoning powers, granted an immediate pardon. *New York Times,* Nov. 21, 26, 29, Dec. 4, 24, 1891. Ironically, at the same time as the pardon, the January, 1892 issue of the *North American Review* was being sold, featuring an article by Hill on "The Pardoning Power." The article had a high moral tone.

93. *New York Times,* Nov. 6, 23, 1891.

94. *New York Times,* Dec. 2, 1891.

95. *New York Times,* Dec. 2, 6, 8, 1891; Theron G. Strong, *Joseph H. Choate* (New York: Dodd, Mead & Co., 1917), pp. 83–84.

96. *New York Times,* Nov. 22, 1891.

97. See Hill Papers, Hill to James Ridgway, Dec. 17, 1891.

98. *New York Times,* Dec. 13, 1891.

99. Hill Papers, Hill to James Ridgway, Dec. 17, 1891.

100. Hill Papers, Hill to A. C. Tennat, Dec. 26, 1891.

101. Hill Papers, Hill to St. Clair McKelway, Dec. 17, 1891.

102. The events occurring on December 21 and December 22 are related by both Isaac Maynard and Storm Emans in a pamphlet, *Judge Maynard: The Facts Relative to the Contested Elections Case.* (N.p., 1892). Hill Papers. It is, of course, an apologia, yet seems to be an accurate account of the actual events. For another view of the incident, see pamphlet by John I. Platt, *The Dutchess County Case: A Unique Story of Crime* (Poughkeepsie, N.Y.: Published by the Author, 1892).

103. Hill Papers, Maynard and Emans, *Judge Maynard: The Facts Relative to the Contested Elections Case.* Maynard's part in this, especially as regarded the repossession of the returns, was not fully known until he testified before Judge Cullen in the contempt proceedings against Storm Emans. Emans was being held in contempt of court because the returns, despite Cullen's order, never got to the state board of canvassers. He was acquitted, however, since they had, in fact, been transmitted. See De Alva Stanwood Alexander, *Four Famous New Yorkers,* p. 161.

104. *People ex rel. Sherwood* v. *Board of Canvassers,* 129 N.Y. 360, Court of Appeals; *People ex rel. Nichols* v. *Board of Canvassers,* 129 N.Y. 395, 449, Court of Appeals.

105. *New York Times,* Dec. 30, 1891.

CHAPTER VIII

1. Marble wrote, "You need to couple, especially now with your recognized 'machine' power and local leadership, a visible grasp and demonstrated mastery of moral and intellectual forces." Marble Papers, Marble to Hill, Nov. 29, 1891.

2. *Supra,* p. 161.

3. Hill Papers, David B. Hill, *The Issues for 1892; Speech at Elmira, New York, December 4, 1891.*

4. Regarding this part of the address, Marble had written, "Of course it seems to put all at stake, because few reflect that your Senate vote would put all at stake much more inconveniently. That is its merit. You will not thereafter, be dragged

up to vote on the Senate bill—an aye or no alike entailing disaster either upon the party or upon you." Marble Papers, Marble to Hill, Nov. 29, 1891. Also, see Hill Papers, Marble to Hill, Dec. 16, 1891.

Moreover, Marble insisted, failure of a coinage bill, once introduced in the Democratic House, could result in the loss of Farmers' Alliance support, upon which Marble was counting heavily. As matters stood, Alliance men might well favor Hill because of his coinage views. Failure of a free coinage bill, however, might lead them to feel that their goals could not be achieved within the Democratic party, and they might boycott the state conventions, costing Hill support.

5. Hill Papers, Marble to Hill, Dec. 16, 1891.

6. New York *World*, Dec. 7, 1891; Jan. 7, 1892.

7. Marble Papers, telegram, [Hill] to Fritz [Marble], Dec. 7, 1891; Marble to Hill, Dec. 7, 1891. Marble frequently used the names "Fritz" and "Neuchatel" in his correspondence with Hill.

8. Hill Papers, Marble to Hill, Dec. 16, 1891.

9. New York *World*, Dec. 8–31, 1891.

10. George H. Knoles, *The Presidential Campaign and Election of 1892* (Stanford, Calif.: Stanford University Press, 1942), p. 16. This work is invaluable for this period of Hill's career, and the author has leaned heavily upon it.

11. New York *World*, Dec. 7, 1891; Hill Papers, Hill to John T. Morgan, Dec. 17, 1891.

12. Hill Papers, Hill to Samuel A. Beardsley, Nov. 27, 1891; Hill to Hugh McLaughlin, Nov. 30, 1891. The fact that Hill wanted Sheehan on the national committee further discredits the widely circulated stories that Sheehan had been nominated for lieutenant governor over Hill's objections.

13. Hill Papers, Hill to Arthur P. Gorman, Nov. 23, 1891; Hill to William A. Wallace, Nov. 27, 1891; Hill to Mortimer Elliot, Nov. 24, 1891.

14. Nevins, *Grover Cleveland*, p. 482.

15. *New York Times*, Nov. 18, 21, 1891; Hill Papers, Hill to H. H. Rockwell, Nov. 27, 1891.

16. *New York Times,* Dec. 31, 1891.

17. Hill Papers, *Farewell Speech at the banquet tendered him by Democratic officials of the State of New York, upon the eve of his retirement from the office of Governor. Albany, December 31, 1891.*

18. It should be noted that Cleveland urged a similar policy on the House Democrats in 1890. At that time, he pleaded with Carlisle to dissuade congressional Democrats from presenting a countermeasure to the McKinley Tariff, lest it enable the enemy to shift the issue from a defense of its own high tariff bill. Nevins, *Grover Cleveland,* p. 462.

19. *New York Times,* Dec. 17, 1891; Jan. 8, 1892.

20. Marble Papers, Hill to Marble, Jan. 11, 1892.

21. Marble Papers, Hill to Marble, Jan. 10, 1892.

22. Williams Papers, Hill to Williams, Mar. 10, 1892. See also *New York Times,* Dec. 10, 1891; and Hill Papers, Hill to Hugh McLaughlin, Dec. 17, 1891.

23. *New York Times,* Jan, 20, 1892.

24. Nevins, *Grover Cleveland,* pp. 467, 468; *New York Times,* Jan. 11, 1892.

25. W. Bourke Cockran to Stephen White, Feb. 15, 1892, quoted in Knoles, *op. cit.,* p. 17.

26. Marble Papers, Hill to Marble, Jan. 22, 1892. Also, Knoles, *op. cit.,* p. 15.

27. Hill Papers, John Martin to Hill, Jan. 21, 1892. The only danger Martin envisioned was that friends of Cleveland's might have time to unite on a western man. But this danger was slight, he added, for in the end, the "bread and butter brigade" would flock to Hill.

28. Nevins, *Grover Cleveland,* p. 483.

29. Marble Papers, Hill to Marble, Jan. 17, 1892. It has been generally accepted that the snap convention was called in an effort to catch Cleveland men off-guard. With bad roads and little time to organize, they would have little chance against the prepared Hill machine. But Cleveland was already considered out of the picture by the Hill camp. It appears that the chief reasons for the snap convention were to exert an in-

fluence on other conventions and to head off possible combinations for a western candidate. See Marble papers, Marble to Hill, Jan. 25, 1892.

30. *New York Times,* Jan. 17, 20, 1892; Knoles, *op. cit.,* p. 18.

31. *Ibid.,* p. 18; Willis F. Johnson, *George Harvey: "A Passionate Patriot"* (Boston: Houghton Mifflin Company, 1929), p. 51.

32. Marble Papers, Marble to Hill, Jan. 25, 1892.

33. Knoles, *op. cit.,* pp. 18, 21; *New York Times,* Jan. 26, 1892; Fairchild Papers (New York Historical Society, New York, N.Y.), "Committee of Democrats Opposing the February Convention," circular letter, Feb. 5, 1892.

34. Hill to Dallas Sanders, Jan. 31, 1892, quoted in Knoles, *op. cit.,* p. 19.

35. New York *World,* Jan. 29, 1892.

36. Quoted in New York *World,* Feb. 6, 1892.

37. New York *World, New York Times,* Feb. 23, 1892. On one matter there was backstage disagreement. Marble had drafted the platform for the convention and had included in it an appeal to the Democrats in Congress not to pass a free coinage bill. Such a bill was soon to be introduced by Bland, and Marble hoped to head it off with a minimum of harm to Hill. He suggested instead that the Democrats pledge to call a special session after the November elections, when, in full control of the government, they would deal with the currency problem. Cockran, Sheehan, Murphy, and the others felt this an inadvisable move, and it was not brought up at the convention. Marble Papers, T. S. Williams to Marble, Feb. 23, 1892; Marble to [Henri Cernuschi], July 23, 1892.

38. *New York Times, New York Herald,* Feb. 23, 1892.

39. New York *Sun,* Jan. 22, Feb. 22, 1892; New York *World,* Feb. 27, 1892.

40. *New York Times,* Mar. 4, 1892.

41. Some of those who expressed themselves as favorable to Hill's candidacy were Senators Daniel and Barbour of Virginia, Pugh of Alabama, Gibson and Gorman of Maryland, Coke of Texas, Vance and Ransom of North Carolina, Colquitt

of Georgia, and Brice of Ohio. *New York Times,* Feb. 23, Mar. 4, 5, 1892; New York *World,* Feb. 26, 1892.

42. New York *World,* Feb. 22, 1892.

43. *New York Times,* Feb. 11, Mar. 3, 1892.

44. *New York Times,* Mar. 2, 1892.

45. Arthur Krock, *The Editorials of Henry Watterson* (New York: George H. Doran Co., 1923), pp. 72–74.

46. *Nation, Harper's Weekly,* New York *Evening Post,* New York *Times,* Feb.–June, 1892, *passim.*

47. Marble Papers, R. Honey [?] to Marble, Feb. 27, 1892; George Miller to Marble, Mar. 15, 1892; Knoles, *op. cit.,* p. 24.

48. Nevins, *Grover Cleveland,* p. 486.

49. *Ibid.,* pp. 448–49, 460–79 *passim.*

50. Nevins (ed.), *Letters of Grover Cleveland,* p. 214.

51. *Ibid.,* pp. 217–18.

52. *Ibid.,* p. 258.

53. *Ibid.,* p. 261; Nevins, *Grover Cleveland,* p. 477.

54. Nevins (ed.), *Letters of Grover Cleveland,* p. 273.

55. Nevins, *Grover Cleveland,* p. 485.

56. Knoles, *op. cit.,* pp. 12–13.

57. Hill, of course, was tending his interests in other areas as well, but he was relying mainly on the South and the four key states in the North to give him the nomination.

58. Nevins, *Grover Cleveland,* p. 483. On January 31, 1892, Michigan's Don Dickinson wrote to Charles S. Fairchild that an "influential New York politician" had offered him the Vice Presidency on a ticket with him. Fairchild Papers.

59. For example, see Fairchild Papers, Joseph Hull to Fairchild, Mar. 21, 1892; Cleveland Papers, B. M. Blackburn to Cleveland, Mar. 20, 1892; Lucius Q. C. Lamar to Cleveland, Apr. 3, 1892.

60. Marble Papers, Hill to Marble, Mar. 23, 1892.

61. Marble Papers, Marble to Hill, Mar. 6, 1892; Hill to Marble, Mar. 8, 1892; Marble to [Cernushi], July 23, 1892.

62. *New York Times,* Mar. 25, 29, 1892; Nevins, *Grover Cleveland,* p. 482.

63. It is difficult to assess accurately the amount of damage

caused by this bill. Marble undoubtedly exaggerated its importance in a campaign post-mortem to a friend: ". . . It convinced the Farmers' Alliance men of the South and West, falsely, that nothing could be hoped for in behalf of free silver from the Democratic party." The Alliance men, as a result, deserted the state conventions in the South, he continued. ". . . That desertion of the Democratic primaries by anti-Cleveland Dems. converted the small Cleveland minority in several states into effective majorities of the non-deserting factions." Marble Papers, Marble to [Cernushi], July 23, 1892.

While Alliance men of the West did desert both major parties, there is no substantial evidence that a desertion also occurred in the South, where the one-party tradition was strong. A state-by-state study of the southern Democratic state conventions would probably shed further light on the Alliance movement and the campaign of 1892.

64. Hill Papers, Association of the Bar of the City of New York, *Report of the Committee Appointed under the Resolution of March 8, 1892, on the Action of Isaac H. Maynard* (New York: Association of the Bar of the City of New York, 1892).

65. *New York Times,* Mar. 3, Apr. 1, 1892; Knoles, *op. cit.,* pp. 25–26.

66. *New York Times,* Apr. 9, 14, 15, 1892.

67. Marble Papers, George Miller to Marble, Feb. 8, Mar. 25, 30, 1892.

68. *New York Times,* Apr. 21, 1892.

69. *New York Times,* Apr. 21, 22, 1892.

70. *New York Times,* May 11, 19, 1892; Knoles, *op. cit.,* pp. 28–29.

71. *Ibid.,* p. 29; *New York Times,* May 5, 11, 26, 1892.

72. *New York Times,* May 30, 31, June 1, 1892.

73. *New York Times,* May 12, 18, 19, 20, 27, June 9, 1892.

74. Marble Papers, Marble to [Cernushi], July 23, 1892; Williams Papers, Williams to Hill, June 3, 1892; Knoles, *op. cit.,* p. 75.

75. Marble Papers, Hill to Marble, June 16, 1892.

76. *Ibid.*

77. *New York Times,* June 19, 1892.

78. Marble Papers, Hill to Marble, June 16, 1892.

79. Knoles, *op. cit.,* pp. 76–78, 80; Nevins, *Grover Cleveland,* pp. 489–90; Everett P. Wheeler, *Sixty Years of American Life, 1850–1910* (New York: E. P. Dutton & Co., Inc., 1917), pp. 204–206.

80. Marble Papers, Marble to [Cernushi], July 23, 1892.

81. *Ibid.,* Knoles, *op. cit.,* p. 78.

82. *Ibid.,* Chap. IV.

83. Hill Papers, Hill to T. S. Williams, July 2, 1892.

84. Marble Papers, Hill to Marble, June 24, 1892.

85. Knoles, *op. cit.,* p. 158.

86. Nevins, *Grover Cleveland,* p. 495.

87. Hill Papers, Hill to T. S. Williams, July 2, 1892.

88. Copy of speech in Hill Papers.

89. Hill Papers, Carter Glass to Hill, June 25, 1892.

CHAPTER IX

1. U.S. *Congressional Record,* 53rd Cong., 2nd sess., 1894, pp. 6719–20; 53rd Cong., 3rd sess., 1894, pp. 387–91. Hill later proposed a constitutional amendment giving the president the power of an itemized veto, which Hill had used so well as governor. *Ibid.,* 54th Cong., 1st sess., 1896, p. 6042.

2. De Alva Stanwood Alexander, *Four Famous New Yorkers,* pp. 194–97; Nevins, *Grover Cleveland,* pp. 568–69.

3. *Ibid.,* pp. 569–72.

4. U.S. *Congressional Record,* 54th Cong., 2nd sess., 1896, p. 355.

5. For example, *ibid.,* 53rd Cong., 2nd sess., 1894, pp. 6611, 6617, 6637. Hill never believed that he had bolted the party on the income tax. Since it was not mentioned in his party's platform, he said, "every man had a right to vote as he pleased upon the question and [still] be loyal to his party platform." *Ibid.,* 54th Cong., 1st sess., 1896, pp. 611–12.

6. *Ibid.,* 53rd Cong., 2nd sess., 1894, pp. 5321, 5470–71, 6443, 6465, 6674–77, 7811. Many of the arguments used by Hill

were identical with those on which the Supreme Court was to base its decision invalidating the income tax in 1895. Carl B. Swisher, *American Constitutional Development* (Boston: Houghton Mifflin Company, 1943), pp. 443–44.

7. De Alva Stanwood Alexander, *Four Famous New Yorkers,* pp. 198–202; Nevins, *Grover Cleveland,* pp. 486–87, 571.

8. Perry Belmont, *An American Democrat: The Recollections of Perry Belmont* (New York: Columbia University Press, 1940), pp. 410–11; De Alva Stanwood Alexander, *Four Famous New Yorkers,* pp. 220–22, 225.

9. Nevins (ed.), *Letters of Grover Cleveland,* p. 370.

10. Hill Papers, campaign documents, 1894; De Alva Stanwood Alexander, *Four Famous New Yorkers,* pp. 225, 227, 228. Ironically, one of the men who stumped the state for the Republicans was William McKinley, whose district Hill had invaded in 1890.

11. U.S. *Congressional Record,* 53rd Cong., 2nd sess., 1894, pp. 3560, 6768; 54th Cong., 1st sess., 1896, p. 4462.

12. *Ibid.,* 53rd Cong., 3rd sess., 1895, p. 2277.

13. *Ibid.,* 53rd Cong., 3rd sess., 1895, pp. 2281–82; 54th Cong., 1st sess., 1896, pp. 468, 472, 4041–44, 4049.

14. De Alva Stanwood Alexander, *Four Famous New Yorkers,* pp. 261–71. Hill was severely criticized for waiting until June, two weeks before the national convention, to hold the New York State convention. Cleveland felt that an early convention, expressing a firm stand for gold, might have sobered the Democracy and tempered the silver craze. Of course, Hill had been criticized for an early convention four years earlier. Apparently the criterion for deciding whether or not early conventions were fair depended upon which interests would be served. Moreover, Hill feared the third-term talk for Cleveland, which the President did nothing to stop, and therefore held off the convention as late as possible, lest a sound money expression give impetus to the third-term talk.

15. Hill Papers, Hill to Lamont, Sept. 14, 1896.

16. De Alva Stanwood Alexander, *Four Famous New Yorkers,* p. 280.

17. *Ibid.*, pp. 310–15.

18. Irving Cobb, quoted in Philip C. Jessup, *Elihu Root* (2 vols.; New York: Dodd, Mead & Co., 1938), I, 429.

19. Samuel T. Williamson, *Frank Gannett* (New York: Duell, Sloan & Pearce, Inc., 1940), pp. 63–64.

20. *Albany Argus,* Sept. 26, 1890.

21. Oswego *Daily Times,* July 6, 1897. Clipping in Hill Papers.

22. Speech to the Democratic Editorial Association of New York, May 24, 1895. Copy in Hill Papers.

23. *Messages from the Governors,* VIII, 897.

24. Elmira *Star-Gazette,* Sept. 21, 1910. Clipping in Hill Papers.

25. *Supra,* p. 244.

26. Hill Papers, apparently notes of an interview, Frank White to Bixby, n.d.; Williams Papers, Irving F. Cragin to H. J. McCartney, Sept. 27, 1889.

27. Hill Papers, Hill to R. H. Moore, June 18, 1891; speech to the Democratic Club of New York, Jan. 26, 1895; Don C. Seitz to Bixby, July 14, 1920.

28. Hill Papers, Hill to R. H. Moore, June 18, 1891.

29. Hill Papers, speech to the Democratic Club of New York, Jan. 26, 1895.

30. Hill Papers, Hill to William Graney, Dec. 16, 1890.

31. Hill Papers, apparently notes of an interview, James Manning to Bixby, n.d.

32. Hill Papers, speech at the Academy of Music, Brooklyn, N.Y., Sept. 19, 1892.

33. *Albany Argus,* Mar. 16, 1895.

34. *Ibid.*

35. Hill Papers, speech to Young Men's Democratic Club of Brooklyn, Feb. 22, 1887.

36. Hill Papers, campaign speech of 1890.

37. Address of Dr. C. S. Carr of Columbus, Ohio, to the Thurman Club, Mar. 8, 1892. Copy in Hill Papers.

Bibliography

MANUSCRIPT COLLECTIONS:

Grover Cleveland Papers, Library of Congress, Washington, D.C.
Charles S. Fairchild Papers, New York Historical Society, New York, N.Y.
David B. Hill Papers, New York State Library, Albany, N.Y.
Daniel S. Lamont Papers, Library of Congress, Washington, D.C.
Daniel Manning Papers, Library of Congress, Washington, D.C.
Manton Marble Papers, Library of Congress, Washington, D.C.
William G. Rice Papers, New York State Library, Albany, N.Y., and New York Public Library, New York, N.Y.
John Boyd Thatcher Scrapbook, New York State Library, Albany, N.Y.
Samuel J. Tilden Papers, New York Public Library, New York, N.Y.
Timothy Shaler Williams Papers, New York Public Library, New York, N.Y.
William C. Whitney Papers, Library of Congress, Washington, D.C.

OFFICIAL RECORDS:

Congressional Record, 1893–97.
Documents of the Assembly of the State of New York, 1872, 1876, 1885–91.

Documents of the Senate of the State of New York, 1876, 1885–91.
Journals of the Assembly of the State of New York, 1872, 1885–91.
Journals of the Senate of the State of New York, 1885–91.
Messages from the Governors, Vol. VIII (1885–91). Edited by Charles Z. Lincoln.
Public Papers of David B. Hill, Governor, 1885–91.
Statutes of the State of New York, 1885–91.

PAMPHLETS:

Address of the Merchants and Business Men of New York City. N.p., 1885.
Association of the Bar of the City of New York. *Report of the Committee Appointed under the Resolution of March 8, 1892, on the Action of Isaac H. Maynard.* New York: Association of the Bar of the City of New York, 1892.
Governor Hill and the Aqueduct Frauds: The Story Related by the Witnesses before the Fassett Investigating Committee. N.p., 1888.
Governor Hill and the New York Aqueduct: Abstract of the Testimony Taken before the Senate Committee. N.p., 1888.
Ivins, William M. *Machine Politics and Money in the Elections in New York City.* New York: Harper & Brothers, 1887.
———. *Questions for Governor Hill.* New York: King, 1888.
Maynard, Isaac, and Emans, Storm. *Judge Maynard: The Facts Relative to the Contested Elections Case.* N.p., 1892.
New York Reform Club. *"What Are You Going to Do about It?" Third Annual Record of Assemblymen and Senators from the City of New York in the State Legislature.* N.p., 1888.
New York State Board of Health. *Report on the Potable Water Supply of the City of New York,* N.p., 1889.
Platt, John I. *The Dutchess County Case: A Unique Story of Crime.* Poughkeepsie, N.Y.: Published by the Author, 1892.
Society for Political Education. *Electoral Reform.* N.p., 1888.

PERIODICALS:

Century
Forum
Harper's New Monthly Magazine
Harper's Weekly
Nation
North American Review
Public Opinion
Review of Reviews

NEWSPAPERS

Albany Argus
Albany Evening Journal
Albany *Evening Times*
Elmira Gazette (later, *Star-Gazette*)
New York *Evening Post*
New York Herald
New York *Sun*
New York Times
New York Tribune
New York *World*

ARTICLES:

Barnes, James A. "The Gold-standard Democrats and the Party Conflict," *Mississippi Valley Historical Review*, XVII (Dec., 1930), 422–50.

Collin, Charles A. "David Bennett Hill: A Character Sketch," *Review of Reviews*, V (Feb.–July, 1892), 19–26.

Hoyt, Albert. "Politics in the Days of David B. Hill," *State Service*, IV (Apr., 1920), 313–15.

Parker, George F. "How Grover Cleveland Was Nominated and Elected President," *Saturday Evening Post*, CXCII (Apr. 24, 1920), 22–23.

————. "Some Decisive Quarrels and Jealousies in American Politics," *Saturday Evening Post,* CXCIII (Sept. 4, 1920), 6–7.

PUBLISHED LETTERS, AUTOBIOGRAPHIES, AND MEMOIRS:

Bancroft, Frederic (ed.). *Speeches, Correspondence and Political Papers of Carl Schurz.* New York: G. P. Putnam's Sons, 1913.

Belmont, Perry. *An American Democrat: The Recollections of Perry Belmont.* New York: Columbia University Press, 1940.

Bigelow, John (ed.). *Letters and Literary Memorials of Samuel J. Tilden.* 2 vols. New York: Harper & Brothers, 1908.

Breen, Matthew P. *Thirty Years of New York Politics, Up-to-date.* New York: Privately printed, 1899.

Brockway, Beman. *Fifty Years in Journalism.* Watertown, N.Y.: Daily Times Printing and Publishing Co., 1891.

Bryan, William J. *The Memoirs of William Jennings Bryan.* Chicago: John C. Winston Co., 1925.

Clark, Champ. *My Quarter Century of American Politics.* 2 vols. New York: Harper & Brothers, 1920.

Cox, James M. *Journey through My Years.* New York: Simon and Schuster, Inc., 1946.

Depew, Chauncey M. *My Memories of Eighty Years.* New York: Charles Scribner's Sons, 1922.

Dunn, Arthur W. *From Harrison to Harding.* 2 vols. New York: G. P. Putnam's Sons, 1922.

Foulke, William D. *Fighting the Spoilsmen: Reminiscences of the Civil Service Reform Movement.* New York: G. P. Putnam's Sons, 1919.

Griffin, Solomon B. *People and Politics Observed by a Massachusetts Editor.* Boston: Little, Brown & Co., 1923.

Heaton, John L. *The Story of a Page: Thirty Years of Public Service and Public Discussion in the Editorial Columns of the New York World.* New York: Harper & Brothers, 1913.

Hoar, George F. *Autobiography of Seventy Years.* 2 vols. New York: Charles Scribner's Sons, 1905.

Hudson, William C. *Random Recollections of an Old Political Reporter.* New York: Cupples & Leon Co., 1911.

Krock, Arthur. *The Editorials of Henry Watterson.* New York: George H. Doran Co., 1923.

Lodge, Henry Cabot (ed.). *Selections from the Correspondence of Theodore Roosevelt and Henry Cabot Lodge, 1884–1918.* 2 vols. New York: Charles Scribner's Sons, 1925.

Nevins, Allan (ed.). *The Letters of Grover Cleveland, 1850–1908.* Boston: Houghton Mifflin Company, 1933.

Parker, Alton B. *In Memoriam, David Bennett Hill.* Albany, N.Y.: n.p., 1911.

Parker, George F. *Recollections of Grover Cleveland.* New York: Century Co., 1909.

Platt, Thomas C. *The Autobiography of Thomas Collier Platt.* New York: B. W. Dodge & Co., 1910.

Riordan, William L. *Plunkitt of Tammany Hall.* New York: Alfred A. Knopf, Inc., 1948.

Roosevelt, Theodore. *Theodore Roosevelt: An Autobiography.* New York: Macmillan Co., 1913.

Stevenson, Adlai E. *Something of Men I Have Known, with Some Papers of a General Nature, Political, Historical, and Retrospective.* Chicago: A. C. McClurg & Co., 1909.

Stewart, William M. *Reminiscences of Senator William M. Stewart of Nevada.* New York: Neale Publishing Co., 1908.

Stoddard, H. L. *As I Knew Them: Presidents and Politics from Grant to Coolidge.* New York: Harper & Brothers, 1927.

Wheeler, Everett P. *Sixty Years of American Life, 1850–1910.* New York: E. P. Dutton & Co., Inc., 1917.

BIOGRAPHIES:

Acheson, Sam H. *Joe Bailey, the Last Democrat.* New York: Macmillan Co., 1932.

Barnard, Harry. *"Eagle Forgotten": the Life of John Peter Altgeld.* New York: Bobbs-Merrill Company, Inc., 1938.

Barnes, James A. *John G. Carlisle: Financial Statesman.* New York: Dodd, Mead & Co., 1931.

Bigelow, John. *The Life of Samuel J. Tilden.* 2 vols. New York: Harper & Brothers, 1895.

Cate, Wirt A. *Lucius Q. C. Lamar.* Chapel Hill, N.C.: University of North Carolina Press, 1935.

Coolidge, Louis A. *An Old-fashioned Senator: Orville H. Platt.* New York: G. P. Putnam's Sons, 1910.

Cortissoz, Royal. *The Life of Whitelaw Reid.* 2 vols. New York: Charles Scribner's Sons, 1921.

Dennett, Tyler. *John Hay: From Poetry to Politics.* New York: Dodd, Mead & Co., 1933.

Dobie, Edith. *The Political Career of Stephen Mallory White.* Stanford, Calif.: Stanford University Press, 1927.

Flick, Alexander C. *Samuel Jones Tilden: A Study in Political Sagacity.* New York: Dodd, Mead & Co., 1938.

Fuess, Claude M. *Carl Schurz: Reformer, 1829–1906.* New York: Dodd, Mead & Co., 1932.

Gosnell, Harold F. *Boss Platt and His New York Machine.* Chicago: University of Chicago Press, 1924.

Hibben, Paxton. *The Peerless Leader: William Jennings Bryan.* New York: Farrar and Rinehart, 1929.

Hirsch, Mark D. *William C. Whitney, Modern Warwick.* New York: Dodd, Mead & Co., 1948.

Jessup, Philip C. *Elihu Root.* 2 vols. New York: Dodd, Mead & Co., 1938.

Johnson, Willis F. *George Harvey: "A Passionate Patriot."* Boston: Houghton Mifflin Company, 1929.

Lewis, Alfred H. *Richard Croker.* New York: Life Publishing Co., 1901.

McElroy, Robert. *Grover Cleveland, the Man and the Statesman.* 2 vols. New York: Harper & Brothers, 1923.

———. *Levi Parsons Morton: Banker, Diplomat, Statesman.* New York: G. P. Putnam's Sons, 1930.

Mayes, Edward. *Lucius Q. C. Lamar: His Life, Times, and Speeches.* Nashville, Tenn.: Publishing House of the Methodist Episcopal Church, 1896.

Nevins, Allan. *Abram S. Hewitt: With Some Account of Peter Cooper.* New York: Harper & Brothers, 1935.

——. *Grover Cleveland: A Study in Courage.* New York: Dodd, Mead & Co., 1933.

Nixon, Raymond B. *Henry W. Grady, Spokesman of the New South.* New York: Alfred A. Knopf, Inc., 1943.

Paine, Albert B. *Thomas Nast: His Period and His Pictures.* New York: Macmillan Co., 1904.

Post, Louis F. *The Prophet of San Francisco.* New York: Vanguard Press, 1930.

Pringle, Henry F. *Theodore Roosevelt: A Biography.* New York: Harcourt, Brace & Company, 1931.

Richardson, Leon B. *William B. Chandler, Republican.* New York: Dodd, Mead & Co., 1940.

Robinson, William A. *Thomas B. Reed, Parliamentarian.* New York: Dodd, Mead & Co., 1930.

Seitz, Don C. *Joseph Pulitzer: His Life and Letters.* New York: Simon and Schuster, Inc., 1924.

Simkins, Francis B. *Pitchfork Ben Tillman, South Carolinian.* Baton Rouge, La.: Louisiana State University Press, 1944.

Stephenson, Nathaniel W. *Nelson W. Aldrich, a Leader in American Politics.* New York: Charles Scribner's Sons, 1930.

Stoddard, Lothrop. *Master of Manhattan: The Life of Richard Croker.* New York: Longmans, Green & Co., Inc., 1931.

Stone, Candace. *Dana and the Sun.* New York: Dodd, Mead & Co., 1938.

Strong, Theron G. *Joseph H. Choate.* New York: Dodd, Mead & Co., 1917.

Williams, Wayne C. *William Jennings Bryan.* New York: G. P. Putnam's Sons, 1936.

Williamson, Samuel T. *Frank Gannett.* New York: Duell, Sloan & Pearce, Inc., 1940.

Winkler, John R. *W. R. Hearst: An American Phenomenon.* New York: Simon and Schuster, Inc., 1928.

Woodward, C. Vann. *Tom Watson, Agrarian Rebel.* New York: Macmillan Co., 1938.

OTHER PUBLISHED WORKS:

Alexander, De Alva Stanwood. *A Political History of the State of New York.* 4 vols. New York: Henry Holt & Co., Inc., 1906–23.
————. *Four Famous New Yorkers.* (*A Political History of the State of New York,* Vil. IV.) New York: Henry Holt & Co., Inc., 1906–23.
Alexander, Margaret C. *The Development of the Power of the State Executive.* ("Smith College Studies in History," Vol. II, No. 3.) Northampton, Mass.: Department of History of Smith College, 1917.
Bidwell, Frederick D. *Taxation in New York State.* Albany, N.Y.: J. B. Lyon Co., 1918.
Brown, Henry C. *In the Golden Nineties.* Hastings-on-Hudson, N.Y.: Valentine's Manual, Inc., 1928.
Callcott, Mary S. *Child Labor Legislation in New York.* New York: Macmillan Co., 1931.
Carman, Harry J. *The Street Surface Railway Franchises of New York City.* New York: Columbia University Press, 1919.
Cherrington, Ernest H. *The Evolution of Prohibition in the United States of America.* Westerville, Ohio: American Issue Press, 1920.
Child, Hamilton. *Gazeteer and Business Directory of Chemung County.* Syracuse, N.Y.: Printed at the Journal Office, 1868.
Collier, William M. *The Civil Service Law of the State of New York.* Albany, N.Y.: Matthew Bender & Co., Inc., 1901.
Colvin, David L. *Prohibition in the United States: A History of the Prohibition Party and of the Prohibition Movement.* New York: George H. Doran Co., 1926.
Commons, J. R., *et al. History of Labour in the United States.* 4 vols. New York: Macmillan Co., 1921–35.
Evans, Eldon C. *A History of the Australian Ballot System in the United States.* Chicago: University of Chicago Press, 1917.
Fairchild, Fred R. *The Factory Legislation of the State of New York.* London: Macmillan Co., 1905.

Flick, Alexander C. (ed.). *History of the State of New York.* 10 vols. New York: Macmillan Co., 1933–37.

Ford, Henry J. *The Cleveland Era.* New Haven, Conn.: Yale University Press, 1919.

Gibson, Florence E. *The Attitudes of the New York Irish toward State and National Affairs, 1848–1892.* New York: Columbia University Press, 1951.

Hicks, John D. *The Populist Revolt.* Minneapolis, Minn. University of Minnesota Press, 1931.

Hurwitz, Howard. *Theodore Roosevelt and Labor in New York State, 1880–1900.* New York: Columbia University Press, 1943.

Josephson, Matthew. *The Politicos.* New York: Harcourt, Brace, & Company, 1938.

Kent, F. R. *The Democratic Party: A History.* New York: Century Co., 1928.

Knoles, George H. *The Presidential Campaign and Election of 1892.* Stanford, Calif.: University Press, 1942.

Lincoln, Charles Z. *The Constitutional History of New York from the Beginning of the Colonial Period to the Year 1905.* Rochester, N.Y.: The Lawyers Co-operative Publishing Co., 1906.

McAdam, David (ed.). *History of the Bench and Bar of New York.* 2 vols. New York: New York History Co., 1897.

McClure, A. K. *Our Presidents and How We Make Them.* New York: Harper & Brothers, 1900.

McGuire, James K. *The Democratic Party of the State of New York.* 3 vols. New York: United States History Co., 1905.

Melone, Harry R. *History of Central New York.* Indianapolis, Ind.: Historical Publishing Co., 1932.

Merrill, Horace S. *Bourbon Democracy of the Middle West, 1865–1896.* Baton Rouge: Louisiana State University Press, 1953.

Morison, Samuel E., and Commager, Henry S. *The Growth of the American Republic.* 2 vols. New York: Oxford University Press, 1940.

Mott, Frank L. *American Journalism.* New York: Macmillan Co., 1941.

Myers, Gustavus. *The History of Tammany Hall.* New York: Privately printed, 1901.

Myers, William S. *The Republican Party: A History.* New York: Century Co., 1928.

Nevins, Allan. *The Evening Post: A Century of Journalism.* New York: Boni and Liveright, 1922.

Oberholtzer, Ellis Paxson. *A History of the United States Since the Civil War.* 5 vols. New York: Macmillan Co., 1926–37.

O'Brien, Frank M. *Story of the Sun.* New York: George H. Doran Co., 1918.

Paxson, Frederic L. *Recent History of the United States.* Boston: Houghton Mifflin Company, 1921.

Peck, Harry Thurston. *Twenty Years of the Republic, 1885–1905.* New York: Dodd, Mead & Co., 1906.

Peirce, Henry B. *History of Tioga, Chemung, Tompkins, and Schuyler Counties.* Philadelphia: Evarts & Ensign, 1879.

Santen, Vernon B. *The Administration of the New York State Civil Service Law, 1883–1917.* Syracuse, N.Y.: Maxwell School of Citizenship and Public Affairs, Syracuse University, 1952.

Schlesinger, Arthur M. *Rise of the City, 1878–1898. (A History of American Life,* eds. Dixon R. Fox and Arthur M. Schlesinger, Vol. X.) New York: Macmillan Co., 1933.

Schneider, David M. *The History of Public Welfare in New York State.* 2 vols. Chicago: University of Chicago Press, 1938–41.

Sowers, Don C. *The Financial History of New York State from 1789 to 1912.* New York: Columbia University Press, 1914.

Swisher, Carl B. *American Constitutional Development.* Boston: Houghton Mifflin Company, 1943.

Thomas, Harrison C. *Return of the Democratic Party to Power in 1884.* New York: Columbia University Press, 1919.

Walker, James B. *Fifty Years of Rapid Transit, 1864–1917.* New York: Law Printing Co., 1918.

Werner, Morris R. *Tammany Hall.* Garden City, N.Y.: Doubleday, Doran & Co., 1928.

Whipple, Gurth A. *A History of Half a Century of the Management of the Natural Resources of the Empire State, 1885–1935.* Albany, N.Y.: J. B. Lyon Co., 1935.

Whitford, Noble E. *History of the Canal System of the State of New York.* 2 vols. Albany, N.Y. Brandow Printing Co., 1906.

Winton, H. C. *Glen Sketches at Havana, New York.* Ithaca, N. Y.: Andrus, McChain & Co., 1868.

Woodward, C. Vann. *Origins of the New South, 1877–1913.* Baton Rouge: Louisiana State University Press, 1951.

Index

Abbot, Leon, 179
Alabama, 146, 231
Albany, N.Y., mentioned, 7, 13, 25, 30, 33, 39, 45, 89, 91, 92, 126, 133, 141, 146, 178, 191, 197, 198, 211, 215, 221
Albany Argus, 143
Albany County, N.Y., 142
Albany Evening Journal, 71
Albany Evening Times, 143, 171
Albany Express, 80
Alexander, De Alva Stanwood, 268n*10*
American System, the, 161
Anderson, E. Ellery, 218, 219, 220
Anti-Cleveland Democrats, support Hill for gov. (1885), 32–33, 39, 43; Hill as a vehicle for, 76, 79, 81, 82; support Hill for pres., 146–47
Anti-Pinkerton bill, 176, 177
Anti-snappers, 221–22, 224, 231, 232, 234, 235
Apgar, Edgar K., 5
Aqueduct commission, 102, 103, 108
Aqueduct investigation, findings of, 102–108; political impact of, 108–109, 114, 115
Arbitration Act, Hill proposes, 23, 67; enacted (1886), 67, 264n*38;*

extended, 69; Hill seeks amendment to, 176–77; mentioned, 120
Armstrong, William, 69, 70
Arnot, Steven, 3, 5, 9, 11, 255n*13*
Arthur, Chester, 11
Assembly ceiling investigation, 137–38
Associated Press, 9
Atlanta Constitution, 179, 230
Atlanta, Ga., 146, 227
Attorney general (N.Y.), 59, 192
Australian ballot. *See* Ballot reform

Bacon, Charles, 31
Ballot reform, need for, 96–98; bill of 1888, 98–101; and Democratic party, 101, 116, 135, 148; as election issue, 116, 119, 127; Hill's proposals on, 1889, 128–30; bill of 1889, 133–35; growth of movement for, 147–48; compromise bill enacted (1890), 151–53, 274n*54;* amended (1891), 178; mentioned, 93, 114, 159
Ballot Reform League, 151
Banking, Committee on (U.S. House), 227
Bar Association of City of N.Y., 228–29
Barnard, George G., 4

303

State Liquor Dealers' Association, 118, 177
State Trades Assembly, endorses Hill, 37, 47; influence on legislation, 69–70; commends Hill, 73; mentioned, 67
Steal of the Senate, 191–200, 215
Steuben County, N.Y., 192–94, 198
Stock-watering, 56
Straus, Oscar, 280n82
Strauss, Isador, 220
Syracuse, N.Y., 32, 72, 195, 231, 232

Tabor, Charles, 138, 139
Tammany Hall, power of in state party, 8, 18, 143–44, 167–68, 171, 245–46; rivalry with County Democracy, 28, 34–35, 111, 188; and Hill, 29, 37, 81–82, 143–44, 245–46; and Cleveland, 81–82, 84, 86; in 1887 state committee struggle, 84, 86; and choice of U.S. Senator (1891), 167–68, 171; mentioned, 40, 42, 43, 45, 92, 139, 163, 242. See also Croker, Richard
Tariff reform, 1885 Democratic platform on, 40; Cleveland's message on, 88–89; and Hill, 89–90, 161; and 1890 election, 163; Cleveland identified with, 165, 180; mentioned, 109, 113, 147
Taxation, Hill on, 132, 155, 175–76
Tenement-house bill, 69
Ten-hour day, 74
Tennessee, 146, 227, 231
Territories, Committee on (U.S. Senate), 214
Thompson, Hubert O., 28, 29, 34, 35, 38, 41, 42. See also N.Y. County Democracy
Thurman, Allen G., 113, 125, 216

Thurston, Hart, and McGuire, 2
Tidd, Horton, 46
Tilden, Samuel J., as Democratic leader, 4–5; befriends Hill, 5–11 passim; endorses Hill for gov., 35; mentioned, 2, 76, 83, 160
Tillman, Benjamin R., 231
Tioga County, N.Y., 59, 60, 254n7
Troy, N.Y., 87, 110
Tweed, William M., and Hill, 4, 45–46; mentioned, 18, 28, 54, 96

Ulster County, N.Y., 39
Union Labor party, 72–73
United Kingdom, 47
United Labor party, 72–73, 87–88, 120
U.S. Constitution, 133
U.S. Supreme Court, 288n6
Urban-rural conflicts, 14, 16–18
Utica, N.Y., 32, 70

Van Renssalaer, William B., 273n24
Varnum, James M., 273n24
Vedder bills, 65, 94
Virginia, 145, 227, 231
Voorhees, Daniel W., 234, 236
Voting registration laws, 19, 46, 96, 155

Walker, Charles, 11, 83, 193–94, 199
Warwick, John G., 276n16
Washington, D.C., 33, 43, 126, 144, 145, 166, 213, 219
Waterbury, Nelson, 133
Watkins Glen, N.Y., 1
Watterson, Henry, 165, 223, 234
Weed, Smith M., aspirant for Senate, 166–67, 168, 171; embittered toward Hill, 172; mentioned, 12, 110
Wemple, Edward, 138, 139
West, the, 161, 182–83, 204, 206

This book may be kept

FOURTEEN DAYS

A fine will be charged for each day the book is kept overtime.

GAYLORD 142